# Studies in Ethnicity

**In association with the Social Science Research Council**

*Editorial board*
Professor Michael Banton, Professor Percy Cohen,
Dr Sandra Wallman

'Studies in Ethnicity' emerges out of the work of the Social Science Research Council (S.S.R.C.) Research Unit in Ethnic Relations, whether directly or indirectly. It treats ethnicity as both an empirical and a conceptual problem, reporting new studies in ethnic relations and new approaches to the study of ethnicity.

The first titles in the series are:

Sandra Wallman (ed.): *Ethnicity at Work*

Verity Saifullah Khan (ed.): *Minority Families in Britain*

# Ethnicity at Work

*Edited by*

Sandra Wallman

*First published 1979 by*
THE MACMILLAN PRESS LTD
*London and Basingstoke*
*Associated companies in Delhi Dublin*
*Hong Kong Johannesburg Lagos Melbourne*
*New York Singapore and Tokyo*

*Printed in Great Britain by*
LOWE AND BRYDONE PRINTERS LIMITED
*Thetford, Norfolk*

**British Library Cataloguing in Publication Data**

Ethnicity at work. – (Studies in ethnicity).
  1. Industrial sociology  2. Race awareness
  I. Wallman, Sandra  II. Series
  301.45'1042     HD6955

  ISBN 0–333–23511–8
  ISBN 0–333–23512–6  Pbk

# Contents

## Contents

# Notes on Contributors

DENNIS BROOKS is Research Fellow, S.S.R.C. Industrial Relations Research Unit, University of Warwick.

DAVID CLARK is Research Associate in Sociology/Anthropology (Ethnicity Programme), S.S.R.C. Research Unit in Ethnic Relations, University of Bristol.

HAZEL FLETT is Research Associate in Social Administration (Housing Programme), S.S.R.C. Research Unit in Ethnic Relations, University of Bristol.

HARRY VJEKOSLAV HERMAN is Assistant Professor of Anthropology, University of Waterloo, Ontario, Canada.

BARRY KOSMIN is Research Director, Board of Deputies of British Jews; and Consultant to the Ethnicity Programme, S.S.R.C. Research Unit in Ethnic Relations, University of Bristol.

JOHN MACRAE is Senior Lecturer in Economics, University of Auckland, New Zealand.

JUDITH OKELY is Lecturer in Anthropology, University of Durham.

VERITY SAIFULLAH KHAN is Research Associate in Anthropology (Ethnicity Programme), S.S.R.C. Research Unit in Ethnic Relations, University of Bristol.

MILTON SANTOS is Professor of Geography and Architecture, Edward Larocque Tinker Chair, Columbia University, New York.

KARAMJIT SINGH is Research Associate, S.S.R.C. Industrial Relations Research Unit, University of Warwick.

DAVID STYMEIST is Assistant Professor of Anthropology, University of Manitoba, Winnipeg, Canada.

SANDRA WALLMAN is a social anthropologist, presently Research Director for the Ethnicity Programme, S.S.R.C. Research Unit in Ethnic Relations, University of Bristol.

# Foreword

It is our objective in this volume to throw some light on an important area of practical enquiry. Given this objective it is essential that the central notions *ethnicity* and *work* are made plain. The meaning of work is, in these times, variable but not problematic. Ethnicity is more slippery. The reader may be surprised to find the term 'ethnic' applied here to so many different kinds of social grouping, and the term 'ethnicity' used to unite the range of us/them distinctions described in these papers. Some summary points on ethnicity and on its relation to work are therefore in order.

Ethnicity refers generally to the perception of group difference and so to social boundaries between sections of a population. In this sense *ethnic difference* is the recognition of a contrast between 'us' and 'them'. While some analytic attention has been paid to the terms of that contrast – to colour, citizenship, competition and so on as markers of social boundary – too little has been given to the flexibility of that boundary, to contextual shifts in the line between 'us' and 'them', and to the fact that both advantages and disadvantages can accrue from keeping that line intact. We are proposing, therefore, that the value of ethnicity varies. It can be regarded as a resource which will, for some purposes and in some situations, be mobilised to the advantage of a social, cultural or racial category of people; will have no meaning or value at all in other situations; and will, in still others, in which other needs and objectives are paramount, be construed as a liability to be escaped or denied as far as possible.

Ethnicity is not, therefore, the same as culture or 'race'. It is not simply difference: it is the *sense* of difference which can occur where members of a particular cultural or 'racial' group interact with non-members. *Real* differences between groups of people are no more (and no less) than *potential* identity markers for the members of those groups. This potential is taken up and mobilised only where it suits the purposes of a particular encounter. In this volume the encounters at issue all occur in the context of work. Where ethnic differences are used in that context they can be seen to coincide with differences in the way in which work is allocated or organised or experienced – although no priority of ethnicity over work or of work over ethnicity is established: systems of work and of ethnicity feed back on each other in ways which are dependent on the overall logic of the context described.

It follows that ethnicity is not always relevant to social relationships in which people of different 'race' or culture interact; and that when it does count it does not always count in the same way. It is not always the most appropriate principle around which social activity or identity may be organised. In some situations it has so little relevance that participants may simply set it aside, acting without reference to their 'ethnic' affiliations. Where it is imposed on them willy-nilly, or is used in a context for which any of the participants deems it inappropriate, it becomes *for them* a crippling liability. Since all parties to an encounter do not necessarily want or get the same out of that encounter, the ethnic boundary that constitutes a resource for one party may turn out to be a liability for the other. Ethnicity need not have the same kind of relevance for all the parties involved: the boundary which identifies and includes 'us' also serves to deny and exclude 'them'.

The modern world is fraught with circumstances in which fixed or frozen ethnic boundaries deny people access to particular spheres of power, status or activity – sometimes because they are boxed in by constraints and obligations of the ethnic group to which they belong; more often because they are boxed out of the mainstream by the discriminatory attitudes and practices of ethnic groups to which they do not belong. Racist exclusion, in these terms, is a version of ethnic boundary-keeping which constitutes a fixed liability to the racial minority designated 'out', whatever the advantages expected or gained by those designated 'in'.

It is important to recognise how difficult it is to observe ethnicity in action. The observer may see a difference between two batches of people which is *to him* a significant difference. If he then assumes ethnicity to be relevant to all encounters between them, he may seriously misinterpret the meaning or the purpose of events observed. Conversely, but with the same effect, the observed similarity of 'others' does not guarantee their mutuality in any respect. Where similarity and togetherness, difference and differentiation are confused, popular, political or managerial interpretations of conflict and consensus in any context will be wide of the mark.

For all these reasons it is essential that ethnicity be analysed and understood in a context which can itself be delimited. The sphere of work is very well suited to this purpose. In the sphere of work it is possible to identify circumstances in which ethnicity is used as a resource managed for specific occupational goals and in which it is also possible to see ethnicity as a refraction of the cultural traditions and symbolic values by which a particular people defines itself in relation to or by contrast with 'others'. Further, the topic *work* now has a significance which goes well beyond its relation to pluralism. The availability, experience, organisation and function of work is now changing throughout industrial society and, whether independently or by contagion, in non-industrial settings. The problems created are widely recognised, but still have not been sufficiently clearly defined.

The inter-relation of the two themes allows us to consider the extent to which systems of work are (also) ethnic systems, and to explore the logic of variations in the organisation and experience of work in relation to the marking, maintenance and shifting of that sense of 'us' which is the basis of ethnic identity.

Each of the ten papers which make up this volume constitutes a complete case study of the relation between ethnicity and work. The collection is nevertheless integrated by an introduction which sets out the main themes, and by brief abstracts which are inserted at the beginning of each paper to point out the particular theme or themes illustrated by it and to link it directly to the whole.

The contributors are all professional social scientists, although not all of a single discipline or of a single theoretical or political persuasion. They are all writing on the basis of their own research and according to their own views of its meaning. All but the last chapter was prepared expressly for this volume, using the framework expressed in its title. None has been published before.

I am indebted to the contributors for allowing their separate efforts to appear in this collective form, for their generous response to my editorial demands and for their tolerance of the generalised interpretation which I have imposed on their material.

Ultimate responsiblity for the volume is of course my own. It does not represent the views of the Social Science Research Council, nor does it necessarily reflect those of all members of the S.S.R.C. Research Unit in Ethnic Relations.

*London*                                                    S. W.
*February 1978*

# Introduction[1]

# The Scope for Ethnicity

## Sandra Wallman

### Ethnicity at Work

Two observations of ethnicity at work – one demographic, the other privileged – set the scene for this volume. The demographic observation is readily made in any good-sized cosmopolitan city. It is that individuals of the same ethnic origin are not evenly distributed across the employment map. Particular 'ethnic groups' tend instead to be clustered in or around particular occupations, jobs or spheres of work, and these 'ethnic' concentrations are only rarely the effect of explicit job restrictions or of formal *apartheid* rules. Nor are they confined to single class or status levels: it is often the case that a definable ethnic category has moved in and occupied an entire industry, top to bottom. But the pattern of these concentrations is consistent only in principle, not in detail: while it is generally true that some 'ethnic groups' specialise in some jobs in any urban economy, it is not specifically true that any one such group occupies the same work niche everywhere, every time. The first observation therefore suggests both that the urban economy typically offers scope for 'ethnic' economic organisation in particular niches, and that the same niche is either not always available or not always appropriate to the same people.

The second observation was made, quite unexpectedly, in the course of a private conversation with a Trinidadian in Toronto. The man worked as a spot-welder in a manufacturing industry. As such, he was part of a moving-belt assembly line, responsible for one short but crucial operation in a continuous process, cheek by jowl with the men on either side of him. He described the job with enthusiasm: *It was skilled work. It paid enough to house and feed his family while his children went to school in Canada. Nobody interfered with him. He led a good and proper life – compared to those 'Wops' he did, anyway* . . . The 'Wops' were his Spanish or Italian or Portuguese co-workers. He did not find it necessary to distinguish one southern European immigrant from another. He seemed to use them collectively to sharpen his contentment, his sense of satisfaction with himself. *They were not men*, he said. *They ate raw vegetables and bread for lunch* . . . *If the foreman said they should all take twenty minutes' break, the 'Wops' were back at work in a quarter of an hour* . . . *They broke their backs to pay off mortgages on houses in the immigrant suburbs which the long, twice-daily rush-hour commute made them too tired to enjoy* . . . *They bought household appliances and goods for their wives and children on credit accounts which trapped them in a standard of living they could neither pay off nor give up* . . . *They had no time and no energy to be husbands and fathers* . . . *Their lives were only work, and the work, for them, bore no fruit* . . .

He described himself by contrast: *He always ate, slowly and with talk, a tasty snack lunch prepared for him by his wife. He gave his employers a fair day's work, no more. One time, months before, the foreman had hassled him 'for nothing' and he had threatened to break the foreman's head. He saw no risk to his job: he was good at it and there was always another. He lived in a rented apartment twenty minutes from the factory and normally made the journey to work by streetcar, reserving his automobile for weekend excursions or visits with his family. He did not aspire to buying a house; to moving up the job hierarchy or out of the central city; to a better credit rating; or to saving for his retirement. He saw the future in terms of his piece of 'the family land' in Trinidad. It was no bigger than a garden,* he said, *but it was big enough to build a small house and grow some rice. When they were finished in Toronto, they would go back* . . .

This second observation suggests that not only will different sets of people perceive and use a given urban environment in fundamentally different ways, but that they may, when conditions are right, define themselves by the differences. Thus two men working together may eat different food, spend their money on different things, relate differently to others and to the job they do, and have different ambitions for themselves and their families. But the differences become significant only in circumstances in which one or the other uses them to identify the right way, 'our' way, in contrast or opposition to what 'they', the others, do.

In the terms of this volume, ethnicity is the process by which 'their' difference is used to enhance the sense of 'us' for purposes of organisation or identification. The ambiguity of the title is therefore deliberate. The volume deals with the ways in which ethnicity 'works' to differentiate and identify groups of people for particular purposes, and to mobilise their symbolic and material resources to particular ends. At the same time, it deals with ethnicity in the specific context of work. The inter-relation between these two elements is explored in the following sections, and each of the chapters included in the volume provides a case in point.

## 'Them' and 'Us'

Ethnicity is the recognition of significant difference between 'them' and 'us'. Neither the difference nor its significance is set. In broad group terms it will normally be couched in terms of culture, race, nation or religion. In a more narrow, individual perspective the same difference may be described in terms of the minutiae of behaviour. At both levels, ethnicity is about the organisation of society *and* the organisation of experience. The social structure, let us say, ensures that members of group X are more likely to work, marry, interact with other Xs than with members of group Y, and that they are more likely to do these things in different ways. The structure is 'felt': *'We' of group X are not like the Ys . . . 'they' do not work, marry, interact with us, the Xs, or in the way that Xs do . . . We feel them to be, know them to be, different from ourselves.*

Because it takes two, ethnicity can only happen at the boundary of 'us', in contact or confrontation or by contrast with 'them'. And as the sense of 'us' changes, so the boundary between 'us' and 'them' shifts. Not only does the boundary shift, but the criteria which mark it change: *The Xs may interact with but not marry the Ys . . . eat the same food but not cook it the same way . . . do the same job but not for the same reasons . . . live in the same street but come from different continents.*

Shifts or changes of ethnic boundary are neither random nor

haphazard. Both the differences between 'us' and 'them', and the way 'we' (and 'they') feel about those differences, vary with the circumstances in which 'we' are using or perceiving 'them'; the criteria of difference and the significance of those criteria are always, in some sense, functions of context or situation: *An X family and a Y family live next door to one another. The two men work together, the children go to school together. On these counts they are the same. They belong, however, to different religions. Perhaps one is Catholic, the other Protestant. Or one is Muslim, the other Christian. Most of the time, neither 'side' minds this difference. Indeed, when it comes to religious festivals, each relishes the excitement of special parties next door . . . But the same religious difference will become a source of antagonism and pain if Miss X and Master Y begin to talk of marrying each other.*

The shifts and changes of context which govern the position and the strength of ethnic boundaries occur both at the level of experience and at the level of structure – whether (ethnic) difference is a resource managed in such a way as to promote 'us' and to deny 'them' in the achievement of short-term or long-term, material or symbolic, implicit or explicit goals; or whether the structure of context or situation exacerbates difference and forces confrontation willy-nilly. It is useful to focus on the interplay between structural constraints and opportunities extrinsic to 'us', and the symbolic or organising potential intrinsic to or inherent in 'our' culture. By virtue of (either or both) the perception of the actors and the structure of the situation in which they act, ethnicity may be of positive, neutral or negative value in the pursuit of individual or collective goals: *Where an X man seeks a job in an industry controlled by or associated with X group, the networks, traditions and prejudices of the X group, and his power over them, will be useful and usable resources insofar as he defines himself and is defined by others ethnically as a member of that group, as one of 'us', not of 'them'; where he seeks a job for which he is well qualified, only his working skills, not his cultural affiliations (should) count; where the 'gate' to the job is a member of group Y who is concerned generally to reserve the job for Ys or specifically to exclude Xs, he may not go after the job at all. If he does apply for it he will certainly not get it. Either way, his working skills will not be relevant because his cultural affiliations are again paramount – but this time because they are the wrong ones.*

Depending on the perceptions of the actors, and the constraints and opportunities of the context in which they act, ethnicity may be an essential resource, an utter irrelevance or a crippling liability. Nor does it necessarily have the same meaning for everybody involved. The ethnic boundary, like any other, necessarily has two sides: 'their' ethnicity as much as 'ours' is at issue. Unlike some, however, no ethnic boundary can remain static throughout history or for every situation. Both 'our' ethnicity and 'theirs' are processes which respond to other things happening, other boundaries, other options pertaining at the time.

Three summary points lead into the next section: *One*: No minority population is simply a bunch of people with characteristics in common. Each is a bunch of people distinguished by characteristics which stand in some meaningful contrast to the characteristics of the classifier. The significance therefore happens at the boundary. *Two*: The difference between two aggregates of people will be *objective* to the extent that an outsider can list items that mark it, but is inevitably *subjective* to the extent that none of these markers has any necessary or precise significance outside the perception of the actors. The perception of significant objective difference is a product of the person perceiving and of the context in which he perceives. *Three*: These statements are true whether the significance put upon a particular characteristic is self-imposed or other-imposed. They can and do pertain to both 'sides' of a boundary.

## The Boundary Process

The boundaries of 'us' shift, the criteria which mark them change, and even the utility of having or maintaining a boundary at all is not consistent. The boundary process is therefore reactive, not independent. It may be happening in response to several different kinds of variable, and on a number of different levels. The factors affecting it may be macro or micro, a function of structure or of perception, of changes in history or of situation. We should not therefore expect social boundary processes to be the same in all societies or among all their constituent minority groups. Nor will two sets of people with common cultural origins placed in similar minority positions necessarily use the same elements of their traditional culture to mark themselves off from non-member 'others'. What they do use will depend on the resources they have, on what they hope to achieve (whether consciously or not) and on the range of options available to them at the time.

In this sense ethnicity, too, is reactive. It is culture in-adaptation-to, in-response-to, up-against 'others' within a context shared by both sides of the ethnic boundary, and it is shaped by the aims, constraints and opportunities of that context as they pertain to each side. This being so, ethnicity does not always 'work' in the same way. Any particular line or confrontation of difference may sometimes be useful to the business in hand; sometimes have no relevance to it at all; sometimes get in the way of one or other 'side'. It may be a resource for 'us' and a liability for 'them'. Even from 'our' side only, it may be an advantage in one context in relation to one set of objectives, and an impediment when the context and/or the objectives change.

The essential points are that boundaries – whether fences or frontiers – necessarily have two sides. And they are probably, or at least possibly, not the same on either side. But a *social* boundary, precisely by virtue of its socialness, has not only two sides: it also has two kinds of meaning.

The first is structural or organisational. It is objective to the extent that outsiders can see it. In this respect the boundary marks the edge of a social system. This edge constitutes an interface between that system and one or more of those contiguous upon it. The analogy is clearest in traffic management: the point at which the flow of traffic changes in speed, direction or vehicular type is the point of interface between two traffic systems. It is also the point at which confusion and/or collision is most likely to occur – as, for example, at the junction between a busy feeder-road and a main highway. By the same logic, a social boundary is the point of interface between two systems of activity, organisation, meaning – or work. Similarly, too, it is a likely point of ambiguity and of danger.

The second kind of meaning inherent in social boundaries is subjective to the extent that it inheres in the experience of participants. Because it is social and not simply mechanical, the boundary marking the ending edge of one social system and the beginning edge of another has significance not only for the observer but also, and more importantly, for the members of those systems. It marks members off from non-members (or non-members from members – the boundary can be read, as we have noted, from either side); it is the point at which, or the means by which, members can be identified. The social boundary identifies 'us' in relation or in opposition to 'them'. More crucially, 'our' identity depends on 'them' and so on the boundary between us.

Unlike a fence or a traffic-light, therefore, a social boundary must be *both* an interface line between inside *and* outside, and an identity line between 'us' and 'them'. The interface element marks a change in what goes on. The identity element marks the significance given to that change and expresses the participants' relation to it. Because a social boundary is about the organisation of society no more and no less than it is about the organisation of experience, neither element has more or less reality than the other. Both the difference and the *sense* of difference count.

'Ethnic studies' have, in English, tended to focus on identity – that is, on group-oriented groups whose instrumental clout is limited to the political sphere. Although the interface of task-oriented groups is only the other side of the same conceptual coin, its part in boundary processes is regularly overlooked. The complementarity of the two elements shows up if systems of identity and organisation are visualised as sub-systems integrated within a socio-economic whole. As such they may vary together or apart or without direct reference to each other, but they are necessarily interdependent: each, at some level, is affected by whatever else is happening.

For the specific purposes of this volume, the group-oriented groups are those normally called 'ethnic', the task-oriented groups are those pursuing a particular job, occupation or livelihood. Each of our contributors examines the process and use of ethnicity in the context of work. Each paper therefore exemplifies the way in which ethnic systems and systems of work interact. The underlying questions in each case are: when, and by what logic, is a system of work made 'ethnic'? How, and by what processes, is an ethnic system converted into a system of work?

**Systems and Spheres**

We know it is theory that determines what we can observe and how we interpret it. We also know that any theoretical model is only as good as it is useful to particular analytic purposes; that none is equally well-suited to all such purposes; and that an 'unsuitable' model can be a real detriment to understanding. So it is with socio-economic models. A model of society as a single and notionally static structure is good insofar as it allows us to observe pattern and continuity in the apparent chaos of social life. It is less good where we are concerned specifically to understand the dynamic of that 'chaos', the process of events happening inside the structural frame. Indeed, where the notion of socio-economic structure is applied uncritically or too literally, any evidence of socio-economic process is, if it is noticed at all, dismissed as an aberration of the normal case.

Exactly this effect has dogged the economic analysis of work. It is reviewed in detail in Milton Santos' contribution to this volume, but can be summarised here. Thus economic activity, notably *urban* economic activity, was said to have, and could clearly be shown to have, a particular formal structure, although not everybody who was economically active seemed to be participating within that formal structure – at least not in the same way or according to the same rules. Some, indeed, were arguably not participating at all. Once the monolithic *formal* economic structure was seen not to account for all those who were observed to be involved in it, the analytic next step was to postulate an extra-structural *informal* sector which *could* account for them. Since this had been defined in opposition to the formal sector, it had either to operate by a different logic and according to quite other rules, or to be 'irrational' and without rules or regularities of any kind.

Neither version is helpful to our present purposes: the latter because it is quite plainly wrong; the former because it ignores the fact that each kind of work is at some level complementary to every other, and because it disallows the necessary interdependence of the 'formal' and 'informal' sectors. In the context of ethnicity at work, we need a theoretical model which recognises that not all socio-economic activity is articulated by the same principles – which is to say that not all work is organised in the same way, for the same reason, or by using the same resources. And we need a theory which can articulate the peculiarly *reactive* nature of ethnic organisation – which is to say that ethnicity only 'works' in circumstances appropriate to it; and that these circumstances obtain in interstices *within* the 'formal' structure, never outside it.

For both these purposes we need a model of co-relating systems which are governed by a single dynamic logic and are complementary to each other. Contemporary systems theory is illuminating. It sees society as a total, unaggregated system whose dynamic nature stems from the interplay of its component sub-systems with each other, and with the external environment.

This, in the terms we have been using, is to say that systems have boundaries which are maintained by other systems, and by the overall framework in which they operate. Because the various systems are inter-related, a change in one allows or entails a change in the others.

Suppose, for example, that some change in the socio-economic environment increases the demand for certain kinds of economic activity, and presents new opportunities for making a living or for earning prestige; and that these opportunities are open to anyone who is aware of them and who is able to mobilise the necessary social and material resources. Suppose further that a particular set of people has in common a stock of symbolic or behavioural items which will serve as a focus for the identification of a new working group, or as a justification for new kinds of economic endeavour. In these circumstances, that set of people may then use its cultural stock to generate new forms of ethnic organisation for the new purposes. Where, on the other hand, existing ethnic forms are inappropriate to the new situation and get, or are expected to get, in the way of success, they will be adapted or rejected by those members of the group who set greater store by success than by tradition. Either way, a change in 'the economic system' can be said to have entailed a change in 'the ethnic system'. And the form of the over-arching system (that is, of the parent structure) need not have changed at all.

Socio-economic sub-systems inter-relate even when they are bounded by or defined by different kinds of criteria; articulated by different principles; operating at different levels of inclusiveness; or appropriate to different frames of perception. Their co-relation probably cannot be consciously engineered. (What small part of any system can reasonably expect to have full control of the whole?) Most often the whole systematic process will be perceived to have come about by chance. Only rarely can anyone claim to have intended it to unfold exactly as it did.

These ramifications make a comprehensive systems model very complex and very untidy. Without an electronic computer it is clearly not possible to analyse all the variables at once. It is expedient, therefore, to concentrate on those sub-systems most likely to be significant to the problem in hand – much in the way that we are here monitoring the relations between ethnic systems and work systems as though no others counted.

One social anthropological variation on the systems theme provides a useful precedent. In it, the innumerable sub-systems are grouped in layers and visualised as spheres – whether of activity, exchange or meaning – to which particular resources, or kinds of resources, pertain, and between which they can be transposed only under very particular conditions. The classic example is that of the man who makes himself a successful entrepreneur by converting status resources from the social sphere into economic resources in the business sphere.

There are similar or analogous 'conversions' observable in the analyses offered here. Traditional cultural resources of obligation, filiation, status, organisation, value and so on are adapted to non-traditional spheres of work, often with the effect of enhancing work-defined objectives; patterns and structures and technologies of work feed back upon traditional culture, affecting, offering – sometimes even enhancing – aboriginal forms and meanings.

Our collective effort is to monitor the feedback relationships between work systems and ethnic systems, and to appreciate the conditions necessary to their occurrence.


## Work and Ethnicity

Systems of work may be created or maintained by ethnicity; ethnicity may be a product of the structure of work. The cases offered here illustrate a number of systems of work, each bounded a certain way and with its own dynamic logic, yet contained within the economic whole. The structure and process of each system is more or less amenable to the admission of informal principles, such as ethnicity, into the organisation of work. The same cases show, on the other hand, that the traditions of a particular culture will lead its members to select certain forms of work out of the options open to them; will allow or require them to carry rights and obligations over from the non-work to the work sphere where the structure of the job permits; and will provide them with idioms, symbolic structures and modes of organisation which may, if they are suitable to it, be adapted to the needs or the opportunities of a particular environment.

Given this range of variables, it is inevitable that our case studies do not fall neatly into one set of comparable categories and that they group quite differently according to the criteria by which they are classified. Taking only the main themes of this volume, we may consider the contributions in terms of:

(i) the focus of each enquiry – whether on ethnicity or on work;

(ii) the interplay between 'formal' and 'informal' systems or elements of organisation;

(iii) the dynamics of the boundary processes involved; and

(iv) the scope allowed to ethnicity – its value as an organising principle relative to other things happening, other options available to participants in *a* or *the* socio-economic environment.

(i) In terms of the emphasis of the enquiry, each of the first five papers (those of Okely, Kosmin, Herman, Brooks/Singh and Khan) focuses on a single ethnic group, on its cultural resources and on the use or adaptation of those resources to the constraints and opportunities of one or more work settings. The other five (by Flett, Macrae, Clark, Stymeist and Santos) come in from the opposite angle to focus on particular contexts of work or spheres of economic activity, on the opportunity spaces within them in which ethnicity can be shown to operate, or on the dynamic logic which effectively denies it usefulness.

(ii) Several of the case studies demonstrate the ways in which 'informal' systems of organisation fit into the interstices of 'formal' occupational structures – whether of factories (Brooks/

Singh, Macrae), bureaucracy (Flett), an urban economic system (Okely, Kosmin, Khan), or the capitalist system as a whole (Stymeist). Not all of these informal principles are 'ethnic'. Clark deals explicitly with other-than-ethnic strategies used by aspiring entrepreneurs seeking the resources of money, organisation or status necessary to success in small business. He makes the point that the structures of any 'formal' political economy must be taken into account if 'informal' systems of economic enterprise are to be effectively manipulated or properly understood. Macrae's economic analysis of the mobility patterns of three different ethnic groups working in the same New Zealand industry demonstrates three different 'informal' systems operating within a single 'formal' structure. Stymeist's account of casual labour in Toronto shows that even workers in a position of least power in the economic system have some scope for 'local' organisation within the constraints imposed upon them by 'outside' structures; but that, given the nature of those constraints – and perhaps also given the diversity of ethnic affiliations represented in the labouring group – ethnicity is, in that context, not often the most useful of 'local' organising principles. Santos' paper deals with the dynamics of 'circuits' in the overall economic system and underlines the essential interdependence of its constituent parts – specifically of the 'formal' and 'informal' sectors, implicitly of the ethnic and work systems with which we are concerned here.

(iii) Boundary processes are signalled in a number of ways. Santos reviews interpretations of the economic system which have imputed unrealistic degrees of autonomy to circuits or subsystems of work because they have mistaken the boundary of the part for the boundary of the whole, the boundary pertaining in one context for the boundary that defines the overall system. Khan discusses changes in the placing, marking and significance of ethnic boundaries 'used' by particular categories of South Asians through historical and situational time, a process illustrating the sensitivity of the boundary process to the constraints and opportunities of the socio-economic context in which it functions in London. The analyses of Okely and Kosmin, dealing respectively with English Gypsies and British Jews, show quite clearly the process by which the exclusion practices of the majority have encouraged or required the creation and maintenance of a minority ethnic boundary or boundaries in each case, and have contributed to specialising the two minority groups into their now characteristic work niches. Flett describes the interplay between boundaries of bureaucratic and moral eligibility to public housing, and Brooks and Singh the fit – or lack of fit – between boundaries marked by traditional Punjabi exchanges of gifts and obligation, and those marked by the technology of work in Midlands steel foundries.

(iv) The final theme recapitulates the general point: a particular ethnicity only 'works' in a particular set of circumstances. It is responsive to and dependent for its effect on the structure and scope of the situation in which it operates, and on other elements in the context – in this volume the *work* context – in which it is used.

The various case studies illustrate this general point in a number of ways. Kosmin, Herman and Okely show very clearly the cultural predilections that have moved Jewish, Macedonian and Gypsy groups into their specialised economic niches and, by the same token, have precluded their participation in others. Clark argues that it is not 'ethnic group consciousness' as much as it is pre-existing habits of organisation that account for the remarkable success of particular ethnic groups in business enterprise. There is no doubt that some forms of traditional organisation are a serious handicap to commercial success; others are readily adapted to entrepreneurial niches.

This latter possibility is nicely illustrated by Herman's democratic and independent-minded Macedonian restauranteurs in Toronto; by the Brooks/Singh analysis of ethnic brokers whose pivotal position in the foundry structure provides the ideal fulcrum for the conversion of tradition into ethnicity, and of ethnicity into a system of work; by Kosmin's account of the reasons for and the adaptation of the self-employment obsession of British Jews; and by Okely's insight into Gypsy enterprise on the margins of the main society.

Two papers look at the 'use' of ethnicity, not in individualistic enterprise but in impersonal places of employment – Macrae's industrial, Flett's bureaucratic – and indicate ways in which a sense of 'us' can be expressed even in work situations that formally preclude personalised or informal styles of organisation. Two papers focus on work settings that escape some of these formal constraints because they are not officially monitored by the outside, and others because of their intrinsic structure. Khan deals with women out-workers in the clothing industry, Stymeist with casual labourers. Both, although to very different effect, show that the use and usefulness of ethnicity varies as the balance between 'inside' and 'outside' alters. Ethnicity is not always the same, nor is it always useful in either setting.

Whatever the readiness of members of an ethnic category or group to pursue particular forms of work, they can only respond to opportunity when it is there. The effect of their ethnicity is therefore dependent upon the state of the economic system and on their bargaining strength within it. Conversely, they will not see, will not accept, will not succeed in the opportunity offered if it is not appropriate to their choice of work and their cultural experience. Their performance at work is therefore similarly dependent on the resources and liabilities inherent in their ethnic system.

In all of this, historical placing seems to be crucial: to be ready and willing and appropriate at the right moment is the start of a successful ethnic work niche. Whether it is the case that economic changes make more or different kinds of work available; whether certain occupational structures always have in them niches which are filled by successive categories of the casual, the transient or the powerless; or whether the hostility of 'others' encourages categories of people to group around a notion of 'us', and so to search for a means by which 'we' can be identified – all the evidence points to the conclusion that ethnicity will only be manifest where it is useful; and that it will only be useful and manifest in contexts appropriate to it. The papers following examine the mutual appropriateness of particular systems of ethnicity and particular systems of work, and describe ways and means by which each affects and is affected by the other.

# 1

*The first example deals directly with our two main themes. It explores the ways in which systems of work and ethnicity interact to the advantage of Gypsies in England. Gypsy economic activity is structured by the Gorgio (non-Gypsy) economy. Gypsy skills and occupations are adapted to the needs of the main 'formal' system, and they operate in those chinks or niches in the system which suit their traditions, and in which 'informal' organisation is feasible and is likely to pay off. To this extent the economic position of Gypsies resembles that of other groups described in the examples following.*

*But the Gypsy version is unique in the way that the prejudices and expectations of non-Gypsy 'others' serve to enhance the Gypsy sense of 'us'; and in the extent to which the Gorgio image of Gypsies is manipulated by Gypsies to suit the idiom of a particular transaction. In this case, both ethnicity and ethnic image are important economic resources.*

# Trading Stereotypes

# The case of English Gypsies

## Judith Okely

The main concern of this paper is Gypsy ethnicity and economic exchange. It describes the Gypsies' special economic niche, showing also why it is more appropriate to refer to economic exchange than to 'work' which in an industrial capitalist system, is closely associated with wage-labour.[1]

## Development Prejudices

A recurrent theme in the literature is that Gypsies' 'traditional' livelihood has gone, and that they will disappear with development. This underestimates their continuing ability to adapt to changes in the larger economy. It assumes that Gypsies have been isolated and cannot survive unless they remain so (Sutherland, 1975, pp. 1–3). It has been said of British Gypsies that:

> isolation, caused partly by the need for protection and partly out of desire to preserve cultural integrity, has kept the gypsy ignorant of the outside world   (Trigg, 1967, p. 43).

> Mass communications have removed the barriers . . . Education, economic pressures and, in due course, miscegenation will do the rest. The long, long history of the gypsies of Britain is coming to an end   (Vesey-Fitzgerald, 1973, p. 245).

Equally misleading observations have been made of Gypsies elsewhere. Some American development sociologists have

classified Spanish Gypsies as 'under-developed marginals' whose
contact with 'modern sectors' is largely through formal institutions likes the police, militia and school (Goulet and
Walshok, 1971, p. 456). Certainly, political contact is imposed
by Gorgios (the Gypsies' word for non-Gypsies), but Gypsies
everywhere also initiate economic contact with Gorgios. Every
day Gypsies seek out Gorgios on their doorsteps, at their factories
and offices, on their farms and at their scrap-metal yards. One
Gypsy put it neatly: 'Work doesn't come to you, but the *muskras*
[police] do.'

Gypsies must and do know exactly what is going on around
them. They are continually adjusting to and participating in
technological and industrial development, although often in
ways unrecognised in orthodox economic terms. Thus the study
of Spanish Gypsies confidently asserts that if Andalusia were to
'develop successfully, Gypsies would be left with no marketable
skills' (Goulet and Walshok, 1971, p. 464). Confining themselves
to occasional visits and questionnaires and imbued with nostalgic
notions of the 'real' Gypsy, Gorgio observers have described only
some of the Gypsy occupations. Other occupations are belittled
or left undiscovered, and the underlying principles behind all
their occupations are ignored.

## Continuity

The Gypsies, or Travellers as they often prefer to be described by
outsiders, are directly dependent on a sedentary or host community within which they circulate, supplying goods, services
and occasional labour. A considerable number of Gypsies in the
British Isles are nomadic, at least for part of the year, living in
caravans or 'trailers' towed by lorries or vans. Even those who
move into houses are not necessarily permanently sedentary: they
could take to the roads again. The Gypsies' shift from horse-
drawn waggons to motorised transport is one example of their
economic adaptation. Modern technology has actually enhanced their nomadism. Larger homes with calor-gas cooking
and heating facilities can now be transported.

Unlike migrant workers who move from place A to place X for

'settled' and wage-labour jobs, Gypsies operate largely independently of wage-labour. The greatest opportunities for Gypsies lie in those occupations which others are less able or less willing to undertake. This is also true of migrant workers moving to the industrialised areas, but they either take up wage-labour employment or operate small fixed businesses (see e.g. the Macedonian and Jewish cases in this volume). By contrast, the caravan-dwelling Gypsy family is both self-employed and actually or potentially mobile with lorry, trailer and minimum overheads. With these advantages, the Gypsies can cater for occasional needs where there are gaps in demand and supply and market forces are uneven; and where any large-scale or permanent, specialised business would be uneconomic or insecure. The character of Gypsy occupations can be summarised as 'the occasional supply of goods, services and labour to a host economy where demand is irregular in time and place' (Okely, 1975b, p. 114).

The descriptive details and history of a particular occupation (for which see Okely, 1975) become less important than the consideration of aspects common to all. A list of the occupations of British Gypsies is indicative. It would include:

(i) The hawking of manufactured Gorgio goods – either small items like brushes and key rings, or larger items like carpets and linen.

(ii) Antique dealing – the Gypsy collects antiques from individual households over a wide area and then trades them to a dealer, sometimes straight to an exporter to the United States.

(iii) The sale of Christmas trees and holly.

(iv) Clearance of discarded goods and waste – old cars, cookers, fridges, boilers, machinery from houses, factories or demolition sites; old clothes and rags. The metal and rags are then sorted and delivered for re-cycling.

(v) External building and gardening – tarmac- or asphalt-laying of small driveways, paving, tree-lopping and external house repairs.

(vi) Seasonal farm work on a contract basis – fruit-picking, potato-picking, beet-hoeing and hop-tying.

(vii) The hawking of Gypsy-made wares – like wooden pegs and wax flowers, the sale of white heather, fortune-telling and knife-grinding. These last are the occupations which Gorgios most frequently associate with Gypsies.

The study on which this paper is based involved direct personal experience of scrap-metal and rag collection from houses, farms and public rubbish dumps; helping to break up and sort the materials and to weigh them in at scrapyards. It involved selling holly to florists and joining a gang of potato-pickers. It also allowed the author the dubious honour of being insulted as a Gypsy by shopkeepers and householders.

The number and variety of occupations reveal the Gypsies' remarkable adaptation to changes in the larger economy. This is most notable in their re-cycling of scrap-metal. The Civic Trust has suggested that 'Gypsies and Didikois contribute 20 per cent of scrap-metal over the weighbridge supplies to scrap yards' (1968, p. 8). Because farmwork and rural-based occupations have declined, those who would fix 'real' Gypsies in this setting will assume there are no alternative economic openings. But the Gypsies, like the sedentary host population, have become concentrated in urban industrialised areas. The 1965 Government Census of Gypsies recorded 43 per cent in the South-East Region and 17 per cent in the West Midlands—compared to 2 per cent in the Northern Region (M.H.L.G., 1967, p. 7). Over a decade later this shift is probably more marked. With it have come problems in finding camping places free of Gorgio interference. This is not because of land shortage as often as it is alleged—there are plenty of temporarily vacated plots—but because of stricter controls on land usage, especially for caravans. On the other hand, motorisation has enlarged the Gypsies' daily work radius from the camp base.

## Self-Employment as Identity

Throughout these changes the Gypsies have retained the preference for self-employment which has always been a crucial defining boundary between themselves and Gorgios. Economic exchanges with Gorgios are, as far as possible, on the Gypsies' own terms. Wage-labour by contrast would entail working to the orders of a Gorgio and would put restrictions on the location, times and type of work. One Gypsy said: '*If we took reg'lar jobs it would spoil us.*'

Like Gypsies in California (Sutherland, 1975), English Gypsies regard welfare as merely a modern equivalent to begging and so not degrading. But wage-labour is contemptible: Gypsies are proud to announce: 'I've always worked for myself.' The Gorgio's stupidity is confirmed by his inability to do so.

> *There's not much to a Gorgio's life – working Monday to Friday the same time in the morning to the same time in the evening. Then the man gets drunk on Saturday. He has sex once a week that night and a lie-in on Sunday. At the end of it all, the man's given a gold watch!*

Even short-term contract work on farms is resented:

> *I like calling for scrap. It's much better than picking 'tatoes all day. I'd rather work for myself than a farmer or someone else.*

But this is as close as Gypsies come to wage-labour. The men of wealthier families dismiss farmwork as 'women's work' and relegate it to their wives (see Okely, 1975b, footnotes).

The Gypsies even avoid wage-labour economic relationships amongst themselves. A Gypsy may work with, but not for, another Gypsy. Economic co-operation occurs in work partnerships: two men might enter a temporary partnership to do some tarmacking jobs together. This often occurs between affines. Always: 'We split the money down the middle.'

In contrast to this egalitarian relationship, Gypsies will willingly exploit Gorgio labour. There are numerous Gorgio tramps or 'dossers' prepared to do the odd day's work for a flat rate. Travellers may call in at doss-houses seeking casual labourers. These dossers, or 'slaves' as they are sometimes contemptuously called, are given the heaviest and most monotonous work in exchange for a fiver and some cigarettes at the end of the day. They may be offered a meal and even a night's sleep in the lorry cab, but always separate from the family, to confirm their permanent exclusion as Gorgios from Gypsy society.

Clearly, the Gypsies' economic activities both express and

reinforce their separateness from Gorgios. Given also the Gorgios' hostility and persecution of them as nomadic caravan dwellers, the Gypsies feel they are entitled to make a living from Gorgios in any way which suits them.

The Gypsies' rejection of wage-labour in their economic niche demands (i) diversification in occupations and (ii) less specific, wide-ranging skills. The non-recognition of these factors in Gorgios' analyses partly explains their historical pessimism.

(i) Occupations noticed and recorded by Gorgios tend to be those such as fortune-telling and rural craftsmanships which confirm the host society's stereotype. With industrialisation, the Gypsies' rural occupations have become exotic in the eyes of Gorgio town-dwellers. They have tended also to exaggerate the extent of Gypsy craftsmanship. It comes, therefore, as a surprise that Gypsies lay tarmac and deal in antiques, and those who break up cars on the highway verges are dismissed as counterfeit. But nor were Gypsies exclusively rural in the past. When Gypsies were first recorded in the British Isles in earlier centuries, it is likely that they did have more occupations than fortune-telling and horse-dealing but that these were not recognised as 'Gypsy'. Ideally, the Gypsies have a multiplicity of occupations both over time and at any one time. Wealthier families have the greatest spread of occupations and over-specialisation is invariably least remunerative. Gypsies are ready to switch occupation from one week to the next and in a single encounter:

> When I went out 'calling' at Gorgio houses with a Gypsy woman asking for scrap metal and rags, among other things, we were given a carpet and some dresses. At the next village my companion encountered a housewife whom she quickly sized up and we were transformed into travelling saleswomen. We sold the housewife the carpet and some dresses from the rag bag.

(ii) Given this absence of specialisation, the Gypsies' wide-ranging skills are appropriate and necessary. Various criteria must be applied to defining a skill. The vast majority of caravan-dwelling Gypsies can neither read nor write. Few have ever attended school. This lack is normally seen only in negative terms. It is said of Spanish Gypsies that:

> Judicious vocational training and the provision of broader job incentives are indicated as a 'must' policy if Gypsies are to be successfully incorporated into development (Goulet and Walshok, 1971, p. 466).

In England, the Plowden Report and the 1967 Government Report on Gypsies described Gypsy children as 'severely deprived' and inhibited in intellectual growth (M.H.L.G., 1967, p. 30). While Gorgio sympathisers are beginning to recognise the ethnocentricism of this stance, the drive for state schooling for Gypsies still pays only lip service to the Gypsies' alternative skills acquired from early childhood. Travellers or Gypsies themselves say:

> *You could put me down anywhere in the world and I could make a living. If there's a nuclear war only the Gypsies'd be able to look after their selves.*

The Gypsies' skills include: knowing the local economy and the local people; manual dexterity; mechanical ingenuity; highly developed memory; salesmanship and bargaining skills (Okely, 1975b, pp. 133–5). More relevant to this paper are their opportunism and ingenuity in choice of occupation, and their flexibility in role-playing.

## Ethnic Identity

Linguistic evidence reveals some early Indian content in the Gypsies' Romany language. Over several centuries it has also incorporated vocabulary from many European languages. English Gypsies use Romany words and phrases. For Gorgios, the Indian origin of Gypsies centuries back has become a mythical charter for acceptance of the Gypsies as a 'genuine' exotic group. For Gypsies this is not relevant. Gorgio proponents of the 'real Romany' may pick out individual Gypsies with dark hair and brown eyes to support their exotic prejudices, they will not 'see' the many others with lighter hair and blue eyes. Gypsies too may note those among them with dark hair and skin, but such features are more distinct among recent Gypsy immigrants from eastern Europe and may actually be a source of stigma. They are certainly not criteria for membership. Like Gorgios, Gypsies entertain ideas of 'pure-blooded' Gypsies, although without the Indian overtones. For both Gypsy and Gorgio, 'real Romanies', perceived as a distinct genetic group, is a convenient metaphor for favoured individuals or groups, depending on context and the specific interests of the classifier. The empirical realities are beside the point. X as a 'real Romany' for one observer may be dismissed as a 'half-caste' or 'drop-out' by someone else.

The Gypsies' dogma of 'pure blood' overlays the continuing threat of marriages across the ethnic boundary. In every generation and in every sub-group, numbers of Gorgios marry in and numbers of Gypsies marry out, but the perceived boundary remains intact. Membership rests on a principle of descent. Anyone claiming to be a Gypsy and recognised by others as such must have at least one Gypsy parent (Okely, 1975a). Membership ascribed at birth must be affirmed by a way of life and commitment to certain Gypsy values. These include self-employment and pollution taboos which express, at a ritual level, the separation from Gorgios (Okely, 1976).

Whatever their alleged racial status, more significant for the Gypsies in their economic and political relations with Gorgios is that, unlike ethnic minorities who are recognisably different from the mass of the resident population, Gypsies are not physically distinct. They can choose to conceal their ethnic identity or to elaborate it.

The Gorgios' categories of 'Gypsy' have a long history and are fundamental constraints on the Gypsies' actions. The Gypsies must become acquainted with these categories in order to manipulate them. They may even have a hand in creating them. The confusion in the literature, and the arbitrariness of Gorgio criteria as to who or what is a 'real' Gypsy, reflect the Gypsies' success in presenting so many separate appearances. The ability is explicitly recognised. One Gypsy woman explained it by saying: '*I have a thousand faces.*'

The image of the Gypsy as presented to outsiders is variable and adjusted to the needs of a particular context. This use of ethnicity is quite apart from the Gypsies' sense of identity and ethnic consciousness which is usually concealed from Gorgios. Whereas economic relations between Gypsies are ideally based on equality and pursued within the framework of certain rules, there are no such rules accepted by both parties in exchanges between Gypsy and Gorgio. Even practices which affront Gorgio codes are therefore considered acceptable. But caution itself becomes a moral principle. There is the story of a Gypsy who made a deal with the Devil:

> *In those days Gypsies traded in salt – it used to be dear. The Devil gave this Gypsy a barrel of salt which never emptied. One day it spilled over and filled the world. It's like that man who touched everything and it turned to gold. The moral of the story, I suppose, is, you must watch what you're getting. Follow through the deal. Think it out.*

The Devil is in essence the Gorgio. Deals with the devil Gorgio must be made with infinite caution. The Gypsy thought the salt barrel would permanently solve the problem of earning a living. The single deal created over-dependence and brought disaster. Whereas a deal with a Gypsy affirms ethnic independence, a deal with a Gorgio risks dependence.

In economic interaction with Gorgios, ethnicity or ethnic image may be handled in a number of ways, each having a different value. It may be:

|  |  |  |
|---|---|---|
| (i) | exoticised | + |
| (ii) | concealed | o |
| (iii) | degraded | − |
| or (iv) | neutralised | + − |

These modes rarely coincide with the Gypsies' own image of ethnic identity.[2]


## (i)  Ethnic Image Exoticised ( + )

The so-called 'traditional' occupations of Gypsies are often those in which it has suited them to present and identify themselves as Gypsies in accordance with an exotic or romantic stereotype.

The word 'Gypsy' derives originally from 'Egyptian', a label often given to persons from the East. As fortune-tellers, the Gypsies exploited the myth of their origins in Egypt, a land once associated with magical arts. Today, Gypsies as fortune-tellers do not claim foreign origins; they need only step into the part bequeathed by their ancestors in England:

> *You have to put on a scarf, show off your gold jewellery and say 'Cross my palm with silver'. Some of 'em says 'Cross my palm with paper money' now!*

The fortune-tellers met in the course of this study rarely believed in any powers to predict the future. Nonetheless, the ability to act the fortune-teller and to read character was recognised as a special skill learnt from childhood. Some of the skill lies in correct sub-classification of the Gorgio client – in matching preoccupations and anxieties with occupation, social class, age, race and gender: '*You can always say to a middle-aged housewife that she's got worries.*' Individual personality is also assessed. Information may be acquired from another Gypsy who, days or weeks earlier, appeared to the client as tarmacker or salesman. The fortune-teller can create confidence by the announcement of this information. If it is followed by ambiguous statements which will be subjectively interpreted by the client, the latter may unwittingly volunteer new facts which add up to a convincing character reading. Several Gypsies interviewed described how they became very frightened when their predictions came true and they gave up fortune-telling altogether. In one case, a Gypsy woman, not being a psychotherapist, did not realise that her predictions had been self-fulfilling. She had imbued her client with the confidence he needed to extricate himself from his difficulties.

Although fortune-telling between Gypsy and Gorgio is seen largely as a con, some Gypsy individuals are believed by Gypsies themselves to have supernatural power, including the power of prediction. These are often older women, classified as *chovihanni* (witch). The Gypsies also associate good or bad luck with some particular items, but those hawked to Gorgios as 'lucky' and 'gold' (really brass) charms are seen amongst themselves as inauthentic trinkets.

Women pose as fortune-tellers more successfully than men (Okely, 1975c), but some older men combine it with the exotic or romanticised occupation of knife-grinding. Old men and women of any age can be exotic without being menacing. Younger men in the same guise may be considered threatening unless disarmed by a violin or guitar. As a consequence, in some parts of Europe it is lucrative for a young Gypsy to present himself to Gorgios as an exotic musician.

Other occupations with romantic if not exotic potential include the production and sale of rural handiwork such as clothes pegs, wax or wooden flowers and 'hand-made' lace – the latter bought by the yard from Nottingham factories. Although manufactured by men, the clothes pegs and wooden flowers are distributed by the women.

## (ii) Ethnic Image Concealed (o)

Gypsies can 'pass' more easily than some other ethnic groups. This may be a permanent or long-term choice when an individual Gypsy becomes sedentarised and abandons his ethnic group (Barth, 1955). More significant for those who continue to identify themselves as Gypsies is the day-to-day practice of passing. Whereas Gypsy women find exoticism remunerative, Gypsy men profit from concealment of ethnic difference. They must disguise themselves as 'ordinary' and 'normal' in terms of the host society. Daily contact gives the Gypsies insight into the Gorgio. Here there is an asymmetrical exchange of information: the Gorgio is permitted very few insights into the Gypsy way of life. The majority of Gorgios who seek out Gypsies are those intending to impose their own laws – police, public health inspectors, teachers and missionaries. The Gypsies have devised responses appropriate to satisfying the Gorgio invader but leaving him ignorant of the Gypsies' view of the encounter.

As tarmackers, landscape gardeners, travelling salesmen or antique dealers, Gypsy men put on 'respectable' clothing – clean trousers, shirts and expensive cardigans:

> *When we goes tarmacking, we don't say we're Gypsies. No. We call ourselves businessmen and say we've got a company.*

Touches of normality and semblance of literacy are communicated by headed notepaper, deviously acquired from employees of building firms or local councils:

> *We don't tell them the price the first time. We say we'll make an estimate and come back later.*

These 'estimates' are typed on the headed notepaper by a Gorgio associate or literate Gypsy. Advertisements are placed in the local newspaper giving the phone number of an obliging house-based relative or, in one case, of a pub pay-phone with set times during opening hours, arranged without the knowledge of the landlord. Antique dealers may lay hands on cards from a local antique shop and use them as passports of goodwill. Both men and women can successfully operate as sellers of linen and carpets. No addresses are necessary, only immediately visible authenticity and trustworthiness. Here the men wear good-quality suits: *Two Traveller women described how they used to call on the local vicar and ask to hire the church hall. They would arrange for specially printed cards announcing the date and place of the sale.*

The selling of second-hand goods also demands a respectable appearance. Preparing to go out selling second-hand clothes, a Traveller woman first removed her ubiquitous apron, then put on a smart dress and imitation pearls (*not* gold jewellery), declaring: 'We mustn't look Gypsified.' The very word 'Gypsify' reveals an awareness that a person can make him or herself more or less a Gypsy in the eyes of a Gorgio.

### (iii) Ethnic Image Degraded ( − )

Gypsies may choose to degrade their image for the Gorgio, as scavenger, beggar, pauper or fool: *Tom, who regularly called for scrap-metal and rags, said he always put on shabby clothing for the purpose. 'You 'ave to look poor, else they don't give you anything. If I 'ad on a smart suit they'd think " 'es doin' alright, I'm not gonna give anything away."'*

A woman posing as a destitute wife makes a better beggar. Irish Traveller women often carry a bundle made to look like a babe-in-arms. If men made such persistent demands as do women beggars they might be accused of assault. Gypsy women outside a fashionable London store may grab men and push sprigs of 'lucky white heather' (white ling) at them. This is the exotic stereotype gone sour. The men pay up to rid themselves of embarrassment. Social security may in future become the modern and more lucrative alternative to begging. It is not, as we have said, considered degrading by the Gypsies, although it does require a degraded image – especially on the local-authority living sites which are ill-suited to the Gypsies' needs for mobility and non-wage employment. Salaried Gorgio wardens on the new official sites assist in getting state benefits as it is in their interest to recuperate the high local government council rents. Illiteracy may be turned to advantage insofar as it precludes some Gypsies accepting certain jobs available at the labour exchange. The Travellers appear suitably mortified:

> *If only I could read and write, I'd be able to do lots of things. I'm not a scholard like you, I've 'ad no egication.*

The degraded image of the helpless illiterate is accompanied by earnest wishes to conform, to 'settle down' and send the children to school 'so they can 'ave a better life', thus reassuring the Gorgio of the superiority of his system. The few literate Gypsies often conceal their ability, preferring to seem deprived. Illiterates can casually screw up or burn official forms, free from the intimidation of their texts.

When there are no further returns to a degraded image and the Gypsies have had enough of Gorgio contempt, they will retaliate by reverting to the Gorgio idiom of respectability.

*I was out with Myra and Aunt Janie. They had been given two batteries by a lady on a luxury estate, with neat hedges and lawns to the private road. Aunt Janie stuffed the newspaper wrapping from the battery in the hedge. The lady, watching from her window, ran out and asked what we'd done with the newspaper:*
Aunt Janie: *'I've put it in the 'edge so it's out of sight.'* Lady: *'Have you indeed! That's the trouble with you Gypsies, living on rubbish dumps you don't care what the place looks like.'* Aunt Janie: *'Be careful who you're talking to, madam. I'm not a Gypsy and I don't live on any rubbish dump. If you'd like to know, I'm working for a charity. I'm giving up my time for this.'* The lady retreated.

*(iv)  Ethnic Image Neutralised  ( + — )*

In other interactions, the ethnic identity of the Gypsy is known by the Gorgio but is largely irrelevant to their business transaction (cf. Wallman, 1974).

In such cases exoticism, concealment or degradation are inappropriate. Relations of this kind occur between the Gypsy as client to some regular patron: the tarmac manufacturer; the antique dealer higher up the distribution ladder; the scrapyard owner or employee at the weighbridge; the builder giving sub-contracts; the linen wholesaler; the Gorgio horse-dealer; the farmer. The Gypsy will make efforts to individualise or personalise the relationship, so winning special favours. The man at the tarmac yard will reserve small quantities at a lower price; the man at the weighbridge will fiddle the amount and the farmer will give priority to particular families each season. The Gypsies may not be above pulling a fast one and are certainly ready to exploit their bargaining skills, but the Gorgio will be on the alert: *A Gorgio horse-dealer said that in contrast to other customers who would ask the price of a horse and take it or leave it, the Gypsies invariably tried to beat him down. They 'made a thing' of the occasion, he said. They would walk away at least three times feigning disinterest before anything was finally clinched. Whereas a non-Gypsy would come back and complain about a second-rate horse, the dealer found: 'I can always count on Gypsies to get rid of a bad horse. They never complain, they just pass it on to someone else.'*

Some economic relationships between Gypsy and Gorgio are based on equality and more mutual trust than between patron and client: *Albert sells old cars to Tony, a Gorgio who specialises in repairs of specific parts. Tony has contacts who specialise in other parts. Albert is always on the alert for a buyer of the renovated vehicle as he will get a percentage from Tony. Albert said: 'I've known him for years. He's like my own brother.'*

These few examples in which the Gorgio is given the category 'brother' in no way undermine the ethnic boundary. Liberal Gorgios seeking 'friendships' with Gypsies believe that their specific relationships with Gypsy individuals will 'break down the barriers of prejudice'. They assume that such friendships can be multiplied, but to the Gypsies they remain exceptions: *A Gypsy discussed a Gorgio woman who believed that her 'Christian love' could*

*destroy suspicion and hostility between Gypsies and Gorgios. 'It's no good,'*
*he said, 'there'll always be Gypsies and there'll always be Gorgios. We'll*
*never mix.'*

In some long-term relationships with Gorgio philanthropists,
the Gypsies do not need to play up the exotic image: the Gorgios
are permitted some amount of insight and their craving for the
exotic is satisfied. It is enough that Gypsies are known and
perceived by others as 'secret strangers'. The Gorgios see the
relationship as political: they are working towards the schooling
and integration of Gypsies. The Gypsies find their own political
advantages: they may ask the Gorgio to appear on their behalf in
court or to delay an eviction. But unlike the Gorgio, they also see
the relationship as economic. Charitable loans have been
obtained on a scale far exceeding the returns from a one-off
customer and 'friendship' may inhibit the demand for re-
payment.

## Ethnic Identity Affirmed

Another ethnic image operates in economic exchanges within the
Gypsy society. Internal exchange takes the form of bartering for
lorries, trailers, horses, dogs, gold jewellery and antique china,
both between kin and between groups distant to each other. Men
rather than women exchange all but the last two items. An
exchange is publicly clinched when the two parties slap their
right hands together. The gesture is called 'chopping hands' and
the exchange is referred to as a 'chop'. Prestige is attached to a
Gypsy's ability to make a good 'chop'. The procedure is
ritualised. At the annual national gathering at Appleby and, to a
lesser extent, at Epsom and at regional fairs like Barnet and Stow,
Gypsy men engage in horse-dealing. This is not only a commercial activity but a form of communication and affirmation of
Gypsy identity. Gypsies who may be strangers to each other,
without a history of competition for land, work or allies, can
establish a relationship, albeit ambiguous, over a 'chop'. The
exchange is usually in front of witnesses but, in any case, a
common code is observed. In contrast to economic exchanges
between Gypsy and Gorgio, those between Gypsy and Gypsy are

symmetrical: each should be aware of the other's tricks and ruses. If a Gypsy makes a poor deal with another, he cannot cry shame. It is shame on him. (Compare the Gorgio who returns to complain to the dealer in the example above.) At a large fair with hundreds of Gypsy participants, each transaction will affirm or diminish an individual's prestige. In establishing contact with someone from a distant region, a Gypsy is also protecting his status in his own region.

The horse is given special status among Gypsies. It is considered ritually clean, not *mochadi* (ritually polluted) as are cats, dogs and some other animals. The horse is an important intermediary between Gypsy and Gorgio as an item of exchange, and between Gypsies it has special significance. Since both parties should be experts in the judgement of horses, its exchange affirms their identity and skills as Gypsies. The ability to make a 'chop', and especially a 'chop' of horses, is an art to be learnt from childhood: *Billy and Sylvie took me with them to a regional fair. Billy, recently housed, had taken his six-year-old son out of school that day. 'My son's got to learn. Gypsies don't need to be educated like the Gorgios are. A Gypsy has to learn to chop; know what to say. Did you notice that old man with the waistcoat and gold watch chain? He said: "Look at this horse, if you take her you can have my wife for the night." Now you couldn't learn that in school! Can you see a Gorgio doing that? He wouldn't know what to say!'*

Readiness to have a 'chop' is linked with manliness. It is a humiliation to refuse, an admission of incompetence before the first round. Having a 'chop' is often the first overture between families meeting on the road. A Gypsy man might say, 'What do you have about you?', 'If I'm half a man for this', or 'I'm a man for exchanging this'. It is no answer for a man to say he will not part with something: *Albert told me he had been approached by Ned, a man of great fighting ability and political stature, to do a chop over Albert's black and white horse. Albert wanted neither to risk dealing with Ned nor to exchange the horse. He said it wasn't his horse but belonged to his five-year-old son. Ned accepted this, and Albert's dignity was preserved.*

The Gypsy woman's ethnic and sexual identity is not affirmed by internal economic exchange as much as by the observance of female pollution taboos (Okely, 1975c). Ideally, like the Gypsy man, she is self-employed in earning a living from Gorgios. Traditionally, it is the woman's responsibility to acquire food for the family. Gypsy women often remark that Gorgio men do not make their wives go out to work.

## Conclusion

Ethnicity should be distinguished from ethnic identity. The first refers to the sense of difference and the image presented to the outsider and may be either repressed or elaborated. Ethnic identity rests on group self-ascription (Barth, 1969, p. 14) in theory and in practice. The Gypsies maintain an ideology of racial purity which is made to work by a biased selection of ancestors. The Gypsies' self-image contrasts with the image offered to others, but the two are interconnected. The Gypsies are and, indeed, must be alert to Gorgio expectations of Gypsy ethnicity and normality and must supply them, while maintaining intact their own view.

Many Gypsy economic activities have been overlooked because Gorgios have needed to define Gypsies only as exotic and/or degraded in their terms. For the Gypsies these are only two out of several available alternatives. Even the host society's concepts of exotic or degraded will change. In the early nineteenth century the Gypsy was considered 'depraved' (Hoyland, 1816, p. 158) as a heathen, rather than 'deprived' (Plowden, 1967, App. 12) as an illiterate. But whereas charitable financial resources once centred in the churches, they tend now to be concentrated in bureaucratic departments of the state. The Gypsies may have access to these resources in the name of development and education if they are willing to adapt their degraded image to the idiom of bureaucratic allocation (see Flett, in this volume). In the United States (Sutherland, 1975) and in Sweden[3] the Gypsies have successfully accommodated to welcome welfare provisions and have exploited suggestions for training programmes – although not necessarily in the manner or with the effect that Gorgios intended.

An American newspaper item is indicative:

While many of the nation's women seek to break away from the housework role, 10 young gypsy women here are learning to use sewing machines and dress patterns. And some are learning to read as they sew.

Many of the women can't read or write. 'For 2000 years gypsies have avoided education because of traditional mistrust of outsiders', said N, a gypsy leader who counsels and arbitrates disputes among his people. There are about 500 gypsies in the area. 'Their society is closed and the women have a role of wife and mother and that's it,' said Sue, a sewing instructor. 'To let the young girls out to go to class is a real breakthrough.'

The $17,000 program, financed by the federal Comprehensive Employment Training Act, is administered by a federal-city agency called Work Experience of Adults. Most of the women are teenagers or young adults. They attend classes 30 hours a week and are paid $2.30 an hour to participate in the sewing classes. 'Those girls aren't doing it for the money,' N said, 'it's for the education.'   (Kansas City Times, 20 October 1976.)

Paradoxically, Gypsies have thrived both on paternalist–liberal efforts to absorb them and on the host society's craving for exotic differentiation. Non-Gypsy observers have failed to understand that Gypsies have an alternative and sometimes contradictory model of their own actions. And they cannot, by definition, see Gypsies at all in situations where Gypsy ethnicity is either neutralised or invisible. Gorgio confusion has been Gypsy survival.

# 2

*This paper reviews the history of Jewish immigration into Britain and demonstrates that Jews too use their minority group status as an economic resource. They have consistently adapted their cultural heritage to the opportunities and constraints of the host economy. Their survival as a people and an ethnic group has long depended on their being able to do so. But Jewish work and occupational choices have not, as in the case of the Gypsies (above, in this volume), been governed by the need to keep clear of the 'formal' sector. Their effort is instead to move into areas of work – whether 'formal' or 'informal' – in which they can maintain the individual autonomy and cultural integrity required by Jewish tradition and yet compete for status and success in the majority society. The following analysis accounts in these terms for the fact that, in Britain at least, the favourite 'Jewish occupations' are those of doctor, lawyer, chartered accountant – and taxi-driver.*

# Exclusion and Opportunity

## Traditions of work amongst British Jews

Barry Kosmin

The work orientation and behaviour of any social group reflects both the experience, goals and values of that group, and the constraints and opportunities of a particular setting. Jewish ethnicity as a dependent variable in work situations in Britain can be considered in two parts. First, the specific cultural traits which can be generalised for the group and which distinguish its members from the majority of the host population. This distinctive social philosophy, the Jewish *Weltanschaung*, may be termed *the expressive factor*. Second, the using of this common culture as a focus for solidarity and identity in actual social situations. This may be termed *the utility factor*.

We are concerned with both aspects of ethnicity in relation to occupation and economic activity among British Jews: their philosophical and cultural inheritance, and their use of ethnicity as a tool or resource (cf. Wallman, 1974). We are dealing with a concept that is time, area and situation specific, and the two aspects of the concept are themselves differently affected by the immediate environment. This paper, therefore, reviews those aspects of Jewish culture most directly relevant to the organisation of work, and considers how and why they have been adapted to the changing British experience. The case is illustrated by the reference to the 'Jewish professions': medicine, law, accountancy and taxi-driving.

## Traditions and History

Jewish attitudes towards occupations and economic life have been formed over a long period, but the present cultural inheritance of British Jews has evolved from three main sources. The first is the body of religious and philosophical literature embodied in the Talmud and Torah. The second is the distinctive Jewish culture which arose in central and eastern Europe as a result of oppression and discrimination there. This experience formed the background to perceptions and attitudes of Jewish immigrants into Britain from the eighteenth to the twentieth centuries. The third influence has been the environment in Britain: its economy, its social structure and the general attitude towards immigrant and minority group participation in society.

In Biblical times the Jewish people in ancient Israel formed a pastoral and agricultural society and their religious life was largely built around harvest festivals. Only after the expulsion of the Jews from their homeland by the Romans were they to find themselves primarily in an urban environment. Thus Talmudic literature from the Roman period shows an awareness of the problems of wage-labour and commercial life. This is especially evident in the field of industrial relations where there are detailed discussions of the rights and relationships of employers and employees. Such a body of literature was influential because it was expected that all Jewish males should learn and know it. This learning was not just for an élite. The ethical foundation of the whole society was open to the masses for their information and use. In later years, concentration on Torah learning grew and literacy was expected even of unskilled workers and labourers. This in turn affected the attitude towards work: study was prescribed as a respite from ordinary daily labour:

> An excellent thing is the study of the Torah combined with some wordly occupation, for the labour demanded by them both makes sin to be forgotten. All study of the Torah without work must in the end be futile and become a cause of sin   (Mishnah, Tractate, *Aboth*, ii, 2).

Home study thus became the accepted form of personal relaxation. This precluded other forms of leisure activity and, more important to the present arguments, enhanced the value of mental stimulation and intellectualism which were to affect the Jewish approach to many other aspects of life.

One can see in Torah learning and in open access to it an early and sophisticated attempt to create social conformity by means of a common educational curriculum and process. Its influence was persuasive for hundreds of years. Until the rise of secular education and the mass media, it had no real competitor for the minds of the Jewish people. Perhaps as a result, Jewish attitudes towards many moral and social matters are surprisingly uniform throughout the world – despite the diversity of environments of the various diaspora communities.

The attitude towards work and earthly riches of the Talmud was quite clear. 'Great is work for it honours the workman' (Babylonian Talmud, Tractate, *Nedorim*, f. 49b) is the theme, and the Rabbinic dictum was 'Love Work' (*Aboth*, 1.10). Austerity and hedonism were both censured as harmful and no virtue was attached to poverty. 'Where there is no meal, there is no Torah' (*Aboth*, iii. 21). It was assumed that God wanted his creatures to be happy so that it was sinful deliberately to shun physical happiness and material well-being. The definition of a rich man was 'He who derives pleasure from his wealth' (Babylonian Talmud, Tractate, *Shabbat*, f. 25b). In its basic approach, therefore, Judaism was an unworried and optimistic religion with little emphasis on sin and damnation.

The Jewish cultural tradition can be said to have entailed an early variant of the 'protestant' work ethic. It attached merit to the work performed and to the material rewards it produced. It also rejected the pursuit of leisure and the idea that the function of work is to provide the means with which to increase and enjoy leisure time.

In eastern Europe until the twentieth century the Jewish experience was a segregated but autonomous existence. Restrictions on Jewish land ownership and other primary production and consumption activities confined the Jewish population to narrow range of service and commercial occupations, and to residence in market towns and the small cities. In such *shtetl* communities, life was oriented towards the rigorous fulfilment of the commandments as reported in the Torah and expounded in the Talmud.

This Yiddish-speaking society maintained its allegiance to the late-classical attitudes regarding work and reward. The good things of the world continued to be recognised as good in themselves; enjoyment of them was seen as both a right and a duty. A common toast was *gezunt un parnaseh*, 'health and livelihood'. Idleness came to be seen as a sin and loafers were scorned. Though the sabbath day of rest was central to the culture, work revolved around it and was equally highly valued.

It was in this environment that new attitudes of a non-religious nature arose. Centuries of victimisation, discrimination and relative powerlessness led to an innovative style and the development of a supportive sub-culture which devalued the dominant ethic – in this case the religion and life-style of the Slav peasants and aristocracy. This Jewish deviance became an integral facet of ghetto sub-culture. One effect was that sobriety, learning, deferred gratification and other bourgeois qualities became more valued; but, on the other hand, activities which are best described by the urban slang term 'hustling' were enhanced. Hustling became popular since it emphasises the use of guile and persuasion in inter-personal relations as a means of minimising personal advantage in financial and status terms. Like some contemporary black Americans, these Jews saw themselves at war with wider society. Economic activity was seen by many as a suitable sphere of opposition or guerilla warfare against the gentile oppressors. This often took the form of evading the state's restrictions and taxes and manipulating its venal officials. One outcome of this was a reinforcement of the trend whereby a Jew who used his head (*kop*) now had a higher status than one who used his hands: the latter did not resist but rather served the enemy.

As a result of this rejection of the norms and values of the dominant society, Jewish communities developed a more democratic and meritocratic ethos. They began to emphasise financial success as the key to social status and respect. Money became good and important. Rewards and gifts took the form of money and rabbis imposed punishment with fines. Manual labour became more closely associated with ignorant and brutal peasants and was increasingly rejected. One indication of the prevalance of this attitude was the revolutionary Zionist commitment to the dignity of manual labour. The emphasis put on a Jewish labour policy in their settlements evolved directly from their rejection of and antagonism to *shtetl* life and values.

Money, however, was scarce in Tsarist Russia and most business establishments had to be joint enterprises, partnerships or operations on borrowed funds. The family was essentially of a nuclear type but reciprocal ties with kin, particularly those of a direct economic nature, were encouraged since this enhanced the status or *yikhus* of the patron or senior partner. As in most pre-industrial societies, economic responsibility was a matter of family membership rather than sex or age, and wives and children were expected to aid in the business. It was also acceptable for a woman to work to support her husband if he was a scholar. The desire to 'make it' led people to try any activity or occupation. Such a man was known as a *Luftmensch*, 'a man of air' – a person who lived on hope and dreams. Moreover, in this inhospitable economic environment many men had to have more than one occupation in order to make a living. The same man might double, for example, as carpenter and coachman. The general pattern is reflected in the expression that 'the best cobbler of all the tailors is Yankel the baker'.

## Immigrants to Britain

The cultural baggage of the majority of Jewish immigrants into Britain after 1850 included these various inclinations and aptitudes, technical knowledge and skills. Its importance in this discussion stems from the fact that these immigrants were the ancestors of more than two-thirds of present-day British Jewry, and that they, like most immigrants, clung tenaciously to their cultural heritage, particularly to the religious element, and attempted to transmit it to future generations. Compared to many immigrants, however, they were extraordinarily adaptable. They came from a pre-capitalist agricultural society into the strange environment of urban and industrial Britain, but brought with them energetic habits of work and an orientation to the future which was almost universally positive.

In effect, they were willing to throw off their past and all ties with their homeland except family ones. This capacity for adaptation was crucial. Though they undoubtedly appreciated the freedom from oppression and the increased opportunity for economic betterment which Britain offered, these poverty-stricken Jewish immigrants were not free to choose their occupations without regard to constraints of the current labour market, or of their own lack of capital resources and facility in the English language. Moreover, they did not enter a virgin territory. There was already a small resident Jewish community with an established niche in British society and the British economy, and there were as a result established attitudes and stereotypes among the indigenous inhabitants of jobs and work appropriate to Jews. This situation can be better understood against an outline of the occupational history of the Jews in Britain.

The wave pattern of Jewish immigration into Britain since the Resettlement in 1653 has gradually transformed the Jewish occupational experience from that of impoverished aliens in marginal jobs, which could be classed as 'immigrant occupations' rather than 'Jewish occupations', into higher status positions. The sole exceptions to this trend were the earliest seventeenth-century immigrants from Holland who entered originally as merchants or financiers. In terms of status these would not fall into the 'immigrant' class of peripheral jobs, but their occupations follow the immigrant pattern in the way they made use of skills acquired in their old environment. The Jews in Holland had had a traditional association with finance and trade. Their success in Britain depended on this expertise and on their maintaining contacts with and access to European markets.

During the eighteenth century, as a result of expulsions of Jewish populations and other political upheavals in Germany and eastern Europe, a larger-scale immigration of Jews from these areas began. At about the same time there was a small drift of Jews from Mediterranean countries seeking their fortunes in London. Many of these immigrants depended on the charity of their wealthy predecessors. Some scratched a living selling old clothes or peddling small goods such as spices and slippers – all occupations which required neither capital nor skill.

In the late eighteenth century, Jewish pedlars and tinkers began to move out of London and to sell their goods and services up and down the country. Of those who stayed in London, some rose in status from hawkers to stallholders. Any progression to shop-owning was closed to them by virtue of the fact that they were, until 1831, denied the necessary qualification of Freedom of the City of London. This barrier had two consequences for the pattern of Jewish activity: newcomers unable to find jobs in London were forced to seek them in the provinces; and, within London, Jews made an attempt to widen their occupational options. The Jewish charities associated with the Neve Zedek Orphan Asylum and the Great Synagogue tried to teach poorer Jews a trade, establishing apprenticeships in shoemaking, tailoring, pencil-making and glass-cutting. Those who had engraving skills turned their hands to watch- and jewellery-making.

In the first half of the nineteenth century there was another influx from Holland, this time predominantly of poor urban Jews who had been involved in the tobacco and entertainment industries. The latter applied their skills to setting up pleasure gardens and public houses while the influence of Dutch Jews in tobacco manufacture in London became so great that it soon had the reputation of being a Jewish trade. Those who were not absorbed into legitimate activities turned to the 'informal' economy, including crime: the Jewish element in London's criminal sub-culture was epitomised by the character Fagin in Dickens' *Oliver Twist*.

The immigrants of the period 1881–1914 came in as a mass migration of some 200,000 persons. In such numbers they overwhelmed the existing community which, in 1880, totalled around 70,000. These newcomers fleeing the Tsarist pogroms were alien in outlook and manner to the resident community. The latter had become anglicised and was beginning to enter the respectable middle class, progressing through the economy into the manufacturing sector. Moreover, there were few existing social or family ties between the newcomers and British Jewry. The resident community was unable and often unwilling to absorb the new arrivals into existing commercial firms, nor was there a large number of available places for them in the informal economy. Irish immigrants had now taken over jobs such as peddling and slop-selling, done earlier by Jews. In addition, existing industries such as agriculture, mining, textile manufacture, iron and steel, transport and construction, and bureaucratic service occupations already had established labour forces with traditional recruitment practices. Jewish immigrants to London, for instance, stood no chance of being employed at the docks or in the London produce markets: the indigenous labour force was violently hostile to foreign competitors.

Unable to find work in basic or traditional industries, the new immigrants had to seek openings in areas which did not compete with native workmen. These they found in producing consumer or luxury goods. Such peripheral consumer-oriented industries were arising as a result of higher living standards in Britain and the growing spending power of the masses. The only existing Jewish industrial niche capable of absorbing labour in this sphere was the seventy-six Jewish East End tobacco factories, mainly producing cigars. Openings here were rapidly filled since there were good wages and strong unions. The new fashion in ostrich feathers supported an industry able to absorb limited numbers of willing workers, but it was clothing which became the main immigrant niche.

The upward progression of Anglo-Jewry in the clothing industry had taken many of the descendants of eighteenth-century immigrants from peddling to market-stall owning and on to ownership of outfitting shops. Clothing merchants such as Montagu Burton were now anxious to move into the manufacture, through mass production, of ready-made clothing such as suits, overcoats and caps, and saw an opportunity for this in the surplus labour of their co-religionists. The advantage of this particular labour pool was that it could be more easily organised to accept the seasonal nature of the work, long hours, job fragmentation, new processes and poor working conditions. The results were the sweat shops of the needle trades and the formation of a Jewish industrial proletariat in the overcrowded London slums of Whitechapel and Stepney, and in similar areas such as Cheetham in Manchester or the Leylands in Leeds. This situation renewed the association between Jews and the 'rag' or *Schmutter* trade. Similar patterns of motivation and development occurred in the furniture trade of Shoreditch and in the footwear industry. In the boot and shoe trade 'skilled Jewish home lasters and finishers took unskilled "greeners" as assistant and made of their homes . . . workshops' (Gartner, 1973).

In London in 1901, approximately 40 per cent of male Jewish

immigrants of Russian and Polish origin were employed as tailors, about 12 per cent were in footwear and 10 per cent in furniture. Surveys done between 1895 and 1908 on 9000 recent immigrants showed that, even before emigration, 29 per cent had been making clothes, 9 per cent had worked in boot and shoe trades, and 7 per cent had been carpenters, suggesting a certain amount of continuity of occupation from their original homeland. It was, therefore, for both economic and social reasons that Jewish immigrants settled in areas of established Jewish communities, predominantly in the cities of London, Manchester, Leeds and Glasgow, where with few financial resources of their own they applied the skills they knew from their home countries, or took jobs in workshops already established by Jews.

New immigrants facing new customs, a new language and a certain amount of hostility from the local population, usually look to their fellows for assistance. The denial of access to other job opportunities was not the only incentive to work for a Jewish employer. The east European Jews' distrust of gentiles was such that they automatically turned to their co-religionists for aid and comfort. Moreover, a Jewish employer was more likely to be able to communicate with them and was usually more amenable to accommodating the sabbath, religious festivals and food taboos.

The gap between immigrant and indigenous workers and the segregation of Jews at work was very evident at the time. Immigrants established trade unions separately from the English workers. There were twenty-two Jewish trade unions in Edwardian London, both because of the social and cultural gulf between Jewish and English workers and the separateness of the Jewish sectors in the main immigrant trades of garment and boot and shoe making.

## Aspirations

The lack of working interaction with the locals was not the only barrier. The Jewish workers had more bourgeois cultural aspirations and in their leisure activities tended to shun the 'pubs'. Neither did the majority of Jews share a conception of themselves as permanent members of the working class. Thus Jewish workers' horizons and strategies were different: the greatest ambition of most of them was to move from the status of employee to that of self-employed worker or employer. This feature is present in all the types of work to which Jews gravitated from their first arrival in Britain as well as in their occupations before migration. It was reinforced by experience of the sweat shops of London's East End which were the scandal of late-Victorian Britain. The folk memory of this episode undoubtedly had far-reaching effects on the Jewish occupational and economic profile: it fostered a general distrust of industrial labour and its associated hierarchies, and a desire for independent economic activity.

But while the most cherished ambition of the immigrant generation was to save their children from their own predicament, movement out of the clothing and associated trades was difficult. Economic pressures were such that young people, like their parents, had to take jobs where they could find them in the established Jewish community, using skills which they already knew or which they could easily learn. Those members of the anglicised Jewish establishment who took an interest in the immigrant young through youth clubs and settlements tended to propel their charges towards developing higher skills in a familiar trade. Jewish boys and girls were therefore encouraged to take up apprenticeships in all areas of garment manufacture. As a result, in the first decade of the twentieth century, most Jewish girls in east London were employed as tailoresses, buttonhole makers, milliners and dressmakers, while boys were predominantly tailors, cap makers and furriers.

As in the late eighteenth century, the community made another attempt to diversify the work options open to the new second generation of British Jews. It encouraged them to use the school system to achieve higher literacy and numeracy standards than their parents. This led to numbers of boys becoming clerks, printers, shop assistants and warehousemen. While the aim was to extricate them from the workshop industries, the results were slower than many had hoped. In the early 1930s it was estimated that there were still 40,000 Jewish workers in the clothing industry; Jewish men supplied half of all male clothing workers nationally. The more numerous female Jewish workers only composed a sixth of the industry's national female workforce, yet they accounted for half of all economically active Jewesses. In the same period the London furniture industry was still estimated to employ 6–8000 Jewish workers.

The sweat-shop experience increased the Jewish bias towards self-employment. It introduced qualitative as well as economic reasons for seeking independent status. At the first opportunity, the London Jewish worker would move over to running a home workshop, doing occasional contract work for a large manufacturer. In the provinces, particularly in Leeds where the clothing industry was on a larger scale, it was more difficult to escape the factory. It often surprised observers to find that among Jews the greatest ambition was not to earn higher wages, but to become a master. What these observers overlooked was the question of autonomy. A worker cannot control his working environment. He has the very real problem that he earns only as long as he is employed.

The home tailors operated at the lower end of the market and, despite their linkage to the formal manufacturing sector, in their actual mode of operation they could better be defined as being part of the informal sector. This does not mean that they were only marginally productive: they had to be economically efficient and profit-making even to survive. Though undercapitalised, small in scale and limited in technology, they provided a basic service for a large, though poor, section of the community (cf. Santos, in this volume). Home tailoring offered the immigrant the advantages of easy family ownership and, since the trade was both erratic and labour-intensive, the opportunity to draw on this pool of resident family labour when, and only when, required. Such family work teams depended on methods and skills acquired and accepted only outside a formally regulated system and they provided the flexibility and independence the immigrant with his *luftmensch* perspective often required. The work was also remarkably well-suited to the back streets of a great port and capital city like London. There was room for the various services of a tailor who owned a sewing machine as well as for the carpenters, masons, cobblers and barbers operating in the same essentially unregulated market.

The tendency to gravitate towards the informal sector can be explained in terms of the opportunities for income maximisation and for the real advancement it was thought to provide. The immigrant could maintain the fiction that he was a 'businessman' and could take hope from the example always available of some entrepreneur who had 'made it'. The attraction of the 'business world' to the lively adventurous immigrant was the freedom and challenge it offered. Any attendant personal disadvantages were alleviated by the Jewish tradition of self-ridicule. Dignity was only for the old. A certain 'thickening of the skin' stood them in good stead in new situations where they had to overcome their heavy accents and poor command of English. Equally, the freedom of the informal economy permitted the Jew to avoid 'others' and to keep social distance without serious cost. It allowed a choice of whom one wished to meet and deal with: really aggressive and bitter xenophobes or anti-semites could be more easily avoided than in a spatially and externally controlled environment. In a factory, for example, an individual foreman or manager could make life very miserable for his victim.

The inter-war generation was more ambitious and had more contact with general society. They shrank from the humiliations they saw their parents suffer in the workshops and in petty trade, and they began to move towards the separation of residence and work. They also began to seek out other sources of employment and, given a choice, were attracted only by the larger family business and 'clean trades' well removed from peddling and *Schmutters*. They tended towards wholesale establishments, light industry, services and the professions. Yet, despite their preference for change and the upward occupational mobility achieved, Jewish attitudes towards work were very slow to throw off the imprint of the informal sector.


## Discrimination

Jewish socio-economic progress in Britain in the inter-war years was slowed not only by the poor economic climate, but also owing to the import into Britain of alien German ideas. The anti-semitic atmosphere of the Nazi era made Jews and gentiles throughout the world very Jew-conscious, and made fashionable not only 'scientific' racism but also crude Jew-baiting. The Jewish population became defensive in all spheres of activity. The small trader was the dominant Jewish image of these years. New Jewish entrants to retail distribution tended to adopt new methods such as cut prices which in turn led to claims of unfair competition and stirred up anti-semitic feelings among the shopkeeping class. In response, a Trades' Advisory Council was established in 1938 with the principal aim of avoiding further friction and misunderstanding in the economic field. This development was a recognition of the fact that the good name of Jewry in the business world was a major concern of the whole minority community.

At the end of the Second World War, this antipathy to the Jew as small trader as well as worker forced many Jews to enter a new or better status career after demobilisation. Some took an alternative escape into new unfettered fields, especially those in which the clear distinction between manufacturer, wholesaler and retailer were not well established. A further incentive to such change was the destruction by bombing of Jewish inner-city neighbourhoods. This caused as much dislocation of Jewish family businesses as did the wartime loss of personnel to the armed forces.

The post-war years provided a much more favourable atmosphere for Jewish ambitions. There was rapid economic growth, and a climate of tolerance and goodwill which was itself a reaction to the Nazi holocaust. In the industrial sphere, the introduction of the five-day week widened the occupational opportunities for the Orthodox by making their sabbath a non-work day across the country. The Jewish economic and occupational profile was, however, still dominated by an uneven geographical distribution. British Jews have remained a highly urban population concentrated in a few large cities. Though they constitute less than 1 per cent of the total population nationally, they form 3 per cent of the population of London, where two-thirds of them live, and slightly more than 3 per cent in Manchester, numerically the second largest concentration.

Although there has been a significant movement towards more integration at work since 1945, this does not deny concentration in certain spheres. (Contrary to popular expectation, however, surveys of economically active Jews have found the number in finance and distributive trades not much different to the national pattern.) It is probable that Jewish employers and Jewish-owned businesses are more restricted to specific industries than are Jewish employees and salaried staff. Among 116 employees interviewed in the north-west London suburb of Edgware, 56 per cent were found to have Jewish employers. Forty of these said it was purely due to chance, eighteen explained it in terms of the number of Jews in their trade and only sixteen admitted it was their preference (Krausz, 1969).

## Specialisation

Jewish businesses are still concentrated in clothing, footwear, timber and furniture, leather and furs. German–Jewish immigrants provide two-thirds of the last-mentioned firms. After the centre of this Jewish speciality was destroyed along with the Jewish community in its traditional home of Leipzig, the world centre for the dyeing, dressing and manufacture of furs moved to London in the late 1930s. In 1945 it was estimated, on the basis of examination of trade directories, that Jews participated in only 24 per cent of the 1040 trades practised in Manchester, 13 per cent of Liverpool's and 8 per cent of Glasgow's. Jewish firms were then still most prominent in textiles, drapery and fashion trades, and it was claimed they owned one-seventh of all furniture manufacturing firms (Barou, 1945). Another popular field which has potentially glamorous contacts with entertainment is the radio, television, hi-fi and electrical industry. Jewish over-representation in the Royal Air Force in both world wars and the fact that electronics was a new growth industry together account for much of this involvement. In London, Jewish firms dominate Tottenham Court Road as much as they do the 'gown' district of Great Portland Street or the market stalls of Petticoat Lane. Despite the growth in the number of manufacturers, the highest proportion of Jewish businesses are today found in wholesaling. Under pressure from multiples, department stores and supermarkets, the independent retailer is a vanishing species and, in the Jewish case, the reluctance of the younger generation to continue in any but the larger firms has quickened the process.

Despite such trends, one can still discern a movement of Jews to occupations in which the intelligent use of small capital makes rapid improvement possible. The most obvious sphere has been that of new or expanding services such as estate and employment agencies, laundromats, hairdressing and beauty parlours, betting shops and small property deals. If a new businessman's personal and family resources were not sufficient to set up a new venture, he had the possibility of calling on communal aid. In the years 1951–5, for example, the loan department of the Jewish Board of Guardians granted 675 interest-free loans to enable small businessmen, handicapped by lack of capital, to carry on or develop businesses in cases where financial help could not be obtained from other sources. Many of these people had trouble with traditional financial institutions because of their progressive approach, new innovations and methods. It is they who have never really lost the outlook of the informal economy, the eye for opportunities and the lack of respect for traditional roles or practices.

The taking up of certain occupations in recent years seems always to have been stimulated by the prospect of early or immediate independence. Hairdressing was very popular for both boys and girls because it offered a short three-year apprenticeship as well as high wages and tips during training. The desire to be self-employed may initially have reflected the need of the orthodox majority to arrange their working hours around their religious observance. Yet, despite a marked weakening in traditional religious observances, the preference for self-employment has remained. In 1945 it was estimated that 15–20 per cent of Jewish males in Britain were self-employed – a rate three times that obtaining nationally (Barou, 1945). Recent surveys have found even higher proportions: 44 per cent in Sheffield and 67 per cent in Edgware worked on their own account, and in working-class Hackney the rate of 21 per cent of working males was still three times the local proportion (Kosmin and Grizzard, 1975).

In Edgware, when the employee minority were asked if they wished to become self-employed, 38 per cent answered in the affirmative. It is interesting that only eight of the forty-four *pro-*self-employment employees wished to change their status in order to earn more: twenty-six wanted the independence it offered and ten the increased social status it might give them. While the pre-war desire had been to avoid potentially discriminating organisations (as Macrae, in this volume), the present tendency appears to reflect instead a disposition towards freedom and lack of external controls. This aspiration is increasingly fulfilled in white-collar work in small companies, in professional practice, or as an independent entrepreneur.

## Independence and Support

These correlations must not, however, be taken too literally. The concept of independence incorporates both increased earnings and independent status. As in the informal economy, the ability to seek work as and when one requires it can produce a maximum income and yet avoid arbitrary constraints such as enforced retirement at sixty-five. Moreover, since extra income makes it unnecessary for a man's wife to go to work, it also increases his status indirectly. All post-war surveys of Jewish populations have shown both above average male economic activity beyond the normal retirement age and below average female workforce participation. In the latter case, the gap has now narrowed relative to 1951, when Jewish female economic activity was only 11 per cent compared to 34 per cent nationally. The reason for this narrowing is probably upward social mobility: in Sheffield, it was found that working wives were more likely to be married to professionals than to businessmen and themselves to have high status careers. The cause of greater female economic activity is therefore career orientation and ambition rather than economic necessity (Kosmin, Bauer and Grizzard, 1976).

The prime contemporary exponent of the non-working wife is the self-employed Jewish businessman of lower middle- or working-class origin. The enhanced social status associated in such circles with the non-working wife reflects more than the traditional emphasis on family responsibility. It was never a question of a woman's place being in the home or, more particularly, the kitchen – even in the time of the *shtetl* this was just not the case. But the recent phenomenon appears also to be linked to the continual striving for middle-class standards. Appearance is all-important, and the working wife is a reminder of sweat shops and East End origins, and low socio-economic status. In his working life the independent businessman seeks a situation in which the harder he works the more he earns; income for conspicuous consumption often appears to be his goal. The price the new 'punter' or 'operator' pays for his independent status is a lack of security, but this does not appear to be a problem. He is quite willing to endure high–low cycles and can move back and forth between semi-detached homes and mansions without losing his aplomb. Temporary changes of fortune need not worry him since, in the past especially, he could often expect material and psychological support from his kin network and friends. It must be remembered that among many Jews even today, a marriage links more than just the couple; it involves also the families of the two spouses. Such enlarged resource networks allow access to capital. In place of the formal security and assets usually required, the creditor has instead the sanction of potential threat to the intangible good name of the family which may be smeared if a debt is not honoured (cf. Leyton, 1965; Wallman, 1974; see also Herman, in this volume).

Friends are another support group. Like relatives, they are often business partners; few Jews enter economic sectors in which they do not already know someone working. These friendships (and sometimes rivalries) are usually of long standing for local Jewish communities are small face-to-face societies. Peers, especially from the pre-war East End, have probably attended the same school or youth clubs together, played in the same football team, dated each others' sisters or cousins. The wartime generation have even served together in the armed forces. The element of sociability in working situations means that favours are frequent, even between apparent business competitors. As a result, any businessman who finds himself in difficulties of any kind is likely to know someone who knows someone who can help him. Communal solidarity and humanitarian concern are both motives for giving assistance in such cases. This whole approach is reinforced by the reluctance of such people to divide their working and social lives, or even to have set periods for work and leisure. Their sense of personal identity – indeed their whole life – is involved in business and work.

## The Integration of Work

These traditional practices and attitudes have had to be adapted or reluctantly dispensed with in recent years. Where post-war businesses have expanded into regional or national chains, or have become public companies, the owners have had to go beyond their in-group for financing, marketing and associated services. This has led to new forms of integration with non-Jewish society since it is at this stage that gentile business partners and associates enter the scene. Many large Jewish-owned concerns now have socially desirable gentile directors or managers who are there to provide the 'image' or even 'a touch of class' as often as an injection of enterprise, skill or capital.

This strategy is the end product of a long process of acculturation to British norms and another example of the adaptability of British Jews. Until this point the dominant trait of the successful Jewish entrepreneur has been a great belief in himself, his ideas and his abilities, and in the service he is performing. Moreover, he usually shows, by British standards, a surprising lack of status concern at work. He has a holistic approach to the running of the business, believes in a do-it-yourself policy, and is quite prepared to *Schlap* – that is, to do physical work – if a job needs to be done. Application of these tenets can be seen in the management training at Marks & Spencer's: every candidate, of whatever social or kinship status in relation to the firm, starts at the bottom of the hierarchy – unloading vans. The Jewish businessman, typically, has no patience with the fragmentation of roles, closed-shop practices, demarcation disputes and people who are too proud to do ordinary work. These attitudes show a distrust of specialisation and expertise and an impatience with hierarchies. They also entail an empathy for employees, a tendency to be on mutual first-name terms with them and an appreciation of worker initiatives and involvement. The Jewish preference for seeing the whole field of operation may be linked to a philosophical belief in free will and man's domination and comprehension of work. There is an evident desire for autonomy and a willingness to take on the burdens of personal responsibility which reflect an essentially optimistic and positive outlook. A favourite Hebrew and Israeli expression in the face of an apparently overwhelming problem is *hiyé-tov*: 'it will be good – it will come right'.

In Britain and the United States, Jews have been proportionately under-represented in large corporations and state bureaucracies. This is no longer due to discrimination and a fear of hierarchies, but involves also a rejection of the fragmentation of work roles. It is a realisation that the techniques of 'scientific management' used by the large corporations have increased the splitting and specialisation of work and have diminished individual comprehension of the whole field of operation. Jews prefer jobs in which they can comprehend and control the whole process and in which an individual controls his environment and is the central actor: where there is a chance for *Yikhus* or personal standing, and one can be a *Mensch* – a real person and not a caricature, number or cog in a wheel. As a result, they are over-represented in careers where these possibilities are open – in medicine, law, entrepreneurship, academia, the arts, research and theoretical science. The traditional dislike for a faceless bureaucracy, the need to know who one is dealing with and the desire for social interaction in the working environment are all evident.

According to a recent survey there is a fundamental difference in the approach to occupations and work between Jews and the English middle class. In their own lives the latter maintain a certain distance from the world of work and 'the career'. Unlike their American and European counterparts, the English do not abolish the distinction between work and leisure but neither do they allow their work time to invade their home and family life. Jews in Britain follow a pattern closer to that of the American and German middle classes (Kumar, 1976). Jews are more willing to invest time and emotion in work and see it as an extension of themselves. They are also less interested in English middle-class leisure activities such as playing sport, gardening or 'doing up the house'. If a contrast is drawn between the leisure orientation of the English middle class and their American counterparts who spend off hours catching up on their work or studying for further professional qualifications, British Jews follow the American pattern. (This may be the basis of their success in America.) The tradition of spare-time Torah learning now legitimises professional study. By training and outlook, Jews have therefore become good students with enquiring minds, but by preference they are intellectual generalists. The converse of this is that they are seldom specialists or 'good company men', nor do they excel as apolitical bureaucrats who must work within a narrow brief.

## Ethnicity, Change and Achievement

After the externally enhanced solidarity of the 1930s and wartime years, there is now evidence of incipient class differentiation occurring among British Jews. This evidence is, however, complicated by the fact that most Jews of whatever socio-economic background see themselves as middle class and subscribe to supposedly middle-class norms and values. On the other hand, Jews in Edgware (London) resisted the idea that wealth should be a criterion of high status and attached little importance to occupation as a determinant of status. In place of these criteria, Edgware Jews suggested that character, behaviour, education and leadership should be the ideal determinants (Krausz, 1969).

That these ideas are similar to those held traditionally in eastern European Jewish communities indicates the tenacity of the culture. And since most of these virtues are linked to minority status and can be seen as necessary for maintaining the integrity and the good name of the community, they can be offered as evidence of ethnicity. This may explain why individual status is increasingly based on the gentile accolade, – consider the delight of those whom the Queen has honoured with knighthoods, peerages and medals. Once in positions of power and influence such people can, if they maintain their group solidarity, become 'gatekeepers', admitting other Jews into the corridors of power and privilege. Just as the position and reputation of 'core ethnics' in the occupational sphere affects the chances and the aspirations of their fellows (cf. Brooks and Singh, in this volume; see also Stymeist, 1975).

The post-war years have seen the Jewish quest for middle-class acceptance come to fruition. The gradual movement of Jews from the immigrant fringes to a position of integration in the centre of society has come to rest with the large-scale entry of Jews into the professional ranks. Over the whole country in 1961, 10 per cent of the male Jewish working population was found to be in professions, and certain area studies such as Edgware (1963) and Sheffield (1975) have found proportions of 16 and 29 per cent respectively.

This has come about primarily as a result of the traditional respect for learning being re-directed towards secular education, and in a climate of tolerance which has allowed Jews to contribute more fully to the society in which they live. Modern technological society increasingly values higher education and has produced a labour market which demands high educational qualifications. Jews have been especially quick to recognise that education and formal qualifications are the secret of occupational success and social mobility in the twentieth century. The shading of class divisions achieved by individual Jews constitutes an important Jewish contribution to British occupational life. They have been pacesetters in the opening up of the professions – traditionally an area of inherited privilege and conservative social outlook – to a new meritocracy. The post-war expansion of the professions coincided with the Jewish community's post-war readiness to exploit any new opportunities (cf. Herman, in this volume).

With a background of respect for learning and desire for self-improvement, Jews have entered this new competition of 'worth not birth' on a better than equal footing with the English middle and working classes. New national policies of free and open access to education through formal examinations enable Jews to use their traditions of work to compete in the professional market. While they were, in the past, prepared to make economic sacrifices to send their children to grammar or private schools and universities and may have even made this a measure of their own financial achievements, little headway could be made in the professions as long as they were discriminated against, either positively or negatively. It has taken over 100 years since the first Jewish university graduate in 1836, the first Jewish barrister in 1843, for Jews to enter the professions in large numbers. What has been required and, to a large extent, achieved, is not just the lifting of quotas in educational institutions such as medical schools, but also the acceptance by the education authorities and fellow students of different customs and beliefs. These range from the recognition of peculiar needs in school assembly, meals and religion classes, to allowing non-attendance on festivals and special arrangements for examinations set on these days. All of these were once a very real barrier to the professional advancement of Orthodox Jews.

The post-war commitment to national 'equal opportunity' and meritocracy has, coupled with the improved economic standing of Jews, favoured the general Jewish ideal of self-improvement. The results were first seen in university attendance. In the 1950s, the proportion of Jewish students at universities was four times greater than that of the population as a whole, though it is unlikely that this gross over-representation survived the general university expansion of the 1960s.

Specific professional and vocational ambitions are still typical. In 1954, it was found that 46 per cent of Jewish males taking up university places did so with the intention of adopting careers in medicine, dentistry, law and accountancy – the so-called 'Jewish professions'. These are all prestigious jobs, with possibilities of high income without sacrificing independence in the establishment of small private practices. The popular career of pharmacist offers the dual advantages of being a professional *and* a businessman. Tradition is evident still in this choice of professions: in those historical periods in which Jews were free to take up high positions in European and Islamic courts, they functioned as physicians, court advisers and financiers, posts which more or less correspond to today's doctors, lawyers and accountants. Possibly the same status and financial motives prevailed then as in modern times. There have been practical considerations too. Until recently, professions in Britain had two kinds of entry barriers: those such as architecture, pharmacy, medicine and dentistry, for which a university degree had long been necessary; and those which, until the late 1960s, one could enter with a school certificate or five ordinary level passes in G.C.E., serving articles of apprenticeship on a small stipend for five years. The far longer period of economic support necessary for university training precluded poorer families sending their children into professions requiring it, however much they may have aspired to do so.

## Doctors

The archetypal aspiration of the Jewish parent, the 'my son the doctor' syndrome, can be traced to the high status and mystique of the medical profession as much as the career and financial advantages it offers. Ordinary people are more aware of the work of a doctor than, for instance, an architect, and are of the opinion that a doctor can never be out of work. Medicine attracted the most promising of the upwardly mobile Jews for many years since it epitomised the Jewish theory of human capital. A medical qualification was considered a self-evident guarantee of the ability to earn a living anywhere in the world – an ability which was a primary attraction for an insecure people. This does not, however, detract from the sense of idealism and the humanitarian outlook which motivates most Jewish medical students; nor from the fact that medicine is a totally absorbing career which can dominate one's life and so has much appeal to the Jewish mind. There are material and social benefits to be gained from engaging in worthwhile and· respected work, and it is undoubtedly hard for the prejudiced to deny skills necessary to them. But even these considerations were often secondary to the sense of vocation.

Before 1939, the average Jewish doctor was more likely to be in an unfashionable general practice than in a hospital. The extra training that was necessary for specialisation and the extra years of deferred income were a barrier to many. The hospital, however, was the ladder for professional promotion to consultant status. At this level it was necessary to have a personal introduction to a well-known consultant for whom one could work. Yet it was common knowledge that some consultants were prejudiced against Jews and supported the unofficial quotas operated by the teaching hospitals. The results were made more severe by Jewish habits of self-protective avoidance: many Jews were not willing to expose themselves to a potentially discriminatory hierarchy. Since the war this situation has changed and the National Health Service now includes a significant number of Jewish consultants.

State grants and scholarships have made postgraduate medical studies more accessible for the economically disadvantaged. However, the distribution of Jewish specialisation still bears signs of the legacy of the pre-war situation. There is over-representation, for instance, in gynaecology and pediatrics, and Jews are under-represented in specialities such as neurology and orthopaedics. The breakthrough was earlier in the first case and relatively late in the second. Jewish interest in pure research has meant that a very high proportion of Jewish specialists can now be found lecturing in university medical schools. In fact, medical staff today comprise about 30 per cent of the total Jewish faculty membership in Britain.

The pattern is similar worldwide. Of 449 Nobel prizes awarded since 1901, seventy have gone to Jews. Of these seventy, twenty-nine are in the category Physiology and Medicine and twenty-two in Physics. Jewish excellence in other subjects is impressive but less striking. It reflects the preferences indicated here. There have been nine Jewish Laureates for Chemistry, five for Literature, four for Peace and four in the new field of Economics (out of a total of eleven).

## Lawyers

The differentiation between the practical, easily accessible professions and the more traditional specialised ones can be seen with reference to law and England's divided bar between solicitors and barristers. Until recent years, five 'ordinary' level G.C.E. passes enabled one to enter five years of articles, and a pass in the Law Society examinations allowed one to practise as a solicitor. Again, Jewish entry increased proportionately following the Second World War, as grammar-school education was expanded and an educational meritocracy established. Before the war an articled clerk had to pay for his apprenticeship a premium of several hundred pounds to a senior partner in a practice. The expansion in the need for legal services after the war reversed this payment and articled clerks began to be paid a small income. This, of course, was attractive to aspirants from less wealthy families.

One attraction of being a solicitor is the flexibility of opportunities and working relationships allowed. The solicitor in post-war Britain is mainly concerned with the conveyancing of property, trustee and divorce work, and most operate from small suburban offices. He or she can also build up links with businesses and may be eligible for advisory posts in big corporations and governmental authorities. Jewish solicitors, however, prefer to be self-employed in small local practices in which they can retain their independence.

This situation can be contrasted with that of the barrister, where the Jewish penetration was much slower and more difficult. The barrister is involved in the romance of court work, but the profession is controlled by the four traditionally-oriented Inns of Court. An aspiring barrister has to pass a stiff Bar examination and the proportional failure rate is much higher than for solicitors. In addition, the barrister is not attached to a firm while studying and so is engaged in unpaid private study. Even after passing the Bar examinations, new barristers must serve an unpaid pupilage for one year. They can then only get work if they are members of a Chambers and to do this they must be acceptable to an already existing practice. Limited accommodation and the competition of numbers makes this branch of the law very much a gamble and unsuitable for people without some private income or support. It is, therefore, the more traditional area of law and, if the amount of occupational inheritance is any measure, among the more archaic of the professions.

## Accountants

In terms of the total numbers involved, accountancy is the most popular Jewish profession, though it is very much a London and Manchester concentration. It is not a demanding vocation like medicine, nor does it require the aesthetic outlook and real talent of something like architecture. Both the profession and its practitioners tend to be regarded as practical and matter-of-fact, even dull, like the subject matter. Its examinations reflect this. They are not so stiff as to exclude the average moderately intelligent person who was able to pass 'O' levels and is willing to apply him or herself to the subject. In return for hard work it offers a financially secure and promising career; there are few restraints on the raising of professional fees.

The large-scale entry into accountancy is a postwar phenomenon and indicates a great expansion in the demand for the service. This has occurred as a result of the vastly increased pressures of governmental taxation in all areas of society. The bread and butter of the profession is the annual audit of a firm's books, but many middle class people now seek the services of an accountant for their own personal income tax return. The demand for labour grew in the 1950s and accountancy was the first profession to pay its articled clerks a living wage. This attraction resulted in one London welfare organisation (the Jewish Board of Guardians) alone apprenticing over 200 boys in the profession during the years 1952–7.

There are four recognised accountancy qualifications each offered by one of the four accountancy bodies: the Institute of Chartered Accountants, the Association of Certified Accountants, the Chartered Institute of Public Finance and Accountancy, and the Institute of Cost and Management Accountants. Jews have tended to gravitate towards the first two, which cater for the independent practitioner: the last two are concerned with the public authority and industrial fields. Again we see a bias in terms of occupational choice. The majority of qualified, certified or chartered Jewish accountants choose to buy their way into the practice of the firm in which they were articled, or set up their own practices. Initially, they often work from the box-room of their suburban house. The more ambitious, in terms of career orientation, seek out more challenging business problems such as forecasting and become finance directors of large companies. One way this is done is through the business contacts one can establish and through which an astute person can join a board of directors of a growing company.

Some Jewish observers have described accountancy, albeit derogatively, as the 'home tailoring of the late twentieth century'. The small accountant operating from his own home resembles the East End tailor in the sense that he keeps his options open and works at the less prestigious end of the market. He has also kept and can capitalise on many of the virtues of his grandfather: an optimistic outlook, a desire for respectability and a penchant for hard work are equally well-suited to success in both occupations.

Since the 1960s, Jewish interest in the professions has begun to normalise. This has taken two different paths. On the one hand there is a movement into new fields with Jews becoming physicists, industrial chemists, engineers and actuaries, and entering teaching and welfare work; on the other hand, they are using their traditional professional qualifications for jobs in industry, commerce and government. These trends suggest that young Jews are now less diffident where hierarchies are concerned and that they consider discrimination by the establishment less of a threat. The change may also reflect a general British trend away from the independent status of professional people. This is an aspect of the overall decline of the independent middle class and has similar origins to the decline of the shop-keeper and small businessman. It is one of the realities of contemporary Britain and its 'corporate state'. As independent middle-class economic activity is discouraged, membership of large hierarchies and interest groups, on the contrary, affords a good bargaining position, financial returns, coveted fringe benefits and security of employment – all of which are parti-cularly desirable in an unstable economic climate.

## . . . and Taxi-drivers

A brewery advertisement recently prominent on London under-ground trains suggests a package of excuses that a (beer-drinking) husband might use to explain his late arrival home: 'Raining. No taxis. Jewish holiday.' This symbolises a situation well known among Londoners: the Jewish representation in taxi-driving is estimated at around 30 per cent of the capital's 15,700 licensed drivers. There are also significant numbers in provincial cities with large Jewish populations. Given the trends towards the professions and other high-status spheres and industries, the very large Jewish participation in this service industry might seem anomalous. But certain elements of the history and structure of the trade are in keeping with our general observations of occupational demands.

The hackney carriage trade burgeoned with the economic expansion of the mid-eighteenth century, which brought the growth of towns and a consequent increased demand for public urban transport. The introduction and large-scale use of the motorised cab occurred in the first decade of the twentieth century. This was also a period of Jewish immigration and Jews were able to take advantage of the demand for labour in new fields in which they could compete on equal terms with the indigenous population.

Not only were they able to apply their own skills in open competition but, as newcomers, they had a distinct advantage. London's taxi trade had been officially organised much earlier. A

rigorous and controlled examination established by the Metropolitan Police's Public Carriage Office in 1853 tested not only
physical fitness and knowledge of routes, but also enquired into
the candidate's background and character. Since immigrants did
not have police records and their backgrounds were unknown,
they were accepted on the basis of their good conduct in England.
Furthermore, a large proportion of applicants were refused
licences on the grounds of convictions for alcoholism – and here
the reputation of Jews for sobriety and the fact that few of them
have had records of drunkenness must have stood them in good
stead. The examination of routes has always been an oral test of
knowledge of roads and public buildings. A driver has to know
the location of all theatres, hospitals and museums in London, as
well as the quickest route between any two points within a radius
of six miles from Charing Cross. These things were learnt by
travelling around the city by bicycle with a clipboard on the
handlebars for approximately six months. Although the test was
a difficult one, it required no other knowledge or qualifications
and could be passed by a newcomer with little formal education
and no written skills. The candidate who successfully completed
the medical, the 'blue book' (routes) and character tests was
granted a licence which was kept for a lifetime. Only a series of
convictions (or one extremely grave one) could result in
suspension. Even today a licence can only be revoked by the
Commissioner of Police, and the penalty is rarely applied.

An additional attraction was the location of stables before
1900. Until twenty years ago the trade was carried out almost
exclusively in the West End and prosperous suburbs, but most of
its bases were situated in East End working-class areas. These
locations, where property was cheap, were also those of high
Jewish settlement, and many garages are still to be found in the
Jewish quarters of Aldgate, Mile End Road and Bethnal Green.
Apart from the convenience of working locally, geographical
proximity facilitated the practice of 'wangling', whereby a
candidate borrows a cab from a garage for training and testing
purposes on the understanding that, once qualified, he would
work initially for that garage. A prospective licencee who was
known in the area would find it easier to 'wangle' than an
outsider.

These then are some historic reasons for the large-scale entry of

Jews into taxi-driving throughout the nineteenth century. In the early part of the century their influence was already reflected in the Yiddish terms used in the trade. In the 1830s, adaptations of the Hansom cab led to counterfeits commonly known by the Yiddish word *Shofuls*. Today, Jewish jokes and phrases are as familiar to the non-Jewish taxi-driver as to the Jew. The taxi meter has become known as the *Zeiger* (Yiddish for clock, watch) or 'Jewish piano'.

It is, however, in the structure and day-to-day working of the trade that we can see why, when Jews have branched into new occupations and have adapted traditional ones, they still continue to provide such a large proportion of taxi-drivers. The historical connections still obtain in part. Among Jews and gentiles, taxi-driving is often an inherited taste, like medicine or the sea, where an individual is influenced by father, grandfather or uncles to follow the same career. Several Jewish families are known to have been in the trade for over 100 years. A large part of the attraction, now as a century and more ago, must be the opportunities offered for independence, freedom from routine and supervision. There are also the possibilities (albeit remote) of high earnings in a respectable, honest trade in which one can take pride in having command of a body of knowledge and in which initiative is rewarded. The training is still rigorous and a prospective driver has to find means of support during the 12–18 months it now takes. But once in possession of a licence the driver can choose whether to become a journeyman and work for someone else, hiring a cab on weekly or mileage rates, part-time or full-time, or to 'go mush' and become an owner-driver. There is little to choose between the two, for even a journeyman may select his own working hours and routes and may even keep the cab at home when not in use. There is no questioning of reasons for taking time off, an obvious advantage to the observing Jew. All drivers are classed as self-employed and are responsible for their own income-tax returns and national insurance. Most will 'go mush' at some period in their working lives, buying a cab on their own or in partnership and then forsaking this for the fewer responsibilities attached to working for someone else. This accords well with the Jewish ideal of democratic working arrangements: there is little status difference between being 'boss' or being 'worker'

A disadvantage of self-employment is the complete lack of security in sickness and old age. Some drivers, therefore, work in the trade only part-time, having a more secure job either at night or daytime. A currently popular second string is a G.P.O. overseas telephonist. On the other hand, taxi-drivers are not subject to any enforceable retirement age as long as fitness can be proved. In 1972, one driver, Jack Cohen, was known to be working at the age of seventy-seven. The chances of acquiring great wealth are slight, but taxi-drivers are free to choose whether to work long hours or to sacrifice earnings for the sake of leisure time. The number of taxis parked outside houses in the popular 'Jewish' middle-distance suburbs, such as Wembley or Ilford, testify to the economic potential realised by some 'cabbies'.

The trade itself bears some characteristics of Jewish work patterns, whether because of the large Jewish influence or as factors contributory to its compatibility with the Jewish attitude to work. Taxi-driving in London affords opportunities for gaining status through charitable work, for the mixing of work and social activities, and for the expression of traditional attitudes towards unionisation.

The trade has an outstanding reputation for giving aid to children in need. The London Taxi Drivers Fund for Under-privileged Children provides outings, collects toys and holds fund-raising functions. Similar organisations exist in cities like Glasgow. In addition, members of the trade are quick to identify and respond as a group to needs of the Jewish community. During the Middle East Wars of 1967 and 1973, many taxi-drivers freely offered their services in driving volunteers and medical supplies to London Airport, bound for Israel. Sports and social activities are diverse, ranging from those associated directly with taxi-driving, such as the Taxi Driver of the Year competition and the Cab Trade Exhibition, to inter-city angling and golfing contests and, recently, to support of the London Backgammon Society. Trade associations abound, some purely social, others aiming at protecting the interests of their members in, for example, demands for tariff reform or in combating the activities of 'pirates' and minicabs. The informal 'camaraderie' of the shelters is well known: waiting for business provides good opportunities for gossip and card-playing.

The large number of diverse associations acting as pressure

groups reflects a weak participation in trade unions. The Transport and General Workers' Union is favoured by journey-men, while owner-drivers generally prefer the Licensed Taxi Drivers Association. But only about one-third of London's taxi-drivers are members of either union, and this conforms with what is, with some notable individual exceptions, a generally low record of trade-union participation among Jews.

In summary, taxi-driving is the Jewish trade *par excellence*. It offers a wide variety of working relations, relatively easy entry and complete independence. It is democratically organised. It demands initial perseverance to obtain a licence, but then has great scope for initiative and gives maximum financial return for work invested. It can be a full- or part-time occupation, allowing those who seek improvement in material status to use their skills to their own advantage and at their own convenience. From first entry into the trade, the driver has the self-employed status sought by so many Jews. Taxi-drivers are socially classless: earning capacity is open, patterns of residence and consumption can vary accordingly, and the occupation itself encourages social mixing.

## Conclusion

The work attitudes of British Jews continue to reflect the world view and moral values of traditional Jewish culture. Generations of oppression and exclusion have nurtured habits of self-help and mutual support and have maintained boundaries of Jewishness all over the world. The occupational patterns characteristic of Jews have, however, altered according to the opportunities and constraints of different contexts of time and place. Against the general background of social changes in Britain, we have seen the particular move of Jews into and through certain professions and have noted their persistent association with the London taxi trade.

But it is not only developments within the host or home country that affect the options and aspirations of a minority group. Since the establishment of the state, Israel has had a marked effect on the occupational outlook of diaspora Jews. About 1000 young British Jews emigrate to Israel each year.

They are most often motivated by socialist and ethnic ideals and rarely – if ever – by the prospect of job advancement. In the adopted country they take up jobs which may be unusual or socially undesirable in Britain: they become pilots, police officers, bank clerks, farm and manual labourers . . .

The disdain with which family and community would view such a career at home turns to admiration for the 'pioneer'. For the young person involved this is often a way out of the respectable suburban life demanded by the parental generation and despised by some of the young themselves. Israel, in effect, provides a safety net for those post-materialists who would like to drop out occupationally, but not socially. Hence there are intellectuals and other highly educated British immigrants employed in trades and skills that their middle-class backgrounds would make it difficult for them to pursue in their country of origin. The reasons for the 'return' to Israel are idealistic and occupational ambition is a low priority. Downward occupational mobility itself may be an ideal. In this way Zionism, a modern manifestation of Jewish ethnicity, exerts yet another influence on the occupational profile and work attitudes of British Jews.

# 3

Like the Jews discussed in the previous paper, Macedonians have suffered oppression and dispersal, and they value the autonomy of self-employment. They have a tradition of migration and a willingness to adapt to exigencies and opportunities arising in the post-migration economy. But while Jews progressed by diversifying, Macedonians in Toronto have concentrated in the short-order restaurant industry. Only one niche is associated with them; their claim to it is very successful.

The Macedonian experience in Toronto illustrates the potential of ethnicity as both collective and individual resource. Macedonians, with many other immigrants, arrived in the city in significant numbers during its early boom years. At that time, rapid ('formal') industrial growth was making new demands in the ('informal') service sector – not least the demand for ordinary rapid-service ready-cooked food which could be eaten in meal breaks away from home.

The first Toronto Macedonians saw the opportunity and organised themselves to take advantage of it, expanding their market by incorporating newcomers into the original 'ethnic' system. The system was also to the advantage of each newcomer. As a dishwasher in a Macedonian-owned restaurant, he might earn less than he could in a factory or saw mill, but he could enjoy the company and support of people who spoke his language and shared his values.

More important, he could, in the long term, expect to move up the restaurant hierarchy into self-employment. His progress from unskilled to skilled worker, from dishwasher to restaurant-owner depended throughout on his being able to claim and keep Macedonian-ness, and to use it in a way that it had not needed to be used in the various countries of Macedonian immigrant origin.

# Dishwashers and Proprietors

# Macedonians in Toronto's restaurant trade

Harry Vjekoslav Herman

This paper deals with Macedonian immigrants in Toronto and with their high concentration as owners and employees in the restaurant industry. Its main purposes are to uncover the reasons for this occupational concentration and the way it is achieved; to assess consequences of such concentration for the immigrants and for their children; and to propose that any study of the coincidence of ethnic and occupational categories in a complex, industrial, poly-ethnic society should include a micro-level study of the members of any specific ethnic aggregate or aggregates. It is argued that ethnic identity can be both an asset and a liability, depending on the logic of the situation in which it occurs, and that it is best understood as a resource more or less consciously used in inter-personal relations (Wallman, 1974).

## Introduction

One striking characteristic of modern, poly-ethnic societies such as Canada is the transformation of rural migrants and overseas immigrants in urban and industrial situations. Closely related to this process is the observed coincidence of ethnic and occupational categories.

The superimposition of occupation on 'ethnic group' has been observed by many anthropologists in non-industrialised societies of Africa and Asia (Cohen, 1969; Leach, 1964; Furnival, 1939). The same phenomenon has been reported for complex, industrial, poly-ethnic societies but, for the most part, by sociologists using macro-level analysis of census data. This kind of study is the basis of much work done in Canada (as by Richmond, 1964; B. R. Blishen, 1973; O. Hall, 1973). All of these works support the statement that '. . . the study of occupations on the Canadian scene today turns out to be . . . a study of ethnic relations and of large scale organisations' (Hall, 1973, p. 46).

The work of Porter (1965) has been particularly influential. On the basis of empirical macro-analysis, Porter demonstrated that the association of ethnic and occupational categories is expressed in terms of ethnic over-representation either in higher or lower occupational classes. 'Occupational class' is used in this context to refer more to a stratum than to a class in Marxian or in Dahrendorf's sense. Porter further associated 'occupational class' with 'social class' and, because of the over-representation phenomenon, social strata within the 'vertical mosaic' necessarily assumed an 'ethnic' character:

> Immigration and ethnic affiliation (or membership in a cultural group) have been important factors in the formation of social classes in Canada. In particular, ethnic differences have been important in building up the bottom layer of the stratification system in both agriculture and industrial settings. If non-agricultural occupations are considered alone, there are ethnic differences in the primary and secondary levels of manufacturing and in service occupations. Depending on the immigration period, some groups have assumed a definitive entrance status   (Porter, 1969, p. 73).

This analysis carries a multiplicity of implications which are yet to be tested and which may or may not be warranted. The over-representation phenomenon implies that ethnic origin is a relevant factor in allocating people within the occupational structure, or that cultural traditions are capable of determining occupational specialisation. If the position of an individual in respect to 'occupational class' is determined by his ethnic identity, this can imply either or both of the following: (i) ethnic identity is a liability for any member of an ethnic aggregate which is over-represented in a low occupational class; and (ii) ethnic identity is an asset for any member of an ethnic aggregate which is over-represented in a high occupational class.

In the Macedonian case, this would mean that the occupational structure in Canada has allocated certain low-level occupations to them and/or that their cultural tradition has not adequately equipped them with the appropriate knowledge and drive to assume positions in high-level occupations.

While sociological macro-analyses do indicate the coincidence of ethnic and occupational categories, they neither explain the phenomenon nor the forces that contribute to its emergence. This gap can be filled only by an understanding of particular ethnic aggregates and of the factors that place them in specific occupational niches. To some extent, of course, the motives of individuals explain what they do: social action is purposeful behaviour oriented in some way towards the future. It is nonetheless constrained by the present and affected by the past (Weber, 1968; Schutz, 1967). The actions of immigrants are directed towards meeting present needs and achieving future goals, but are related to their past experience and even to the experience of their predecessors. Future projects are seen in terms of the past – the goal is visualised 'in future perfect tense' (Schutz, 1967) or (to paraphrase McLuhan, 1967, p. 75) future goals are seen through a rear-view mirror. Having this approach, the present paper combines an analysis of field data collected in Toronto between October 1974 and March 1975 with an overview of the cultural traditions and the economic and social history of Macedonians. The combination explains the concentration of Macedonian immigrants in the restaurant industry in Toronto.

**The Macedonian Situation**

Contemporary Macedonians are originally the Southern Slavic and slavicised population who inhabited the territory that comprised the Macedonia of antiquity: that population that calls itself *Makedonci*. This territory falls today within three Balkan countries: Bulgaria, Greece and Yugoslavia. Through history to the present, it has been a source of controversy and the locus of contradictory political, economic and cultural interests.

It is not clear when Slavic penetration of the Balkans began. It is known, however, that it was a slow process due to the resistance of the local population and to the relative disorganisation of the penetrating Slavs. By the beginning of the seventh century, Slavic tribes seem to have been present throughout the peninsula, occupying the countryside for the most part, but attempting to occupy larger towns as well (Doklestic, 1964, p. 10). They were organised into tribes, with names that remained throughout the centuries, some being used to the present day. Well-known tribes were the Dragovites, Velegezotes, Sagudites, Rinhinites, Struminites, and Smoljanites (*Istoria na Makedonskiot Narod*, 1972, p. 29).

This penetration of Slavic tribes into the Balkans naturally changed the ethnic structure of the area. The surviving local population withdrew into fortified towns on the coast, or was assimilated by incoming Slavs. The Slavs presented a great problem for the Byzantine Empire which was trying to establish absolute control of that area.

The detribalisation of the Southern Slavs seems to have started soon after their arrival in the Balkan Peninsula, but their consolidation into nations occurred only among the Serbs and Croats. The Slavic population that inhabited the territory belonging to Byzantium, although resisting Byzantine rule, did not develop a national consciousness and did not form a nation. Only in the brief period between 976 and 1018 did a local ruler (by the name of Samuil of Trnova) form a kingdom with its centre in Ohrid. He expanded his rule over all of Macedonia, part of Bulgaria and as far north as the Danube. This seems to have been made possible by the temporary weakness of Byzantium and Bulgaria, the great powers in this area at the time (*Istoria na Makedonskiot Narod*, 1972, p. 43).

These facts, like many others involving Macedonians, are a source of controversy among the Macedonian and Bulgarian historians today. There is no doubt, however, that Christianity came to the Macedonian people by way of Byzantium and that it was spread through the efforts of two Greek missionaries, Cyril Constantine and Methody, who translated the holy books from Greek into the Slavic language spoken around Salonica, which became the official church and literary language of all Christianised Slavs. It is today known as Old Church Slavonic.

The territory of Macedonia was constantly under some foreign rule and a source of conflict among Byzantium, Bulgaria and (later) Serbia (Doklestic, 1964, p. 45). The squabbling over Macedonia was halted by the Turkish conquest of the area. By the year 1395 the whole territory of Macedonia was in the firm control of the Ottoman Empire. So it remained until 1912.

Islamisation of the occupied territory by the Turks was especially strong among Slavic feudal lords and in the towns, while the serfs in the countryside remained Christian. An interesting ethno-economic structure developed within the territory of Macedonia. The feudal system was characterised by the Turkish type of tenure (*Timar*). The feudal lords were Turks, while the serfs who engaged in agriculture and cattle-breeding were Slavic Christians. In the towns, oriental-type craft guilds were in the hands of Moslems, while Greeks, Jews and merchants from Dubrovnik controlled commerce (Doklestic, 1964, pp. 52–3).

The weakening of the central Turkish government changed the feudal system of tenure. Overburdened by work and heavy taxes, many serfs abandoned their land and moved into towns, or retreated into mountains where they formed small bands of resistance (*Ajduti*). The towns did not offer many options to these rural Slavic Christians. They could survive only by entering service occupations of very low socio-economic status. Many saw this movement into the towns as only a temporary solution to their problems and so left their families in the villages.

This temporary migration, which came to be called *pecalba* in Macedonia, is central to our later discussions.

Throughout the Turkish occupation, control of the church in Macedonia was in the hands of Greeks. Macedonians were therefore doubly subordinate in the spheres of culture and religion as much as in economics. Towards the end of the Turkish rule, when it was clear that Turkey would have to pull out of Macedonia, the Greeks, Bulgarians and later the Serbs competed for control of it. Greece based its claims over Macedonia on the grounds that the province of Macedonia had in antiquity belonged to Greece, and also on the grounds that the 'Greek Orthodox Church' had saved Macedonians from being totally Islamised. They also emphasised the superiority and prestige of Greek culture and offered to educate and Hellenise Macedonians. Both Slavic nations, Bulgaria and Serbia, based their claims on the fact that the territory in question was inhabited by Christian Slavs who spoke a Slavic dialect and, therefore, should be integrated into their already existing nations. Bulgarians claimed that Macedonians were actually Bulgarians who spoke a different dialect, while Serbians claimed that the Macedonians were actually closer to them.

Towards the end of the nineteenth century a new Macedonian consciousness was expressed in the formation of the conspiratorial Internal Macedonian Revolutionary Organisation (IMRO). It was formed in 1893 and, in 1903, organised an uprising against the Turkish authorities. The organiser and ideologist of the uprising (one Goce Delcev) later became one of the most celebrated of Macedonian heroes. The uprising was a failure and resulted in a split in IMRO, but the Turks did not stay much longer in Macedonia. In the First Balkan War of 1912, Turkey was defeated by the three allies, Bulgaria, Greece and Serbia. These subsequently fought the Second Balkan War of 1913 against each other and split Macedonia into three parts.

After the First World War the situation in Macedonia did not change. Each of the three countries behaved towards Macedonia as towards an integral part of their nation, giving no special consideration to the local Macedonian populations. Only Bulgaria actually used the name Macedonian, meaning by it Bulgarians of a slightly different variety. Serbia treated Macedonia as part of the Serbian nation, calling it 'Old Serbia' and imposing the Serbian language and administration. The worst situation was in Greece. There, Macedonian as a distinct identity was not recognised. The language that the local Macedonian population spoke was called Bulgarian and was forbidden. One decree issued in Lerin (Florina) on 27 January 1926 states that from that day on it was forbidden to use the 'Bulgarian' language in all public places, offices, commercial transactions, meetings, parties, luncheons, weddings and so on. Only Greek was to be used. Parents, teachers and priests were responsible for the actions of their subordinates. Offenders would be treated as traitors and would be prosecuted (Doklestic, 1964, p. 220). And these prosecutions did take place, especially under the dictatorship of General Metaxas (1936–41), whose regime sent thousands of Macedonians to jails on the Greek islands. The assimilation effort included the opening of special schools in Macedonian villages to teach older Macedonians to speak Greek (Doklestic, 1964, p. 93).

In this situation it is not surprising that expressed Macedonian ethnic consciousness was very weak. It actually existed only among young Macedonian intellectuals. The masses either succumbed to Serbian, Greek or Bulgarian propaganda, or ignored it all and just tried to survive the hard times.

Things changed somewhat during the Second World War, when the communist parties of Greece and Yugoslavia became the first to recognise the right of Macedonians to have their own nationality. Macedonian nationality finally became a reality within the Yugoslav federation after the war. But this concession only intensified the suspicion of Macedonians in Greece. Greece suspected that Yugoslavia was aiding the Greek communists, and the persecution of Macedonians in Aegean Macedonia was given a strong anti-communist rationale.

This situation continues unchanged. It may be significant that Macedonian nationality is not recognised by the two countries which are a part of the global division of power: Greece is a member of NATO, while Bulgaria is a member of the Warsaw Pact. Yugoslavia belongs to neither and recognises Macedonian nationality.

## Migration (Pečalba)

Within this historical framework, there developed one of the most interesting features of Macedonian culture: *pečalba*.* All indications are that the word is of Slavic origin and that in its original meaning *pečal* meant sorrow, sadness, melancholy or grief (Sadnik and Aitzetmuller, 1955, p. 85). The Russian language still uses *pečal* in this old church Slavonic sense (Romanov, 1964, p. 169), while in Macedonian and Bulgarian *pečalba* is usually used to describe gain, profit, return or earnings (Macedonian: Crvenkowski and Gruik, 1965, p. 242; Bulgarian: Cakolov, Ljabova and Stankov, 1961, p. 548). The connection between these two meanings is made clear by the realities of *pečalba*.

---

\* č is pronounced like *ch* in *church*.

The word is still used in reference to migration in pursuit of work from one's village into neighbouring or distant towns. A disintegrating feudal economy; the increase in the agricultural and cattle-breeding population in an area of scarce agricultural land; the stagnation of agricultural productivity – these in combination forced many Macedonians to seek income away from their homes. Originally this migration was or was perceived to be temporary, either seasonal or lasting a certain number of years. It involved mostly young bachelors but sometimes married men or even whole nuclear families moved. To leave family and native village is to suffer sadness and sorrow; one makes such a sacrifice only with the expectation that it will compensate by gain or profit.

Men engaged in this type of migration were called *pečalbari* (Crvenkowski and Gruik, 1965, p. 242). Towards the end of the nineteenth century their number increased until *pečalba* was an important factor in the socio-economic organisation of the area and a main source of income for many Macedonian families. It became so widespread and so institutionalised that some authors actually referred to it as an occupation (Cvijic, 1966, p. 457). Since none of the areas to which *pečalbars* migrated in pursuit of income was industrialised, *pečalbars* did not become proletarians engaged in industrial production. They had no option but to earn their income through low-status occupations or as small entrepreneurs.

This channelling into low-status occupations was caused by two major factors: the lack of skills that are marketable in towns; and the occupational stratification based on ethnic origin that had existed for centuries in the areas to which Macedonian *pečalbars* went. The consequence was that *pečalbars* took jobs as servants, masons, butchers, peddlers of sweet drinks and candies, and only a few succeeded in owing a small grocery store or a small restaurant. Even by the end of the nineteenth century, Macedonians from different localities became associated with particular low-level occupations. *Pečalbars* from Kostur (*Kastoria*) were milkmen in Istanbul; those from Dgavat and Buf were lumberjacks and charcoal-makers in Turkey, Bulgaria, Rumania and elsewhere; and *pečalbars* from Tetove, Bitola and Kichevo were bakers in Bulgaria, Serbia and Rumania (Doklestic, 1964, p. 164).

It became customary for *pečalbars* from the same locality to leave together and seek jobs such that they might stay together and support each other in times of crisis. This was also a way for young *pečalbars* in *pečalba* for the first time to learn the skills of a particular job, as well as the ways of a foreign land. Men still living remember stories of young boys leaving their families even before puberty to join *pečalbars*. This experience enhanced the solidarity of the village or local group, and the youngsters' early contribution to the family economy strengthened family ties. These loyalties can be seen still to be relevant to Macedonian immigrant organisations in Toronto (pp. 80–1 below).

The departure and return of *pečalbars* were and are special occasions in a village. The first is accompanied by sadness and sorrow, the second by the joy of return. The life of a worker in a service occupation is very hard and strenuous and when it entails also leaving home and family the result is anguish, homesickness and anxiety about the future. This overpowering burden of *pečalba* has left its mark on the whole of Macedonian folk culture. It is a dominant theme in their folk-songs and dances:

| | |
|---|---|
| *Tuginate pusta da ostane* | Foreign lands should be damned |
| *Taja od libeto me razdeli* | Because they separated me |
| *Što go ljubev vreme tri godini* | from my loved one, whom I loved for three years. |
| *A bre vie mladi pečalbari,* | Hey, you, young *pečalbars* |
| *Ne go li vidoste mojto libe* | Have you seen my loved one |
| *Od pečalba doma da se ide.* | coming home from *pečalba*? |

During celebrations of the return of *pečalbars* it was customary for men to dance the *teškoto*. This dance, the name of which means 'difficult' or 'heavy', starts slowly, with restraint, the dancers bent over and supporting each other. The physically difficult steps are supposed to express the hardships of *pečalbars*. Gradually the pace of the dance quickens and becomes fast and full of intricate steps and syncopated rhythms expressing the *pečalbars'* joy at returning home.

Worsening economic and political conditions in Macedonia at the beginning of the twentieth century in effect prevented many *pečalbars* from returning home. In this circumstance, *pečalba* assumed a permanent character and *pečalbars* became emigrants in the true sense of the word. They either took their families with them, or formed families in their new place of residence. The United States, Canada and Australia became the destination for Macedonian *pečalbars*. Many of them found life and work in these new countries equally hard and more alien. There are folk-songs expressing this too:

| | |
|---|---|
| *Bog da bie koj prv spomna* | God should punish the one |
| *Na pečalba tugja zemja,* | Who first mentioned *pečalba* in foreign lands, |
| *Tugja zemja Amerika.* | Foreign lands, America. |
| *Tri godini bez rabota,* | Three years without a job, |
| *Bez rabota em bez pari.* | Without a job and without money. |

## The Toronto Setting

At the beginning of the twentieth century, Toronto seems to have been the place that most attracted Macedonian *pečalbars*. Eventually it boasted the second largest Macedonian population after the city of Skopje. The first known Macedonians to arrive in Toronto came from the village of Zelevo in 1903 (Tomev, 1971, p. 75); and the first *pečalbars* from the village of Oščima followed in 1904 (Anniversary Booklet of the Benefit Society of Oščima, 1957, p. 46).

Since Canadian statistics have never counted Macedonians as such, estimates of their numbers have varied over the years. It is believed that around 1909 there were between 1000–2000 Macedonians in Toronto (Woodsworth, 1972, p. 122), and 6000 in Canada prior to the First World War (*Canadian Family Tree*, 1967, p. 220).

Their low rate of literacy, lack of skills and inability to speak English did not prevent Macedonians rapidly learning the workings of the Canadian system. The traditional loyalties to family and local group that had helped *pečalbars* within the Turkish Empire were transferred to Canada in the form of benefit societies organised by native villages. The first Macedonian church in Toronto was formed on the basis of these benefit societies, which effectively represented separate villages in Macedonia. Donations for the formation of the church were listed as coming from village associations. Individual donors were recognised only when they did not have an association to represent them. Many associations of this type have persisted to the present; the now popular Toronto Macedonian picnics are actually gatherings of people of the same village origin.

In the first phase of immigration, Macedonian *pečalbars* were men without their families who were employed mainly as labourers on the railroad, roads, canals and in the meat-packing industry. Gradually they started bringing their families with them. This forced them to establish permanent residences closer to the place of work, and to seek permanent work in one place. The climate and agriculture of Canada were quite unlike what Macedonians were used to, and work in the agricultural sphere was out of the question. Instead, they concentrated in urban and industrialised areas.

In the beginning, work in restaurants was apparently a last resort to be taken up only if one were unable to find a job in industry. It seems to have become a conscious choice and the preference of many Macedonians during the depression years: work in restaurants assured at least food and a small income sufficient to pay for rudimentary accommodation. Every Macedonian *pečalbar* who worked in a restaurant planned to own a restaurant one day. Each seemed to realise very quickly that self-employment was the only way for an unskilled labourer to achieve upward mobility. Work as a butcher or a helper in a restaurant or a grocery store gave a man the chance to learn useful skills on the job. While working as a dish-washer or a bus-boy one would be given the opportunity to observe and to try the work of a sandwich man or a short-order cook, and eventually to start working as such while newcomers took over the bottom-rung jobs. This was the pattern typical of Greek- and Macedonian-owned restaurants.

Work in restaurants very quickly became the most popular and most desired work among Macedonian *pečalbars* newly-arrived in Toronto. In spite of low wages and long hours, it offered work indoors, in a warm place among fellow ethnics or even with kin. And it offered the possibility of advancement and the promise of self-employment in the future. *Pečalbars* who had some family member who owned a restaurant in Toronto were considered lucky because they could start work immediately upon arrival. Those who did not have relatives but were aware of the possibilities that work in a restaurant offered would look around for a Macedonian- or Greek-owned restaurant to which they could offer their services.

Until very recently, most Macedonian immigrants in Canada were from Aegean (Greek) Macedonia and were bilingual in Macedonian and Greek. They could, therefore, present themselves as Greeks or as Macedonians according to the filiation of a prospective employer. For their part, Greek and Macedonian restaurant owners preferred to employ people with the same ethnic background for two explicit reasons. First, fellow ethnics were ready to work for lower than market wages provided they were given the opportunity to learn the business and, having this opportunity, would stay on the job longer than someone who was using it as only a temporary expedient. Secondly, the owner could place more trust in fellow ethnics who had just arrived in Canada and who depended on him in every way.

The type of restaurants which Macedonians owned and operated varied: the term restaurant is used here very loosely to describe any eating place outside the home. Although many Macedonians started by catering particularly to immigrants, the food that they offered was never 'ethnic' food; it was always North American food that is acceptable to the general public. Their establishments were most often the small, open-kitchen, short-order restaurants which began to prosper when general economic growth and rapid industrialisation encouraged or forced increasing numbers of people to eat outside their homes. Because many of these people could not afford the existing restaurants, a new occupational niche opened. The Greeks and Macedonians were in the right place at the right time and with the right attitudes and skills to appropriate it for themselves.

## Business Organisation

Some Macedonians improved and expanded their businesses into larger and better restaurants. Others opted to specialise in ice-cream parlours. Today, specialisation takes the form of steakhouses and licensed restaurants. Statistical data on the number of restaurants owned and operated by Macedonians in Toronto are not available, but anyone who lives in Toronto may observe that the number of Macedonian restaurant owners is disproportionate to their relatively small number in the population. Estimates of this total vary between 30,000 (*Canadian Family Tree*, 1967, p. 220) and 150,000 (some prominent members of the Macedonian community in Toronto). The real figure is probably somewhere between 70,000 and 80,000 persons. Similarly, estimates of the number of restaurants vary between 600 (according to some) and two-thirds of the total number of restaurants in Toronto (*Canadian Family Tree*, 1967, p. 221). *The Canadian Macedonian Calendar and Commercial Directory* of 1961 gives an incomplete list of restaurants in Toronto owned by Macedonians. While the list cites 313 restaurants, I am personally aware of a number existing at that time which are not included in it (1961, pp. 43-7). Whatever the case, no one disputes the high representation of Macedonians and Greeks among restaurant owners in the city.

Not all Macedonian *pečalbars* who try to start a restaurant succeed, nor do they all succeed on the first try. Probably the majority of owners have had at least one failure – bearing in mind that success and failure are relative concepts and most often defined in narrow monetary terms.

In financing a restaurant, kinship and ethnic ties, and traditional patterns of borrowing and lending money play a very important part. In most cases, the Macedonian *pečalbar* who wants to start a restaurant or any business of his own does not have sufficient funds. But this does not prevent his proceeding with his plans because loans from relatives and friends are always available. Lending and borrowing money is a common practice between Macedonians and especially among kin. Neither receipts nor interest payments are required, although the sums lent are sometimes in the tens of thousands of dollars. But no case of a bad debt between Macedonians has been reported: all debts are apparently honoured sooner or later. For the young entrepreneur, this form of financing is easier and cheaper than borrowing from a bank or finance company. And since it is available only to Macedonians who are known to hold traditional cultural values, the person who wants to make use of such financing must identify himself as Macedonian. For the purpose of borrowing money in this way, ethnic identity is a necessary asset. The majority of the people employed in any Macedonian-owned restaurant are Macedonians. Even in larger restaurants that require more than one cook, a chef and a variety of expert hands, all the jobs are done by Macedonians supplemented, when necessary, only by Greeks. Further, the owner or owners are always in the restaurant during working hours and there is no separation between ownership and management. The owners take an active part in the operation of the restaurant.

There is a recognised hierarchy of jobs, and job status is reflected in income. In large restaurants the income and status order runs downwards from owner-manager to chef, cooks, sandwich-man, bartender, waitresses, bus-boy, dishwasher and so on. Despite this hierarchy, interpersonal behaviour among all staff including the owner is normally egalitarian – a style evolved by Macedonians living in societies such as Greece, in which economic strata were coincident with ethnic origin and in which they occupied the lowest stratum or strata. In these circumstances, it became a tradition to regard all Macedonians as equal even though some were financially better off than others. The restaurant owners themselves interpret stratification in terms of a balance between income and work. Since, despite their relatively higher income, most owners worked more than any staff member, they saw themselves as equal to others working in the restaurant who earned somewhat less. Had they been able to have an income from the restaurant without actually working, the owners might have considered themselves 'better' and so kept a social distance. Given this logic, Macedonians want their children not to become restaurant owners, but to better themselves by entering white-collar professions.

## Work (Rabota)

Work and the attitude towards work are well-defined in Macedonian tradition. The ideology of work is consistent but fixed; its meaning varies with context and even contradicts itself (as Wallman, 1974). Both the meanings and the contradictions are expressed in Macedonian folk sayings. Sayings like *Rodi me majko so k'smet, pa me frli na buniše* (Only bear me lucky, mother, and then you may throw me on a garbage dump), or *Ako e, od Boga e* (If it is given it is from God) express certain degrees of fatalism. On the other hand, sayings like *Kaj što treba motika, ne treba molitva* (The one who needs a shovel does not need a prayer) and *Ako kopaš lozje, ke jadiš grozje* (If you work in a vineyard you will eat grapes) express instrumentality and realism.

In many of the Macedonian folk sayings, work is seen as the ethical enhancement of man, as more than a means of survival. *Rabota go krasi čoveka* (Work enhances man), *Trudot e za čovekot zdravje i život* (For man work is health and life) and *Ne e sramota od rabota* (It is not shameful to work) are examples of this attitude. In other sayings, success and wealth are said to come only through work: *Ako e raboten, ke bude imoten* (Diligence brings wealth), *Ima rabota – ima pari; nema rabota – nema pari* (If you work, there is money; if you do not work, there is no money). There are also sayings which express a profound dislike of work outside the native place: *Ržen labac da jedam, tuginata da ne odam* (I would prefer to eat dry rye bread than go to foreign parts) or *Tugina fali, sam ne odi* (Praise foreign parts, but do not go there yourself). On the other hand, when one is forced to leave one's native village for self-employment the preference for an urban setting is expressed in a famous Macedonian folk-song:

| | |
|---|---|
| *Što mie milo em drago* | How nice it would be |
| *Na Struga dukian da imam,* | To have a shop in Struga, |
| *Na Struga dukian da imam,* | To have a shop in Struga, |
| *Na kiepencite da sedam* | To sit in its window. |

The work ideology and occupational preferences expressed in Macedonian folklore are doubtless relevant to the overrepresentation of Macedonians in the restaurant industry in Toronto. In this context, the sanctions surrounding work are important, but the range and adaptability of the notion are probably crucial to Macedonian success as migrant entrepreneurs.

## Ethnicity

Any discussion in which ethnic identity is seen only as a liability that constrains a man in all his activities, especially economic ones, would be misleading. The coincidence of ethnic and occupational categories within a poly-ethnic, industrial society is more complicated.

By ethnic identity is here meant a category that is a combination of self-identification and identification by others. It is an identity that is very flexible, without clearly defined boundaries, which in some instances and, according to the logic of particular situations, can be manipulated by the incumbent to his own advantage. While the basis of self-identification is the belief in common descent, common cultural traditions and memories of emigration (Weber, 1968, p. 389), identification by others is based primarily on physical and behavioural characteristics that are most obviously different from those of the identifier. Self-identification and identification by others can, but very often do not, coincide, especially at the initial stage of contact of two ethnic aggregates. At the initial stage of their immigration to Toronto the ethnic identity of Macedonian *pečalbars* was expressed more in terms of their native village, while Canadians identified them, or rather lumped them together with, 'Greeks' or 'people from the Balkans' or 'foreigners'.

It must be stressed that persons with the same ethnic identity do not automatically constitute a social group, although they might use this identity as a basis for the formation of a variety of social, political, economic or recreational groups (Weber, 1968, p. 389). Thus ethnic identity is potentially a resource. It is a resource not only in that it facilitates some kind of group formation, but in that it can be utilised in inter-personal relationships. An individual can reinforce or shift his ethnic boundary to suit the demands of a specific situation.

It must also be said, however, that ethnic identity can have both positive and negative implications. Its successful manipulation is not always possible. Identification by others can sometimes impose ethnic boundaries that are excluding and impossible to shift or manipulate – especially when it serves the particular interest of a powerful identifier.

When individuals engage in economic competition, they may

use their ethnic identity in situations in which they see it as an asset, or they may minimise or try to hide it in a situation in which they see it as a liability. Macedonian *pečalbars* in Toronto minimise their Macedonian identity in situations in which they think this identity might harm them. They maximise their Macedonian identity in situations in which they think it will help them.

Ethnic identity of Macedonians and other 'low-status' ethnic aggregates tends to be seen only as a liability or constraint (as Porter, 1969). Its positive aspects are neglected. This is an effect of macro-analysis, which cannot present a real picture of the role of ethnicity in the economic structure of countries such as Canada. Macro-analysis of this kind should be accompanied by detailed study of the aggregates that compose poly-ethnic society.

The lack of diachronic analysis has also inhibited the understanding of ethnicity. Macedonians (included under 'other Central European') are described as concentrated in the lowest occupational class within the present Canadian economic structure (Porter, 1969, p. 81). But Macedonian immigrants see themselves in relation to their past, present and future rather than to the immediate structural situation alone. Porter, for example, sees them only in respect to Canada. They see themselves also in respect to their country of origin, and to Canada through time – at the time of their arrival, in the present and in the future. Throughout history, Macedonians were in positions where the lowest economic status was superimposed on their ethnic identity. When they came to Canada the majority were uneducated and without skills. Channelling into the lowest occupational class was not on the basis of their ethnic identity but on the basis of their skills, or more accurately their lack of skills. It was not their ethnic identity that was a liability, but their economic situation prior to arriving in Canada that prevented them from achieving immediate upward mobility. If ethnic identity is a liability, it can be hidden: lack of skills cannot. Macedonian immigrants are very aware of the difference.

For the unskilled labourer in times of industrialisation and growth, occupational choices are limited to manual work in a primary resource industry, the building of the infrastructure, or a service industry in a large urban area. Movement out of this occupational class is either perceived as impossible, or is seen only in terms of self-employment. Other studies show that the most likely route out of manual into non-manual occupations is through self-employment (Lipset and Bendix, 1967, p. 171).

The work of a dishwasher is less prestigious and less well paid than work in a mine, lumber camp or steel mill. Nevertheless, many Macedonian *pečalbars* in Toronto chose to be dishwashers. For some the choice was made on the grounds that it was the first step to future self-employment; for others it was simply convenient to follow the tradition of other *pečalbars* from the same area and to enjoy the amenities of a warm workplace where food was provided and the immigrant was close to people who shared his language and values. Whether their goals were short-term convenience, tradition, or long-term plans for self-employment, the work of a dishwasher or a bus-boy carried more potential for self-employment than work in a mine, lumber camp or steel mill. In their own eyes, their situation had improved with respect to the past and they could see it improving even more in the future – for them and still more for their children.

Because economic improvement must be achieved through self-employment, even those Macedonians who succeed in owning small open-kitchen restaurants in which they work hard, long hours for incomes not much higher than those of unionised factory-workers still prefer their own situation: in their own eyes and according to their own standards, they are better off than factory-workers. Their view reflects the Macedonian ideology of work expressed in the term *pečali*, which applies to the management of gain and profit. Work in a mine or factory means too much dependence on others and too little control over one's own situation and one's own resources. Self-employment, no matter how small and insignificant it might be, is better, more *pečali*, because one is in control of one's own resources.

The economic success of Macedonian *pečalbars* in Toronto who have achieved ownership of restaurants and so moved from the position of unskilled immigrant labourer to that of small independent entrepreneur can be attributed partly to their traditional work ideology and partly to ethnic identity and their own ability to utilise it as a resource. The skill – perhaps not always a conscious skill – with which some informants are able to shift boundaries and change their ethnic identity in various interpersonal relationships is marvellous to see. At one moment the owner appeals to one set of ethnic loyalties in the way he uses Macedonian to comfort his rebelling cook; at another he 'shifts' to joke in Greek with a non-Macedonian waitress, or to discuss the latest policy of the Greek *junta*; and in interaction with customers who are neither Greek nor Macedonian he will not be 'ethnic' at all. These are not, as we have noted, 'ethnic restaurants'; they serve only 'American' food. Ethnic identity is not therefore relevant to restauranteur–customer relations as such (as Wallman, 1974).

There are, of course, Macedonians who started as dishwashers and never became self-employed restaurant owners. Of these we might say that the inertia of their ethnic identity brought them to restaurants, but they lacked the entrepreneurial spirit and the necessary entrepreneurial skills to rise to the top of the restaurant hierarchy. Although they might have held the same work ideology, they were not able to control and manipulate their own resources, including ethnic identity, in the same way. If they have remained in restaurants and risen from dishwasher to cook or chef they have, in effect, moved from unskilled to semi-skilled or skilled status. But in the eyes of other Macedonians they could have done better.

There are also those who have disliked restaurant work from the beginning, but had no choice other than to work with kinsmen when they arrived. Some very successful restaurant owners are successful in spite of themselves, still despising the work that they are forced to do every day. Even the more content have reservations: most Macedonians who own restaurants would not wish this to be the occupation of their children and stress the importance of education. Their traditional preference shows here too: they want their children to have the kind of education that will enable them to be self-employed. Consequently, to be a doctor or lawyer is very much in vogue, and many of their children are training to be accountants.

While there are no restrictions imposed by the receiving society on Macedonian immigrants wishing to move from the occupation of unskilled labourer to self-employment or some professional cadre, it is too early to say whether their children will have the same freedom to move further upward into the elite. The question is actually whether their ethnic self-identification will be an asset or a liability on their way up and whether they will be able to manipulate it the way their fathers did. As much depends on the way they will be identified by the people who now occupy positions further up the scale as on the ambition and skill of the next generation itself.

## Conclusion

The coincidence of ethnic and occupational categories within a poly-ethnic society is misleading if studied through macro-analysis only. The impression is given that it is ethnic identity which constrains those who seem to be concentrated in 'low occupational classes'. A micro-study of the same phenomenon allows us to see that ethnic identity can also have advantages, even for the people at the bottom of the stratification scale, and that it is not their ethnic identity which impedes them as much as their lack of occupational skills.

Ethnic identity has been positively useful to Macedonian immigrants to Canada to the extent that it has channelled them into occupations which, although included within the 'low occupational class', provide the most potential for advancement. At the same time, their cultural tradition equipped them with values and resources appropriate to economic advance in the new setting. Ethnic identity was not for them fixed and pre-determined, but a resource which could be used in particular situations and in the pursuit of particular goals. It cannot be assumed that these principles operate in the same way for other immigrant aggregates in Canada, or that it will operate in the same way for the children of these Macedonian immigrants.

# 4

This case shows a particular 'home' tradition operating in a particular workplace 'away'. Punjabi Sikh Jats use a patron–client structure to organise a range of relationships between individuals who are not kinsmen. In the Punjab, these relationships pertain to interstices in the kinship structure. In Britain's Midland foundries, the setting is radically different, but both the principles of reciprocal obligation and exchange, and the process by which a man may compete for gain and subsequently lose power, remain the same.

Two important points are illustrated here: (i) the ('informal') client system flourishes only because it is appropriate to the ('formal') foundry structure. Foundry organisation restricts the enterprising migrants' access to other-than-ethnic resources, but it contains a number of 'pivotal positions' which may be converted into the separate centres of ethnic client systems. (ii) The client system highlights boundaries of loyalty and communication within the foundry and in the population outside it. On the one hand, each client group includes people of only a single, narrowly-defined ethnic group. On the other, both the system and the gift exchange which lubricate it are seriously misunderstood by British foundry supervisors in close contact with Punjabi foundry workers.

# Pivots and Presents

# Asian brokers in British foundries[1]

Dennis Brooks and Karamjit Singh

Our setting is the engineering and metal-manufacturing industries of Britain's West Midlands; particularly metal manufacture, specifically the ferrous foundries. The booming economy of the first half of the 1950s brought subsequently unequalled low levels of unemployment. Pronounced labour shortages developed in some sectors of the economy. So far as the foundries were concerned, these shortages were primarily in the 'least desirable' jobs – the hot, dirty, noisy, physically demanding and often, but certainly not always, poorly paid. But foundries are in basic industry: numerous other sectors of the economy were and are dependent on them. From the foundry owners' and managers' perspectives, output had to be maintained or increased, production targets met. Labour shortages had, therefore, to be remedied. There is then an essential economic dimension to the situation we describe here: it represents an adjustment to labour shortages.[2]

One part of Britain's imperial inheritance has been the availability of almost countless potential extra hands, drawn or driven by the under-development – some would argue the development – of their homelands to man the foundries of the Black Country or the looms of Bradford. Another legacy of the colonial and imperial past was – and is – a pronounced racist value system in the metropolitan country. Apart from other potential handicaps, the job opportunities of black migrants from colonial and ex-colonial territories have been limited by essentially racist considerations. The racial dimension is, then, the second important ingredient in this case.

These two elements provide the context for our detailed analysis: labour shortages in a racist setting. Before proceeding with the analysis it is necessary to sketch the salient characteristics of the major participants and the situations in which they found themselves. The participants are the migrant workers and the foundry supervisors.

The migrant workers who constitute our focus are Punjabi Sikh Jats.[3] With a long history of overseas migration they were no strangers to Britain, though their numbers here were small until after the Second World War. The majority were peasant farmers. Their individual motives for migration, for seeking work in booming British industry, were primarily economic. In this respect they come close to the ideal-typical 'target workers': '. . . someone who goes abroad to earn as much money as possible, as quickly as possible, in order to return home' (Böhning, 1972, p. 62). This motivation is one important characteristic. Another is their lack of skills relevant to the British setting. Most lacked proficiency in spoken and written English; many were illiterate in their own languages. Being strangers to the industrialised world, they lacked any experience of manufacturing industry. Thus while strongly motivated to work hard and long to maximise earnings, they were handicapped by their lack of industrial and linguistic skills. Further, they were perceived as 'black' or 'coloured'. For all these reasons their job opportunities were limited, and their survival depended on the successful exploitation of all available resources.

One such resource derived from their ethnic identity. This comprised a strong set of reciprocal obligations, most particularly within the extended kinship network, but also going beyond kinship boundaries. One way in which obligations could be met and, by the same token, incurred by the other party was in the finding of employment for kinsmen and friends. If a kinsman or friend could be successfully recommended for a job vacancy, present obligations could be met and future obligations incurred. Cultural dimensions are directly relevant to these obligations.

Let us consider now the position of the hard-pressed first-line supervisor in the foundry. His superordinates are pressing him to meet production targets, but he is short of men. He has one or more Asian workers, judged by him to be 'very good': they work hard for long hours on the most rotten jobs without complaining.

They turn up for work regularly – and on time. So when one Asian worker tells him that he has a brother, or a cousin perhaps, who is looking for a job, the supervisor's problem is solved: 'Bring him along – we'll start him tomorrow.' After all, he cannot get suitable white British to do these jobs for long; he *must* meet production targets. In this context his own racial perspectives are largely irrelevant.

These are the bare outlines of the situation we explore here. A combination of economic, racial, ethnic and cultural variables ensured that Asian – in our case Punjabi – workers were not spread at random throughout the foundries. Rather, they were clustered. In some clusters the workers were linked by kinship; in most they knew each other before they were recruited.

## Recruitment Networks and Brokers

Clusters of Asian workers were found in the foundries – in particular departments and in particular occupations. This section deals with the extent to which such clusters or concentrations are brought about by the emergence of recruitment networks organised by particular individuals (as Boissevain, 1974). These networks constitute a particular response to the labour market situation in which job opportunities are limited by exclusion, and by a minority group's initial lack of industrial and linguistic skills. Individual brokers occupy a pivotal position in these networks; without them, the whole mechanism would collapse. This pivotal position emerges at the interface between industry and ethnic groups with certain characteristics. Its basic features are best explained by a description and analysis of the performance of one man, here called (fictitiously) Gurdial Singh. Our evidence is derived from an empirical situation, but in most respects it can be regarded as ideal-typical, and it is presented in those terms.

In Gurdial Singh's section, a finishing shop in an iron foundry, there were twenty-eight men. Ten of these were on fettling and dressing: knocking surplus metal from castings and finishing this operation with a powered grinding wheel. A further sixteen men were engaged in sandblasting and shotblasting: operations which clean the castings. Finally, there were two labourers.

The ethnic composition of these work groups was as follows. Both labourers were Punjabis, as were twelve of the sixteen men on shotblasting and sandblasting; the others being one Jamaican, one Italian and two Englishmen. The shotblasting, generally acknowledged to be the most unpleasant task in the foundry was – except for the one Jamaican – an all-Punjabi job, and one for which it was difficult to recruit or retain white workers. In the fettling and dressing area, three of the ten men were Punjabi, five were English, one Jamaican, one East European.

The arrangement of working hours in the foundry was complicated, with a number of men starting and finishing at idiosyncratic times. The timing of work was largely determined by requirements for moulding and core sand or hot metal. The shotblasters covered the twenty-four hours by two twelve-hour shifts. This made it necessary for the company to employ a third shift; the extra four hours or so each day for each man was overtime work. In effect, they worked a minimum of twenty hours' overtime each week, commonly increasing this by Saturday and Sunday working. Fettling and dressing was covered both by shift- and day-working; and the two labourers worked twelve-hour shifts. Substantial overtime, including weekends, was worked on these tasks also, especially by the Punjabis.

Apart from the two labourers, all the operatives in this section were piece-workers. Earnings were high, relative both to the plant and to the district, especially for those working overtime.

Gurdial Singh was one of the shotblasters. He was a Punjabi in his mid-forties, who migrated to Britain in the late 1950s from a Punjabi village. Without formal education, he was illiterate in both Punjabi and English; his ability even to sustain a conversation in English was limited. He was the first Punjabi to be employed in that section, initially as a labourer, then a fettler, and finally in shotblasting. He had worked there some ten years.

During this period, he had introduced between eleven and fourteen other Punjabis to the section. A precise count is difficult but the minimum figure is certainly eleven. A number of these were related to him: one was his brother-in-law (wife's brother), one his nephew (brother's son), a third another nephew (sister's son), a fourth another brother-in-law (sister's husband).[4] Two more were linked to him through his brother-in-law and nephew: they came from the same *ilaqa*[5] in the Punjab and knew his kinsmen before coming to Britain. Three others were from the same *patti*[6] as Gurdial Singh, and again it is reasonable to assume that they were known to him before migration. Another two came from the same *ilaqa*, but we know of no other link to Gurdial Singh.

For a number of reasons there was little need for constant or detailed supervision in the finishing shop. First, it was largely autonomous in the production process: it relied on the moulding lines for castings, but was not linked to other areas by the production hardware. Second, each operation was relatively simple, easily learned and repetitive: the throughput was a number of standardised castings and there were not constant changes in the design of these products or in the manufacturing hardware. And third, all the production operatives were piece-workers: earnings provided a sufficient inducement to produce the output required.

Excluding plant failures or major changes in product design or production equipment, the men in effect ran the shop with very little supervision – it was not necessary. Much of the contact between the foreman and the Punjabi operatives was via Gurdial Singh, particularly if any instructions were out of the ordinary. Conversely, if a Punjabi operative had a grievance or, for example, wanted to request extended home leave, he would in most cases first approach Gurdial Singh who would then accompany him to the foreman or shop steward. Even where this was not the case, Gurdial Singh would be likely to know the content of any interaction between one of his group and the foreman or shop steward.

The links between Gurdial Singh and the other Punjabis extended into the non-industrial sphere. They met regularly in public houses; they invited each other to weddings and festivals. Gurdial Singh was at the centre of all these activities: he had more drinks bought for him than he reciprocated.

From this brief description of Gurdial Singh and his group it is possible to draw out some generalisations on the nature of such groups. The individuals at the centre of these recruitment mechanisms (Gurdial Singh in this case) act as brokers.[7] They retain their own position through a distribution of patronage in the form of jobs, higher piece-work rates and overtime work. We have noted that the role of such individuals is central in that its continued existence is necessary for the maintenance of such mechanisms for recruitment or other purposes.

Here we are examining a specific type of network both in terms of its function and structure. These networks we call pivotal systems in order to cover all the actors relevant to the situation: the broker, his client group and the supervisors with whom he is in contact. The group which is created by the broker and is dependent upon his patronage can be considered a 'quasi-group'.[8]

Why do such brokers emerge within certain ethnic minorities at the interface between these groups and industry? First, the employment market faced by black – and specifically Asian – workers is conducive to the establishment and maintenance of pivotal systems. The broker would have little or no power if Asian workers were not confined to some industries and occupations by being barred from others.

Second, proficiency in English is operative in a number of ways. Some observers have stressed the lack of fluency in English as a major variable in the establishment of black 'ethnic work groups', and in what we interpret as pivotal systems (Aurora, 1967, pp. 77–8; Marsh, 1967, pp. 18–19; Rimmer, 1972, p. 30; Wright, 1968). We argue on the contrary that the level of ability in English is relatively unimportant: some brokers speak little English and are certainly unable to write it; Asian workers with little or no spoken English may be recruited by the *formal* system and remain outside ethnic work groups; and most Asian workers perform relatively simple and easily learnt repetitive tasks in which the lack of spoken English is unlikely to cause problems. Spoken and written English *is*, however, relevant to the extent that an Asian with these skills is less dependent on *informal* mechanisms and has a greater chance of securing employment unaided. The man lacking them is necessarily more dependent on the informal mechanisms and his alternative opportunities are much more limited.

Third, the objectives of Asian workers themselves foster a pivotal system. While the external constraint of discrimination forces them into certain industries and occupations, their own preferences lead them to search for the best paid jobs within this narrow range. Information about jobs is freely circulated at pubs when Punjabi workers meet each other; their social interaction is based on kinship and village networks deriving from the country of origin, rather than their present work situation. Information about – or the expectation of – better wages at plants where pivotal systems have emerged reinforce the tendency to utilise them and so to strengthen the broker's position.

Fourth, the formal industrial recruitment procedures must be sufficiently flexible to accomodate *some* measure of informality or of discretion. The formal recruitment mechanisms of the industrial West have been contrasted with the informal practices operating in India (Lambert, 1963, pp. 70–9), but our evidence indicates that a clear distinction cannot be drawn. It is more accurate to say that formal systems can be adapted; and that there are degrees of informality and varying amounts of scope for adaptation. Certainly an ideal type pivotal system could not emerge in a highly bureaucratic and, therefore, impersonal recruitment system.

A prerequisite for a pivotal system is that first-line supervision has the power to accept or reject candidates for employment who can effectively bypass any bureaucratic elements in the recruitment procedure. If applicants are first 'filtered' by a personnel department, the foreman's power is very much weakened as, correspondingly, is that of a potential broker. In this situation all a Gurdial Singh could do would be to tell his kinsmen to apply, offering them no guarantee that they would be accepted.

Fifth, some of the necessary conditions inhere in the organisation of work tasks. These cannot be precisely itemised since our data are limited to seven plants, and there is a wide disparity of technical operations between industries. It is clear that a production system employing small, stable work groups is more conducive to the development of pivotal systems than is one of large groups, or one in which there is frequent movement of operatives between work tasks. Pivotal systems are, therefore, more likely in small foundries than in large machine or assembly shops. The 'technology' of the plant, in terms of its production hardware, is clearly important here. It is relevant to the extent that it determines the physical layout of jobs and the intensity of direct supervision: the likelihood of pivotal systems developing is directly related to the degree of work-group autonomy. This in turn is related to the nature of the product: long production runs requiring relatively simple operations need infrequent supervision and hence are conducive to pivotal systems. Simple production operations are also relevant in another sense: these are precisely the jobs initially sought by Asian migrants of rural origins, and the jobs which management had in mind when recruiting them. Payment systems can be coupled with the system of production and level of direct supervision in that the majority of workers in the West Midlands foundry industry are paid by some form of piece-work system (C.I.R., 1970; Rimmer, 1972). Such systems often incorporate group bonus schemes which accentuate the cohesiveness of workers engaged in particular work tasks.

Sixth, ethnicity and cultural expectations are relevant in that pivotal systems can only emerge amongst certain ethnic groups. In British industry, brokers and their networks appear to be a purely Asian phenomenon. The importance of multiplicity of strong mutual obligations between members of an ethnic group is clear in the case of Gurdial Singh. The Asian assumption that there *ought* to be such obligations is not normally operative in the western industrial employment context. It is incorrect to assume that the sole reason for the emergence of the broker and for his continued existence has been his control over recruitment. The broker and his networks may be understood not only as a peculiar response to the interface with industry, but also as the logical extension of cultural assumptions brought in from the migrant's country of origin. Thus the broker on the shop floor with his monopoly of contacts and resources may be likened to individuals who have emerged from the Asian communities within other social and particularly political contexts. Similarly, it can be argued that the hierarchical structure of Asian society lends itself to the emergence of brokers. Pivotal systems among Asian workers can be contrasted with the emergence of informal non-hierarchical work groups amongst the English – both constituting a particular ethnic response to a particular situation. The important difference is the inclusion of Asian workers' pre-migration cultural assumptions that their relationships *should* be hierarchical (cf. Clark, in this volume; and contrast Herman and Kosmin, in this volume).

Finally, there are the constraints operating on, and expectations of, the principal actors within the situation: the foreman or other first-line supervisor, and the broker.

## Perspectives of the Foreman, Broker and Clients

At the embryonic stage of a pivotal system, the foreman desperately needs men to meet his production requirements, particularly men for the unpleasant or low-paid jobs. If the conditions are right, there will be at least one Asian worker already in the department or section who will perceive that more men are required or who may even be asked by the foreman if he knows of anyone looking for a job. This potential broker is under obligations to his kinsmen to assist them, and one way of meeting these obligations is to help them find employment: better-paid jobs than they are in, work nearer to kinsmen – possibly *any* employment.

The combination of the constraints on the foreman and the obligations of the potential broker entails that the latter introduces a kinsman or other acquaintance. He will not bring just anyone: apart from selection by obligation, he will introduce only those whom he assesses as capable of performing the task for which labour is required. Since most jobs at this level are easily learnt, the major constraint is physical ability.

The pivotal system thus provides the foreman with a ready source of recruits. It also offers him other advantages. While most foremen have, in their own eyes, the ability to select a 'suitable' white native applicant, this ability does not extend to these apparently very strange oriental men, many of whom speak little or no English. Of this problem, foremen are usually well aware. If, therefore, a Gurdial Singh can be relied upon to bring along 'good men', the problem is solved. Experience will soon prove whether or not the man *is* satisfactory, and the foreman does have redress. Most commonly he will tell the broker that if any of his nominees prove to be 'no good' he will accept no more, or he may threaten to put any unsatisfactory nominee in the broker's own work gang which, with a group piece-work or bonus system, is likely seriously to affect both his earnings and prestige.

Pre-selection by only one broker avoids conflicts and this, too, has advantages for the foreman. When more than one source of recruitment by recommendation was used for Asian workers, conflicts arose between nominees from the different sources. Foremen were somewhat surprised to be told by one Asian worker that he preferred not to work with another Asian worker:

to the foreman, 'They all look the same'. Whites were far less likely to complain about the presence of another white. These conflicts were seen as disruptive to output and, therefore, to be avoided. Commonly, they were attributed to differences of religion or caste, but it is likely that some reflected a rivalry between two or more client groups of the same ethnic origins. The foreman's solution was obvious either way: he must recruit all his Asian workers through one man. This decision, of course, enhanced the power of the chosen broker and accentuated ethnic separation. Workers recruited through the pivotal system are socialised into the tasks and norms of the workplace by their kinsmen and friends; the system too acts to maintain adherence to these norms.

These are the major advantages to the foreman of recruiting Asian workers through a broker, but there are also advantages in employing Asian workers *per se*. The value system of the Punjabi Jats at least puts great store on the ability to perform and endure hard physical work. They are willing to carry out physically hard, hot, dirty and unpleasant tasks for long hours, and without complaining. Not only do they not complain, but they treat the foreman with a respectful deference he has seldom, if ever, met before. He is treated much like a District Officer in the heyday of colonialism. This he finds not unpleasant: he is appreciated. This is a far more congenial relationship than that he enjoys with his often troublesome white workers. One indication of this appreciation is the drinks pressed upon him; another is the presents which are proffered. Among most foremen there is broad agreement on which presents they ought to accept or reject. Drinks are no problem: anyone can buy someone a drink, and the fact that most of the buying is done by one party in the relationship does not bother them. Similarly, a bottle of spirits is usually acceptable, but commonly only at Christmas, less often on the foreman's birthday. . . . This area of behaviour was difficult to investigate: some foremen were probably less than completely frank. Certainly there existed a large stock of stories, often from credible sources, of presents which had been refused.

Relationships between Gurdial Singh and the foreman were cemented outside of the work situation. Gurdial Singh would regularly buy the foreman drinks in the company's social club or at a public house where the Punjabis regularly met. In the foreman's words, 'You *have* to go for a pint. They insist. You daren't refuse – even when you don't want a pint.' He felt constrained to accept, but clearly he did not regard doing so as an onerous burden. He did feel, however, that a refusal would offend Gurdial Singh in particular and the group in general. Buying drinks for the foreman was recognised as Gurdial Singh's prerogative, although the foreman might be offered a drink by someone else in his presence. The common feature of any such relationship is that the broker and his group do almost all the buying, with the foreman making an occasional reciprocal gesture.

We now turn to the broker's perspective of the pivotal system. He, from his side, is subject to pressures which push him towards making overtures to the foreman. There are the obligations that he feels towards his kinsmen. The Asian ethnic minorities are characterised by a multiplicity of mutual obligations between their members. Since the broker's own status within the wider Punjabi community is to a certain extent dependent upon meeting these obligations, any failure here reflects upon himself. The broker (as in Gurdial Singh's case) is likely to have been one of the first members of his joint family to have migrated to Britain, and it is almost inevitable that demands will be made on him by later comers. There is an expectation that the rewards accruing to the successful migrant will be shared in the form of sponsorship to Britain and help in finding work. This sponsorship may be financial, in terms of assisting with the costs of the journey; more commonly it has involved providing accommodation and sustenance until the kinsman has found work (John, 1969, p. 19).

The achievement of such a system and its attendant client group would itself be considered worthwhile in the Punjabi village (John, 1969; Lewis, 1958). The network of patronage that is created is interpreted by all as evidence of power. The patron receives respect in his own right, a distinction being made between the reality of the patron's power and his ability to demonstrate it (Lewis, 1958).

The perspective of potential or actual clients is complementary to that of the broker: they share his cultural assumptions. We have already suggested that pivotal systems may also be an extension of the migrants' assumptions about the rightness of hierarchical relations. Therefore, the deference with which the foreman is treated by members of the quasi-group is in part a response by them to the broker who has given them a job. It reflects too the Asian worker's awareness that he has a precarious foothold on the employment ladder. His experience or perceptions of recessions may have strengthened this viewpoint (Brooks and Singh, 1972, pp. 226–7).

## The Gift Relationship

Pivotal relationships in the workplace are begun and sustained by a continual round of gift-giving. The giving of gifts (in the widest sense) occupies a major role in Punjabi social intercourse, as it does in many pre-literate societies. Beneath everything, it is argued (Mauss, 1960), is the implicit notion of reciprocity. The giving of gifts – or of returns – is seen as a legitimate means of achieving one's aims, since it places the receiver under an obligation. The items given may be intangible and need not be reciprocated at that point of time. The analysis of gift-giving is advanced by taking into account such variables as power relationships, kinship distance and kinship rank, wealth or command of resources, and patterns of social organisation. A typology of reciprocal exchanges can be drawn up in which their asymmetry is linked directly to the degree of instrumentalism behind the gift and the social distance between the donor and recipient (Sahlins, 1965). A distinction can be made between the gift relationship of the supervisor and the broker, and those between the broker and his client group. In his dealings with the latter, particularly with those related to him, kinship morality tempers any inclination towards severe exploitation.

His dealings with the former, at least in the early stages of their relationship, represent more clearly an instrumental use of gift-giving in which: 'The conditions of exchange determine the status relation; that is, one manipulates the status relations by manipulating gift-giving' (Befu, 1966–7, pp. 173–4).

Taking this perspective, it can be seen that studies which dismiss gift-giving as simple attempts to 'bribe' the foreman are insufficient in their analysis (as John, 1969, pp. 113–14 and 136–8; Marsh, 1967, pp. 28–31; Wright, 1968, pp. 141–3). Cash transactions cover only one small part of the gift relationships. And although similar practices occurred in nineteenth-century European industry (as Hudson, 1970), the Punjabi connotations of such transactions need not be those of an Englishman. Equally, the suggestion that Punjabis may be giving gifts simply to ingratiate themselves and to show signs of conforming has no basis. Even the fact that Punjabis choose such occasions as the foreman's birthday or Christmas to give the gifts cannot be taken as evidence of conforming to British customs. The more tenable explanation is that this reflects an increasing awareness on the part of the Punjabi workers that their foremen are more likely to accept gifts at certain times. Christmas and the foreman's birthday have been identified as two occasions on which it is legitimate to present gifts.

A popular gift to foremen (especially from older Punjabis) is a boxed nylon shirt, together with other articles of clothing such as socks and ties. Younger Punjabis try to widen the range of gifts and, at the same time, to increase the likelihood of acceptance. One informant settled for a pipe after much thought and discussion. Other imaginative presents were pen sets, cuff-links and large packs of cigarettes. Few contemplate giving really valuable presents unless they are sure of their acceptance. The Punjabis themselves are aware of the connotations an expensive gift has for Englishmen.

The most common gift, as we have seen, is buying the foreman drinks. He may also be invited to family occasions such as the marriage of a son or daughter. In the first instance, the buying of drinks over a long period of time may not have an easily identifiable reciprocation on the part of the foreman. He may buy substantially fewer drinks in total, but his continual acceptance of drinks from the Punjabis marks the existence of a relationship based on reciprocity. This relationship is recognised by the Punjabis, who sustain it, and the foreman is usually aware of the implications of acceptance. The buying of drinks for foremen constitutes a use of English means for Punjabi ends. The foreman's acceptance of an invitation and his presence at a Punjabi house is the reciprocation for the gift of invitation. The presence of a foreman at the wedding of a broker's son not only publicly displays the relationship between them, it also accords the broker higher status even in the eyes of Punjabis who do not work in the same plant.

All these various types of gifts are presented to the foreman by the Punjabi workers, either through the broker or in his presence. They may be presented quite openly and in full view of the other Punjabi workers. But this is not always the case: the presence of workers of different ethnic origins (and their reactions) may make giving more secretive. Where there is rivalry among the members of a specific client group, they may present the gifts without each other's knowledge. Any attempt to offer the gift without the broker's knowledge is interpreted (by him) as a direct challenge aimed at upsetting the existing pivotal system. (One informant followed his foreman home in order to find out his address, returning later to present a gift.) Punjabi workers are therefore transposing the concept and functions of gift-giving to the shop floor and in doing so are incorporating the recognised figure of authority on the shop floor – the foreman – within these relations.

It is important to emphasise that while gift-giving underpins the pivotal system, it is not confined to these situations. The offering of presents does occur in a wide variety of situations and is most likely to be secretive wherever individuals are attempting to establish pivotal systems or are simply competing against each other for the foreman's patronage.

The foreman apart, there exists a network of reciprocal relationships amongst the Punjabis themselves. The broker is offered gifts in return for his patronage in the form of jobs or upgrading.

These two sets of reciprocal relationships are symbolised by a variety of gift-giving and -receiving responses. There are relationships based on an exchange of money, which are the most easily identifiable. While Punjabis see these exchanges as legitimate, they are aware of the different connotations attached to them by the native British. There is, however, a point at which a foreman stops merely receiving and begins to expect it: he exercises sanctions if gifts are not forthcoming. The borderline between a gift relationship and an essentially exploitative one is very thin. Similarly, there is a continuum in the relationships between the broker and the members of the client group. These span a range from the deference of younger for older brother at one extreme, to a strictly cash transaction at the other.

## The Broker Compared with other Middlemen

The personal characteristics of the broker himself vary from one plant to another. While the emphasis of this study was on male workers, the emergence of Asian women brokers substantiates the argument that pivotal systems are in part an Asian ethnic response to the circumstances of British industry. Nor are age and the level of education consistent among brokers. Age varied from the mid-twenties to near retirement age; education from illiterates at the one extreme to university graduates at the other. Simple observation suggests that brokers are more likely to be middle-aged or older and with a relatively low level of education. Certainly a broker is more likely to be an older person than a younger one. The reasons for this are twofold: brokers have in many cases been among the earliest members of their ethnic group to start in each plant; and many brokers incorporate the respect given to older people within their role. Literacy is not significant: the broker derives his authority from a non-industrial and non-English sphere. It is not even prerequisite for him to be fluent in English.

Common to all brokers is the method of recruitment to their client groups and of distributing patronage to them. Each broker is identifiable to other members of his ethnic group by his village of origin, his *ilqua*, and his recruitment of nominees along those lines.

The details of the pivotal role need to be distinguished from other types of middlemen in industry who have emerged elsewhere. In Britain, the terms 'straw boss' or 'go-between' are used to designate this role. Often they are used interchangeably (Wright, 1964, 1968; Aurora, 1967; Allen, 1971; Patterson, 1968). In North America, the term 'straw boss' stands on its own (Hughes, 1949; Hughes and Hughes, 1952). The straw boss is not a full member of management; his authority extends only over the members of the minority group. Neither the straw boss nor the go-between need belong to the same ethnic group as that of the workers (Dahya, 1973); and their relationship with them is potentially exploitative. Apart from the power derived from the lack of communication between management and workers, the go-between may also bolster his position by providing living accommodation (Brody, 1960).

Unlike the straw boss or the go-between, the broker in a pivotal system must be a member of the same group. The three roles are different, although they may be filled by one person: a straw boss is a go-between, but a go-between is not necessarily a straw boss; a broker performs the go-between role and could be a straw boss, but usually is not. The roles and power of the straw boss and go-between arise essentially from the industrial situation and are limited to that context. The ties and obligations which give rise to the broker's pivotal role are derived from the traditional, non-industrial community and have meaning outside the industrial context.

## The Dynamics of the Pivotal System

The pivotal system must be dynamic: it cannot continue unchanged because, over a period of time, a number of variables are liable to alter, presenting the broker with challenges which may result in his eclipse. The challenge to the broker can be either *internal* or *external* to the pivotal system.

Internal challenges can occur as a result of schisms within the client group, conflict between the broker and his clients, or conflict between the broker and his supervisor. Conflict between a broker and his clients can occur for a number of reasons. Given a constant scarcity of jobs in relation to the total number of job-seeking clients, the broker faces conflicts of loyalties and obligations to kinsmen or to the group. All members of a client group are linked to the broker, but do not necessarily have links with each other. The greatest strength of the client group – the web of mutual obligations – is therefore paradoxically also its greatest potential weakness. In particular circumstances, one client will decide to eclipse the broker for reasons of ambition or revenge, or the client group will become dissatisfied with the broker's performance and seek to displace him in his industrial role. Alternatively, conflict may be injected into the pivotal system from the non-industrial context: for example, a dispute occurring elsewhere between two kinsmen related to members of the work group. Finally, although least likely, conflict may arise between the broker and his supervisor which has stemmed from the broker's inability to satisfy his clients.

External challenges to the pivotal system may be posed if the supervisor is promoted or leaves the plant, since this destroys the existing web of reciprocal relationships; or the system may be directly affected by decisions imposed by senior management. These may take the form of redundancies or deployment of the workforce elsewhere.

Conflict may also arise between a broker and other members of his ethnic group who are *not* his clients. This has occurred where Punjabis who were not within the pivotal system attempted to unionise a plant, and the broker has perceived this as a threat (John, 1969; Marsh, 1967). Conflict has occurred when members of other Asian groups were introduced into all-Punjabi sections, or into a job previously occupied by a Punjabi (C.I.R., 1970).

Observers of the American and British scene have stressed that the ethnic work group has come into being primarily because of the problems posed by language and integrating the migrant into the mainstream labour force (Hughes, 1949; Rimmer, 1972; Wright, 1964, 1968). But we have seen that knowledge of English is relatively unimportant to maintain production in tasks involving easily learnt repetitive movements. The efficient industrial functioning of ethnic work groups may be only a by-product of strong client groups which have expanded throughout an entire section.

It cannot be assumed that any broker inevitably faces eclipse. What is certain is the high probability of external or internal challenge to his group and network. These pressures vary in intensity. There is a common pattern of events, although the time span may differ at each stage. Assuming a broker emerges, he has successfully established a set of reciprocal relationships with his supervisor and his group. His position remains consolidated until he is unable to accommodate himself and these relationships to any changed circumstances – at which point he faces eclipse and the possibility of being superseded by a new broker.

The existence of recruitment networks in some form or other has been reported among Asian workers in the West Midlands and elsewhere in Britain (Allen, 1971; Aurora, 1967; Brooks,

1975b; John, 1969; Marsh, 1967; Patterson, 1968; Wright, 1964, 1968). These recruitment mechanisms can be differentiated along a continuum beginning with those (merely) providing information to prospective recruits concerning vacancies or rates of pay offered by a specific employer, and culminating in the pivotal systems we have described.


## Conclusions


The job distribution of Asian workers in the Midlands foundry industry can be explained by a combination of economic, racial, cultural, ethnic, organisational and technological variables. No one of these variables by itself provides an adequate explanation: it is their interaction which is significant. Labour shortages were relevant to the extent that they provided the impetus to recruit Asian and other black migrant workers in Britain. But the demands of the labour market were distorted by racial considerations: blacks were acceptable in some occupations, not in others. Race difference exacerbates the lack of industrial development in the colonial and ex-colonial territories, and gives extra meaning to the gap between them and the metropolitan country and to the forces which, in varying degrees, push and pull workers from the former to the latter.

This was not, however, a homogeneous workforce. It consisted of groups of workers with their own distinctive traditions and their own ethnic identities, which in turn influenced their occupational and industrial distribution. In a sense, these specific cultural and ethnic aspects were imposed, perhaps superimposed, on the industrial organisation of the metropolitan country. The forms of this industrial organisation were important to the Asian brokerage system we have described in two respects beyond the purely economic. First, the recruitment mechanisms had to be sufficiently informal or flexible to permit recruitment 'by recommendation'. Second, a technical and organisational structure which provided for small, stable work groups with minimum supervision was most conducive to the establishment of pivotal systems.

Such pivotal systems are one of a number of types of

recruitment networks which could have emerged, and they have a number of distinguishing features. The central role, that of the broker, differs considerably from other forms of shop-floor leadership. This person occupies a pivotal position in the flow of relationships between members of an ethnic group on the shop floor, and between them and the supervisor. Clearly, the pivotal system does not need to incorporate all the jobs within a section, but it normally includes all those held by members of a particular ethnic group. In many respects the broker's role is an adaptation of a pre-industrial function which exists in other facets of the migrants' lives. He controls and distributes resources in the new sphere as he might have done in the old. The broker's role is in this way an ethnic response to a specific labour market situation. In contrast to other forms of shop-floor leadership, it is not a product of industrial organisation as such.

The peculiar ethnic characteristics of the broker are also apparent in the nature of the group dependent upon him and in his links with it. The client group differs from other forms of informal work group: while it is formed on the basis of work tasks, it can also be regarded as the transposition of a village faction on to the shop floor. Cultural assumptions underlining the nature of the links within it and radiating from it to the broker and supervisor are little different from those in the country of origin. The role of culture in reinforcing ethnicity through the flow of gifts further emphasises the peculiarity of the broker's role within his pivotal system. Here he succeeds in transferring a type of relationship legitimate in the village setting in the Punjab into the industrial British context. By doing this he has encompassed non-Punjabis such as the foreman, who is expected to reciprocate in a Punjabi idiom. The *pre*-industrial origins of the pivotal system's character are underlined by the *non*-industrial links within it. These non-industrial links, together with the cultural assumptions involved in gift relationships, distinguish pivotal systems from other forms of recruitment network. They give the broker and his client group an identity which goes far beyond the industrial context. Similarly, the stress laid on non-industrial elements is a considerable factor in securing the relative stability of the pivotal system and ensuring that the broker's role does not wither once his clients are recruited. It is these elements which enhance the broker's impact upon plant industrial relations, and on the nature of relationships between an ethnic group and its constituent individuals.

Finally, while our evidence is necessarily drawn from one area of industry, that of the West Midlands foundries, we have shown that not dissimilar phenomena can be inferred from other studies, in other industries, in other parts of Britain.

5

*This essay deals not with the adaptation of 'our' traditions to a different work setting, but with circumstances in which the very boundaries of 'us' are altered to meet the exigencies of work and work-seeking in a new environment.*

*South Asians in Britain are of very different linguistic, economic and cultural origins. But it is not only in the eyes of the British that they function as a single 'ethnic' category. In the general context of minority group survival in a strange land, and specifically in the sphere of work, the concept of 'Asian-ness' is sometimes a useful addition to the ethnic repertoire. The women home-workers described here have expanded their information and support networks across traditional ethnic boundaries and have made important social resources of contacts which, in their original homelands, they would never have made.*

*The paper illustrates two aspects of our theme. It shows how an exploitative ('informal') system of work may allow the better fulfilment of non-work obligations than any straight ('formal') job could do. And it describes the processes by which the meaning and the relevance of 'ethnic organisation' change with situation and through time.*

# Work and Network

## South Asian women in South London

### Verity Saifullah Khan

The statement that a relatively high percentage of South Asian women (Indian, Pakistani and Bangla Deshi) are involved in home-work or out-work[1] in London is supported by the evidence of research in south London and by verbal and written reports from other parts of the city (Bolton, 1975; Brown, 1974; Shah, 1975). But for a number of reasons it is difficult to prove or quantify such a statement. First, by its nature, the work cannot be officially enumerated. In the terms of the formal economic system, much of it is illicit, and both employers and employees may be unwilling to discuss it at all. Second, the lack of a common workplace for employer and employee and the wide geographical distribution of each employer's work make it impossible to cover an entire firm or even to contact all homeworkers employed by it. Third, direct communication between employer and home-worker is minimal and the tracing of chains of home-workers working for the same employer and/or living in one geographical area is hindered by lack of communication between sections of the Asian population. The Asian population is not homogeneous: there are differences of language, ethnic origin, socio-economic background, country of origin. These are complicated by variations in the time of migration and the motive for coming to Britain (Saifullah Khan, 1975). Within any ethnic or religious category there are sub-sections within which most interaction takes place (Saifullah Khan, 1976c). Fourth and finally, a complete outsider will have no access to this world of women and work, while anyone trusted enough to be 'adopted' by some is not, by definition, acceptable to all South Asian women workers.

These initial comments indicate problems of research, some crucial features of out-work, and some important characteristics of the Asian population. They indicate also that any explanation of the large number of South Asian women doing home-work in London involves several different levels of analysis. Most significant are the overall employment situation, the knowledge that South Asian women have of available jobs and the jobs perceived by them to be appropriate to their non-work obligations. Different sections of the population have access to different information about available jobs and use it in distinctive ways. The old-established know more than new arrivals; middle-class professional people have options and aspirations different from working-class manual workers; men are normally less constrained than women etc. Nor do job-seekers' maps of the options available indicate which jobs will be taken or explain any pattern in the choices made. The contacts, skills, alternative forms of support and the communication network of job-seekers determine their knowledge and perception of the environment, and their ability to manipulate it to particular aims and objectives. Any pattern of work will therefore be governed by these objectives, by the (material and social) resources of the job-seekers, and by their cultural predilections – all operating within the constraints of a particular environment.

Money is the main objective of Asian women seeking work. This paper illustrates how the constraints of the London environment and of the traditional culture coincide in the job-seeking network to limit both economic success and social costs. It stresses the variety of ethnic categories within the South Asian population; it indicates that ethnic allegiance is neither consistently marked nor consistently relevant: in certain settings, at certain points in time and for certain purposes, ethnic organisation will be inappropriate to the task in hand and so ignored; and it demonstrates that the meaning of ethnic group category/identity shifts according to context (as Wallman, 1974).

## Features of the Environment

Apart from the number and type of industries in the area and the number of jobs available, other variables determine the in habitants' use of their environment. The transport system determines ease of access and time taken to get to work. Child-care and pre-school facilities constrain the time available to work, affecting the married woman worker most crucially. A desired standard of living or felt economic need affects the choice of work and, more fundamentally, the decision to start working. The recent great increase in the cost of living has affected sections of the population differently according to their geographic and economic circumstances. These effects may be cushioned or altered by transferable resources available to some sections of the population, and by their differing expectations and priorities in saving and spending.

Nor can processes of change be ignored. It is not enough to know present circumstances; their significance can only be assessed with relation to the past. There are some changes taking place in the wider society and other changes experienced only by minority groups. While the rapid rate of social change and the apparent deterioration of 'race relations' are experienced through-out the country, both have tended to make Asian families particularly insecure, despite their increasing participation in and appreciation of certain aspects of the British way of life.

Although the local employment situation must be clearly distinguished from the women's perception of that situation, it is evident that they affect each other. The work that Asian women are doing (or not doing) at any point in time can, for example, be used by employers as an explanation of 'ethnic' preference or competence, and so to justify excluding Asian women from other work. When the women then interpret this exclusion as an immutable feature of the environment, limitations on the seeking of other work are reinforced.

Certain features of the environment constrain the work options open to all women – including the local indigenous population. The type and number of industries in the area determine the kind of work available (whether part-time, full-time or home-work), the rates of pay, amounts of overtime etc. The majority of jobs in south London are in manufacturing, construction, distributive trades and services and the last decade has seen a decrease of employment opportunities in the area. But while the manufac-turing sector has lost most jobs over the period, it remains the chief employer. Wages in south London are lower than for

Greater London as a whole, and there are greater numbers of small, privately-owned, labour-intensive firms. Over 40 per cent of wage jobs are done by women, but one-third of this figure is involved in part-time work. Although the female activity rates for south London are higher than the average for the rest of London, there is under-enumeration of women involved in any wage employment and of all workers in the non-enumerated 'informal' sector (see Santos, in this volume).

In London generally, women have a wider choice of employment than in many other cities. There is a greater variety of jobs in all sectors. The actual job options depend, however, on the amount of unemployment in different sectors of the economy at the time in question, and on the overall job situation. Following the policy of moving industry out of London and the general recession, the manufacturing sector has seriously contracted. Because women work predominantly in manufacturing, clothing, light industries and office employment and are more likely to be in part-time work, these changes have involved a disproportionate number of redundancies for women. It is possible that the trend has been matched by increases in certain forms of unenumerated casual work, but the excess demand for jobs has prevented any improvement in rates of pay or conditions of work.

Unemployment rates in south London are higher than for Greater London as a whole, greater for 'coloured' men than for indigenous whites, and greater for immigrant women than for women generally. Approximately one-third of all unemployed women are immigrants. Since the registration of unemployment is low among married women and Asians generally, and is particularly rare among Asian women, these figures are almost certainly under-estimated.[2]

The position of Asian women in the job market in south London is compounded by their being migrants, newcomers, dark-skinned and female. Relatively recent arrivals in the area do not have access to established networks of contacts or information to facilitate job hunting. As migrants from a different culture they do not have the social and linguistic skills of the indigenous population. As newcomers they are likely to be excluded from those areas of the employment market in which there is competition for jobs – and this is doubly true where women attempt to enter traditionally male-dominated sectors. As newcomers with a different culture and a darker skin, they may be further excluded on the grounds of 'race'. Discriminatory practices on the job may be rationalised in terms of the popular English notion that Asian women are submissive, never make trouble and do not know their rights.

## The Asian Population in South London

Interaction among Asian groups and between the different Asian populations and the wider society is determined in part by the composition and geographical distribution of the Asian settlement, but it cannot be understood simply by reference to the present situation. Communication networks and the boundaries between different sections of the population also reflect the process of migrant settlement. Although certain parts of London have a concentration of one particular ethnic category (for example, Sikhs in Southall, Bengalis in the East End etc.), most areas of immigrant settlement contain a mixture of many religious and national categories of Asian (Punjabi, Bengali, Gujerati; Sikh, Muslim, Hindu, Jain, Christian; and Pakistani, Indian, East African).

Relatively more migrants to London came without previous close contacts than to other parts of Britain. They had better job qualifications, more experience of urban life and more knowledge of English. Many Asian families came to London earlier than the majority in some of the northern industrial towns: on the whole, south London Asian women have lived in England longer than, for example, Pakistani village women in Bradford (Saifullah Khan, 1976b). The time of arrival affected subsequent settlement in important ways. The earliest male pioneer migrants had no existing support system of kin or ethnic institutions. Some chose or were forced to interact with local people and work-mates, and others looked for support from other Asians. All had contact with the local population in the work situation and did not have the opportunity or the need to work with those of their own cultural group. Many of the earlier arrivals therefore learnt English and English social skills, and developed more confidence in and knowledge of British institutions and culture. All but the very religious could introduce their wives to some of these skills, and even wives whose interaction beyond the home was restricted might share houses with other Asian couples who were not of their own national, ethnic or linguistic background. In this diverse population there was more opportunity and necessity for inter-ethnic and inter-national contact. While it did not necessarily entail identification with the British system, relatively more London Asian families admit that they will spend the rest of their lives in Britain and acknowledge that a determined effort will be necessary if they are to pass traditionally-valued beliefs and customs on to their children's generation.

Such generalisations cannot be proved statistically. But combined with the local employment market and the diversity of the Asian population in the area, they do explain why Pakistani village women in London live very different lives and have work options different from those of Pakistani village women in other parts of Britain. There is a wide variety of 'women's work' in London's labour market, and there is less pressure to conform to 'the traditional' because there are few closely knit, ethnically homogeneous areas of settlement. External factors in the environment are thus crucial determinants of so-called 'ethnic' patterns.

## Perceptions of Work

The external features of the environment and the local population determine the information available about local opportunities, but the assessment of their appropriateness is largely culturally defined. Retention of traditional cultural values depends in turn on pressure from the local Asian population and the degree of contact with the homeland.

Certain general statements can be made about South Asian culture. First, throughout the Indian sub-continent the mother has responsibility for the domestic sphere of activity. This includes child-care, housework and the domestic comforts of her husband. The husband is responsible for gaining the livelihood of the household. The division of labour is clearly demarcated. Second, high-status employment for men (*izzat-wali-kam*) is 'brain' work. It is not manual or potentially dirty work and should not involve dependence on, or taking orders from, another (cf. Kosmin, in this volume). The professions and business activity have therefore high status; cleaning and domestic work very low status. Third, in situations where female employment is acceptable, preference is given to work which does not involve contact with men outside the family.

There are numerous variations on these three general principles both in the Indian sub-continent and in the British situation. There are relatively more women in India than in Pakistan who work beyond the household and in contact with men. The *purdah* system is more strictly adhered to in Muslim Pakistan. Even in the professions the only acceptable jobs for orthodox Muslim women are those in which contact can be exclusively with the female sex (Saifullah Khan, 1976a). In these terms, medicine and teaching are high status but nursing is not: most Pakistani nurses are of a lower socio-economic background, or are Christians. Throughout the sub-continent, village women participate in the farming economy, caring for the domestic animals, cutting fodder in the fields and helping the men in the busy harvest seasons. Restricted interaction between men and women is relaxed in the village setting because fellow villagers can be perceived in terms of brother–sister relationships. But village women moving to cities are subject to stricter seclusion, are unable to contribute to the household economy and unable to take up other forms of employment.

In Britain, rural Asian women have very different opportunities according to their places of origin. Many Sikh and Hindu women from India and East Africa go out to work, mostly in unskilled or semi-skilled factory jobs. Whereas the majority of Pakistani women of rural origin do not go out to work because it is unacceptable for cultural/religious reasons, Pakistani women of urban background are more likely to take wage work. For all categories there is criticism and disapproval of the mother with young children who leaves the house to work. Children, it is believed, should be cared for by their mothers or close relatives until school-going age. In most families, the mother's employment is only accepted as long as it does not prevent her fulfilling the basic household work of cooking, cleaning and child-care. Employment beyond the home can be condoned only if it does not jeopardise the affection and care of young children, nor threaten the husband's position as main wage-earner and his exemption from housework.

Although there are variations in work ideologies and perceptions of available and appropriate opportunities held by the different categories of the Asian population in Britain, the new context highlights the similarities between these categories in contrast to the wider society. In the British situation it is meaningful to talk of a generalised Asian culture. The British context defines the significance of this new boundary: life in Britain involves a gradual appreciation of the crucial and distinctive constituents of Asian culture.

As information about jobs becomes available, it will be assessed by the job-seeker in terms of practical preference as well as traditional values. For most women the first priority is money; for the isolated or bored, work also provides companionship; and for those aspiring to status in the British system, a job allows the acquisition of social skills. The assessment of work options is determined by the job-seeker's goal, and will determine whether she prefers full-time work, part-time work or home-work. Most women in south London only consider home or part-time work while their children are under school age. But those who take full-time employment when their children are young and those who do not have an arrangement to ensure their children's safety between the end of school and the mother's return in the afternoon are equally severely criticised. Mothers with young children seek part-time work, either in the evening when the husband or elder sibling looks after the children, or in the morning while they are at nursery or with a child-minder. Child-minding is itself a form of work acceptable to women with young children who do not want to work outside or who are not allowed to by their husbands. For many, home-working and child-minding coincide with a certain stage in the family life-cycle and are therefore temporary. For others, particularly Pakistani women and older women, they are the preferred or most acceptable forms of employment.

A Hindu, Sikh or East African woman who can organise her domestic situation and has her husband's approval will not be morally condemned for working outside the home. For her, the only social costs of wage work are its repercussions on family life. The Pakistani village woman, however, is aware that employment beyond the home jeopardises the family's status and must be kept secret from the family in Pakistan. Deviations from the norm were in the early days rationalised in terms of migration targets and the intention to return to settle in the homeland. As time passes there is greater appreciation of the difficulty or inadvisability of rigid adherence to traditional notions of appropriate work and patterns of behaviour. Educated fathers explain their factory employment in terms of money to ensure the children's education in Britain. Mothers increasingly explain their desire for work in similar terms. While this gradual redefinition of what is acceptable makes the step to work less traumatic for some women, it may still be necessary to ensure that family members in the homeland do not know the type of work being done in England.

Finding work beyond the home directly affects the traditional division of labour, relationships within the household and the socialisation of children. But whether the husband sees his position threatened by his wife's physical mobility, contact with outsiders, earning of wages and subsequent acquisition of social skills and confidence, will depend on his personality and on the conjugal relationship as much as on religious or ethnic affiliation. There are some Pakistani Punjabi women whose husbands actually insist that they seek work; other women have found work and then informed their husbands. Alternatively, crisis situations or exceptional circumstances cause, or are used to justify, a woman starting work: work is usually taken when its economic advantage is perceived to outweigh its social costs.

At the present time in south London, full- or part-time work beyond the home is valued for its economic gain and any threat to the traditional family structure is likely to be justified by the ability to transfer monetary profits into socially acceptable and valued skills or consumer goods. But for those with young children, for traditional Muslim families and for women with traditional status-conscious husbands, the social cost in terms of family prestige and child-care responsibilities will still be too high. For these women, home-working is the only acceptable form of economic activity.

## Working the Network

All Asian women have very limited options when looking for work. Available jobs are limited to certain sectors of the economy; knowledge of them depends on the work-seeker's information network; and the perception of appropriate jobs depends upon cultural and domestic sanctions. But within these constraints there is some scope for choice and for alternative strategies. At any point in time the job-seeker has more or less explicit incentives to work, and has a set of material and social resources with which she will try to achieve her current objectives. Her evaluation of the costs and benefits of any course of action is determined by moral values as much as by economic considerations.

Highly-educated Asian women whose network of contacts is particularly limited may use the official job-seeking agencies. The majority, however, have limited skills, limited knowledge of the services provided by the agencies, restricted access to the local indigenous information network – but an extended network of Asian contacts.

Even in areas where the local Asian population is large and predominantly of the same ethnic origin, there are some crucial differences in the contacts and information channels open to different sections of it. Although a husband and wife have a common core of relatives and friends in their network of contacts, the peripheries are distinct; the husband's includes work-mates, and the wife, if she is not working, meets other women at the local clinic, shops or in the neighbourhood. Contact is restricted to specific settings (in the case of some women it is confined to the home and only when the husband is out), and useful information is available only in relation to specific spheres of activity. Women use their contacts to find out about child-minding; secondary schools for their daughters; a marriageable partner for a niece or nephew; and channels to home-working. Men keep in touch with the latest house prices, job opportunities and the political situation in the homeland.

The periphery of the network of contacts is distinct to each individual. It is a source of occasional companionship, but members of it are also used for specific purposes at particular points in time. Men in the workplace have the greatest potential for establishing wide links although (in parts of Britain) the contacts of Sylheti restaurant workers, Mirpuri textile workers on 'permanent nights' and Bengali workers in small clothing firms are largely restricted to their own ethnic (sub) category. There are few meeting places beyond the home and the workplace. For the first-generation married Asian migrant, most sociable interaction takes place in the home. The place of worship is a crucial exception, but not all families attend their mosque or temple, nor do all families have one in the vicinity. In any case, few local mosques in English cities cater for women. Men may attend Friday prayers and many young children learn their *Quran* in the evenings or at weekends, but for the more isolated women there is no meeting place in which they might organise social or religious gatherings.

In south London the peripheral network of contacts used for specific purposes such as job-seeking crosses ethnic boundaries. For some families even core network members are of different ethnic origin – although usually of the same religious affiliation. This is particularly true for long-established families who shared accommodation with unrelated South Asians on their arrival in Britain and have few close kin in the locality.

A particular set of six families living in south London illustrate the operation of these various ties. These people are all core members of each others' British-based network of contacts. Core membership implies that the families exchange visits, give each other financial and emotional support, are in frequent physical or telephone contact and have some number of core or peripheral contacts in common. All the families are Muslim and all but one are Pakistani, but two of the adult members were born in what is now India. One family is Bengali from Bangla Desh, three families are Punjabi, one couple is Pathan and the sixth consists of a Pathan man whose wife was born in the Indian Punjab but brought up in Karachi. Only two families are related by kinship ties and not all have the same mother tongue: when vernacular communication is not possible, Urdu is used as the *lingua franca*.

The development of inter-relationships between families of different ethnic origin illustrates the way in which the boundary and significance of ethnic affiliation shifts with setting and circumstance. Half the families have no kin at all in Britain; the two related families have none apart from each other. In the other cases, blood relatives, even when perceived as part of the core network, have no special emotional or financial significance, whereas there may still be loyal involvement with relatives in the homeland 6000 miles away. The alliance of these six families is based on neither kinship nor 'ethnic' criteria. Three of the men had the same occupation in the homeland; four of the families have spent periods in the same town in Britain before coming to London; and four others actually shared the same house at different stages in their first years in Britain. Only two families have not, at some time, shared accommodation with one of the others: . . . *Family A owned their own house and Family B [Mr A's younger brother and wife] shared the accommodation. Family C joined them when Mr C traced Mr A, whom he knew from their years in the navy together. Mr A also knew where Mr D, another old friend from the navy, was now living and the contact was re-established. When Family C moved to their own house [three miles from house A, and a mile from house D], Mr E came to lodge with them. Mr E is from the same home region as Mr C and without family or kin in Britain had found the whereabouts of Mr C before he left Pakistan. Family F lived near Families A, B and C when they shared a house and there were few other Pakistanis in the neighbourhood. When Family C wanted the use of all their house and could afford not to have lodgers, Family E moved into the house of Family A . . .*

Common residence in the early years in Britain is a common basis for continued support and involvement. Each family was able to draw on common network resources in the difficult early years and in periods of bringing up of young children and saving hard to buy a house. When Mr A died, the others rallied to support Mrs A and her four children. This network provided the women with company and support when they had few alternative Asian contacts, limited ability in English and in communicating with the English. It was made more important by the experience of disinterest or discrimination of neighbours and other local contacts. Its ties are strong enough to have survived one major dispute involving three of the families, and a mutual understanding that marriage between all but the two related families is precluded by ethnic, class or caste differences. The families exchange visits and the wives frequently consult each other for advice, support, help in times of crises, and for establishing contacts with others:. . . *Mrs R once lodged in the house of Family C for a year and afterwards remained a close contact. Mrs C was asked to find a 'suitable' girl for the brother of Mrs R's friend. Mrs C then telephoned members of her network whom she judged to be most useful in this context. These were those with family and friends of similar educational, socio-economic and ethnic background. By acting as in-*

*termediary in the subsequent visiting between the families involved, Mrs C
extended her own range of peripheral contacts. Mrs C also helped Mrs E
find her present wage work and is looking for home-work for Mrs D and
Mrs A . . .*

Women seeking work have access to the contacts of core
members of their network and to their own and their husbands'
contacts. The successful mobilisation of these contacts provides
access to information from others who may be several links
removed from the job-seeker.

## Working at Home

Women take home-work either because they estimate the
economic advantage of outside jobs as small and the social cost of
working beyond the home as too great, and/or because they are
unable to find other work which they consider appropriate.

Working at home is the safest option in terms of social costs:
working hours are flexible and can be adjusted to the daily
routine; there is no need to move beyond the house, nor is there
any threat to the husband's role as principal wage-earner. But
even if the home-worker's income is always a supplementary
income, it restores the village woman to the status of a
contributor to the household budget that she had in the
homeland. Whether the money earned is spent on personal
effects, pooled for household expenses or saved, home-working
eases financial pressure and prevents the anxiety of total
dependence which is a source of tension for some couples. In
many instances it makes a crucial contribution to the household
budget.

But home-working provides no opportunity for the acquisition
of social skills, nor any training which might be useful in work
beyond the home at a later stage. Most employers do not count
home-working as 'experience' or as 'previous employment'.
Although home-work may involve skilled performance, it is
never a 'proper' job (cf. Macrae, in this volume). And as a
woman at home has not the opportunity for social interaction
and the speaking of English, there is less likelihood of her gaining
confidence or advancing her position vis-à-vis husband and
family. There is also less likelihood of her fully understanding the

pressures and problems faced by her children growing up in Britain.

Because home-working rarely involves a formal contract or any responsibilities on the part of the employer, home-workers have no security of employment. Many Asian women do not know the name or even the whereabouts of their employer, using a telephone number for urgent messages. Most employers bear none of the costs of an industrial machine or of lighting and heating, and there is no holiday pay or sickness benefit. Some of the work is seasonal, especially in the clothing industry, and this accentuates its casualness: in the slack summer season the supply of work decreases or may dry up altogether. The type of work offered may change without warning but a certain number of articles must still be completed on schedule. Home-workers must make sure they are at home on delivery-and-collection days (often twice a week) or they must arrange to collect and deliver their own work on schedule.

The irregularity and flexibility of home-work is not always a handicap. Although many women do not know when or for how long there will be a slack period, it may happen that those involved in sewing will be laid off for periods which coincide with their children's holidays. Women home-workers with a good work record who go to visit the Indian sub-continent for several months have a greater chance of re-employment on return than do their neighbours in full-time factory employment.

Many features of the home-work system and of the home-workers' perception and organisation of work are reminiscent of early industrial Victorian life . . . 'a wife's responsibility for the well-being of her husband and children always came before her work in social production [but] every member of the family participated and contributed to the family income' (Alexander, 1976, p. 77). For these English workers, as for the villagers of the Indian sub-continent, there was no clear distinction between domestic and farmwork nor a regular, ordered schedule for work. The economic value of the work was perceived in terms of 'the total amount earned each week rather than the number of hours worked to earn it' (Hope *et al.*, 1976, p. 28). The same is true for the following South Asian women: . . . *Mrs J lives in a Victorian terraced house in a quiet street in south London. She is Pakistani, a Punjabi of the Ahmadiya sect. She came to Britain in 1971 to join her husband, who had lived in Britain since 1958. Mrs J is more educated than her husband [she has a university degree] and speaks very good English. Despite his many years in Britain, her husband had neither bought a house nor had he saved much money before the arrival of his wife – both failures being unusual in Pakistanis of this background. Mrs J found their rented accommodation depressing and inadequate. It is for this explicit reason that: 'I worked very hard, never buying any clothes, just saving all I earned.'*

Mrs J's husband is in wage employment, earning about £60 a week. The Ahmadiya sect are particularly strong believers in the *purdah* system and, although unusually highly educated, most Ahmadiya women do not go out to work. Mrs J became pregnant with the first of her two children soon after her arrival in Britain but, having assessed their financial and housing situation, began taking in home-work soon after it was born. During these first few years she worked 'whenever possible' while caring for her two children and the needs of her husband. She earned about £25 a week. While she knows that her 'employer' came from outside the borough, she is not sure where the business was. A few months before her third child was born the family moved into its present home – her savings from home-work providing the deposit on the property. Her first employer would not deliver work to this new locale and so she found other home-work through a friend. This new work she knows to have been supplied by a Cypriot firm in North London. It consisted of sewing dresses sold in a well-known chain of fashion shops. The work was hard but the rate per garment was, at 50 pence, higher than before. Mrs J sewed between sixty and sixty-five dresses a week for nearly two months before the birth of her third child. For the four or five months after his birth she was too busy to sew. When she eventually contacted her old employer he said he would deliver work to her home only if she could guarantee to complete 100 garments a week. Knowing that she would be unable to complete even as many as before, Mrs J tried to find a few friends who would take some of the quota off her hands. At the same time, she realised it would be harder to meet the high standard of work demanded now that she had three small children. She has lately been trying to find different work through friends, and friends of friends:

. . . *Mrs K is a Bangla Deshi woman. She arrived in Britain in 1963 soon after marrying. Her husband has lived in Britain since 1954 and now runs his own business. He bought their house in 1962 and rented half of it until recently. Mr and Mrs K have two explicit priorities; they are concerned to educate their children well and to provide for their families at home in Bangla Desh. This last includes building a house there in case they, or their children, return to settle. Mrs K says: 'We do not spend much on decorating our house and buying luxury things. We think of the future and remember our homeland.'*

*Five years ago Mrs K started home-working. She remembers feeling very bored and that a friend of her husband gave her the phone number of an employer which she thinks is in the East End. Her husband did not want her to work outside the house and, anyway, it could not at that time be seriously considered because of their two young children. Now that the fourth child is starting nursery school, her husband wants her to work behind the scenes in his business. Because he will not allow her to work in the presence of other men, there are few jobs other than home-working which will allow her to earn the independent income she would like.*

*For the last five years, Mrs K has been sewing sleeping bags, earning £10 to £12 a week. The work is dirty and takes up a lot of space, and she has tried to get her employer to give her a different task. She knows he has other items to be sewn, but it is said that her work is not of high quality and he may be tired of her complaints. After the (enforced) break in work over the Christmas period he has not given her more work, despite her many pleading telephone calls. It is important that there are now so many women looking for work that employers with a good network of contacts have a wider choice. A friend of Mrs K's who rang this employer on her behalf was told that he has all the workers he needs.*

*Mrs K is now looking for other work by asking friends. An Indian landlord a few streets away told Mrs K that his Chinese woman tenant was doing simple work at home. He gave her the telephone number of the Chinese woman's employer – a Greek Cypriot firm in North London. On inquiry, Mrs K was told that the dresses had to be completed by each worker and that the job would be too hard for anyone with only experience of sleeping bags. Skilled workers may still be scarce: this employer was said to be keen to engage new workers.*

*. . . Mrs L works for the same employer as Mrs K, who had given her the firm's telephone number a few months after she started there herself. Mrs L came to Britain in 1963 and moved into her own house in 1968. Her husband has stayed in the same wage employment throughout. He earns approximately £80 a week by working an irregular shift system and maximum overtime. Soon after her arrival in Britain, Mrs L worked in a*

*small clothing firm with another Pakistani woman who lodged in the same house. The employees were all women, mainly Asian. Mrs L left during her first pregnancy and became a child-minder for two periods while her children were small. For several years the family rented out rooms in their own house. When there was space for an industrial machine she started home-work. Mrs L is a more skilled machinist than Mrs K and has established a better relationship with her employer. If she takes a few weeks off for a holiday or because of illness he takes her on again after the break, and he gives her (but not Mrs K) a gift at Christmas time. Mrs L considers herself lucky to have found this employer and better off than many friends who have to accept changing styles or even types of garment without notice, and with no demonstration of how it should be done. She works fast and systematically can earn from £16 to £23 a week in only two and a half days' work. Last year she completed sixty to eighty garments each week (collected twice a week) and received 25 pence per garment. This is a 3 pence rise on the rate at which she started five years ago. There was one period of simpler garments during which she was able to sew 100 a week, receiving 23 pence per garment. Recently, a more complicated design has been delivered, paid at the rate of 27 pence per garment. Although it takes her longer to sew, she does not want to complain for fear of jeopardising her supply of work.*

*Mrs L prefers to work very hard on two days a week (which she admits tires her a lot) rather than a little each day. She fits the work into the family routine and the money she earns is spent on luxuries and 'extras' like household decoration, toys and holiday money for the children. She is now also saving for two major house repairs. Mrs L is tired of doing this home-work and complains of occasional backache and sore eyes. She had hoped to take wage work in a year or two but says it is essential that it be near home and finishes in time for her to collect her son from school. She wonders anyway whether it is worth working for a part-time wage of £16 a week when she can earn more than that in half the time doing out-work at home. Some of her friends have told her that it is now harder to find wage work in a factory . . .*

There are signs that some firms have increased their numbers of home-workers. This may mean an overall expansion of firms employing only home-workers, or that firm using out-work *and* factory-based work are increasing their ratio of out-workers. There are even signs of new out-work firms starting up in response to the current economic recession. For the employer of out-workers, the advantages are plain. They cost him nothing in overheads; there is no contract between employer and employee, no record kept which would allow official scrutiny of conditions of work or pay; and there is little likelihood of a cohesive organisation emerging to demand improvements. The advantages to employer and home-worker are in effect complementary.

## Boundaries of Acceptance

It is clear that culture and ethnic affiliation are just one factor influencing work in the local Asian population, and the patterns of communication within and between different sections of it, and with the wider society. The local environment determines opportunities and constraints in terms of housing, employment and social life which influence the mechanics of the migration process, determining the settlement pattern. The composition of the settlement in turn determines the form and content of communication between sections of the population, and influences the efficiency of the information network for specific purposes. The traditional 'Asian culture' constrains the perception and manipulation of the British system, but provides alternative resources in times of uncertainty and hostility. The combination of political powerlessness with high aspirations and the need for protection against the bombardment of British culture tend to mean that options within the Asian system are chosen in preference to the British whenever possible. The alien environment defines previous 'outsiders' as fellow Asians, fellow sufferers and sources of support and identification.

As context determines the significance of social boundaries, so the boundaries shift over time and from one situation to another. Pakistani Punjabis settling in a British city with a large number of kin and fellow villagers from the home locality could, for example, maintain the most significant 'we' group of daily village life, the *biradari* (kin) of co-operation. The move to Britain, however, ensures a gradual appreciation of the externally defined category of 'Pakistani' or 'Asian'. And on certain occasions (as war with India) and in certain interactions (as with English work-mates), common identification and solidarity among Pakistanis is manifest. South Asians perceive themselves as members of several 'ethnic' and non-ethnic groups, whose appropriateness depends on the priorities of each specific context (Saifullah Khan, 1976c).

The concept of 'nesting' of ethnic categories is crucial to an understanding of job-seeking networks in south London. For some purposes, notably those related to marriage and family visiting, it is the narrowest ethnic affiliation which regulates interaction. For other purposes, such as job-seeking, the boundary is extended to envelop a wider network of affiliation which depends on available numbers, on the encumbent pressure to conform and on identification with others in a similar position who share a common label in relation to the wider society. In south London where the ethnic/national/religious mix and physical dispersal is greater than in many other areas, and where families have settled for longer, South Asians have a greater awareness of British society, its restrictions and definitions. Families of Asian origin have maintained their distinctive values and patterns of behaviour by extending systems of support and information beyond traditionally-accepted categories of people.

The category 'Asian' provides a basis of interaction and organisation for an increasing number of first-generation migrants of Asian origin in certain areas of Britain. The emergence of a socially and physically more mobile, British-orientated second generation points to a decrease in significance of the narrower ethnic categories. While the concepts of a 'Pakistani ethnicity' or an 'Asian ethnic' category were meaningless for the Mirpuris, Sylhetis and so on, who comprised most first-generation migrants, the structure, reception and definitions of British society are bound to provoke a sense of Asian-ness in their children. The trend of greater numbers of Asian women going out to work will have fundamental repercussions on relationships within the family, but will not necessarily lead to conformity to the norm of the majority society. As the need for and the consequences of various adaptive strategies change with situation and through time, so the balance of ethnic processes will alter accordingly.

# 6

As in the previous example, the boundaries of 'us' are shown here to shift according to the exigencies of the work context. In this case, however, the context is that of a ('formal') bureaucratic government office whose job it is to allocate scarce public housing resources according to established rules of 'fairness', justice and welfare.

The scope for ('informal') discretion comes in the interpretation and application of those rules; in the individual worker's general notions of a worthy applicant; and in his/her specific assessment of an applicant's worth. In making these assessments, the conceptual line which distinguishes 'us', the members of the moral community from 'them', the non-members who are (or should be) excluded is marked by notions of Englishness. The fact that these notions are idealised and often inconsistent does not make them any the less 'ethnic'.

# Bureaucracy and Ethnicity

## Notions of eligibility to public housing

The setting is the [local authority] Corporation Housing Department in a large industrial city in England. The workers are the
rank and file staff of the department. The materials which
they process are the thousands applying for housing, awaiting rehousing from clearance areas or already living on corporation
estates.

The bureaucratic structure of the department and the constraints upon the organisation and distribution of scarce (housing) resources combine to define Housing Department staff
against those 'others' in local government who have work
objectives and values different from theirs and against 'others' in
the applicant/tenant population whom they feel are making false
or improper claims.

The staff do not consider these reactions 'ethnic'. But in
response to the threat to their basic values posed by a minority of
applicants/tenants, they must define the moral boundary of 'us'
and are driven to articulate Englishness.

This paper considers the bureaucratic constraints on staff and
the particular concerns of key sections of the department; the
values of the staff and their justification; and lastly, attitudes
towards tenants and towards the welfare state. These attitudes
indicate how and where the moral boundary is drawn. The
basis of mistrust in the welfare state is the extent to which it rots
traditionally-valued English attributes and distributes services
without discriminating between those within and those beyond
the moral boundary.

**Staff and Structure**

The first point to be made is that working in the Housing Department is a job: it is not a vocation or a 'profession'. Very few officers went in because they were particularly interested in housing or felt they had a flair for dealing with people. Rather, it was better paid than the Gas Board, made a change from the insurance office, or the advertisement caught their eye when they had come out of the army.

Most staff are not qualified: housing management has not been regarded as a profession. 'Local government is very lucky to have conscientious officers working through the years without recognition', a long-serving officer insisted. Recognition includes a comfortable salary.

Second, the Housing Department is highly bureaucratic. The work is divided into many small routine tasks which can be performed by staff with minimal training. This mode of organisation is significant to performance in three ways:

(i) Initiative is devalued. There is no room for it in a system of this sort: 'You came in here as a new recruit full of ideas and you got squashed. They didn't want to know. They took away all your initiative after a few months.'

(ii) Experience counts for much. The procedures of the section, the precedents set when exceptional cases occurred – both, of course, specific to the department – were the requisite knowledge for those in supervisory positions.

(iii) The scope for discretion is limited. Most of the work entails the use of standard procedures and standard formats. Difficulties are referred upwards to clearly identified positions. Even where there are rules, of course, some judgement is required in applying them and in recognising the exceptional case to refer to a senior, but this scarcely counts as discretion. 'The exercise of discretion occurs when officials are required or permitted to make decisions without being given instructions which would in effect predetermine those decisions' (Hill, 1972, p. 62).

The jobs which require considerable judgement are those entailing selection or assessment of applicants/tenants. Selection may be for offers of properties or for the transfer list. Assessments must be made of applicants' housekeeping standards and the sort of tenants they are likely to make; of evidence of eligibility for housing; of the truth of tenants' 'stories' both over eligibility and over arrears. This is where the work becomes 'psychological', as one officer put it. Again experience is emphasised. Although these tasks are less rule-bound than, for example, rent collection and the classification of cases, there is a stock of section wisdom for the guidance of the individual officer.

If this description makes the Housing Department approach the ideal type of a bureaucracy, we may expect it to be criticised for the ideal typical bureaucratic faults of rigidity and impersonality. Whereas those tasks built into the routine are routinely performed, other tasks may be overlooked, and needs outside the defined tasks of the organisation ignored. Cases are duly processed, but it is nobody's business to ensure that residents receive the full information about clearance or rehousing, or about the choice of estates: that their conditions during the emptying of the area are as tolerable as possible: that their introduction to the new estate is welcoming. When the Department has been criticised for disregarding people's needs, the cry has been for social workers – *not* for a broadening of housing officials' roles.

Impartiality could be construed by applicants as impersonality. If all applicants get much the same sort of deal, it might seem no one cares much about any of them. This is, of course, the classic bureaucratic dilemma. Too much formalisation creates rigidity and impersonality; too little means inconsistency and loss of that impartial rationality which is bureaucracy's defining feature.

Three results of formalisation may be mentioned. First, most staff do not individually have very much power over the life chances of applicants/tenants. Second, staff feel they have little power and are obliged to carry out policies they dislike. Third, the rules, in some sections, take on absolute character.

It also follows from the bureaucratic nature of the Housing Department that staff in one section know relatively little about the work of those in another (especially if either is outside the Town Hall). It is not necessary for them to know the functions of other sections in order to carry out their duties, so they are not

told of them. When staff at the area offices accuse the Town Hall
sections of indifference, or when lettings staff mutter at the delays
over their enquiries at the area offices, they are complaining
about sections they do not understand and very likely have never
visited.

Similarly with the policy of the council. Most staff know only
the policies which affect their own work. Staff in the clearance
section are informed of changes in eligibility rules but not of those
covering management. When policies alter, staff affected are
notified of changes in procedure, but the reasons for the changes
are not explained. Thus policy changes appear as capricious,
vote-catching devices, needlessly complicating the work of the
staff. Only at the top of the department do staff have an overall
view of the functioning of the department and its objectives.

Beside a limited view, the work of each section breeds a specific
set of concerns.

The Waiting list and Transfer sections (jointly, Registration)
spend practically all their time classifying and reclassifying
applications, and maintaining the filing systems. They deal not so
much with people as with application forms. What surprise, then,
that the classification system tends to take on 'natural' moral
value? It has continued almost unchanged since the early 1950s.
The interpretation of older councillors is indicative: it had
worked all that time, so it must be all right – 'worked' being
judged, presumably, by the fact that people do get housed.

Though staff assure applicants that cases were given priority
according to need, they do not enquire whether the scheme in
fact measures need *accurately*, measures *all* relevant needs or ranks
them *appropriately*. If one asks these questions, one is told they are
not qualified to say: the council decided many years ago.

The Medical Officer of Health has power to advance cases
considerably. Officials are sometimes surprised by his gradings,
but then 'we're only laymen'. They have great faith in the
possibility of assessing medical needs objectively (on the basis
of a scrawled doctor's note) but are sceptical about assessing
social needs and about including them as a consideration for rehousing.

These staff are the servants of the classification system. They
have operated it for years, meticulously, uncritically. They are
also its guardians. The system which is *The System*, the system to

whose maintenance they have devoted years of their lives, must be kept pure. What is the point of having a system, they ask, if it is not rigidly adhered to?

Seniors, of course, having greater scope for discretion, also have more scope for generous interpretation, for mercy. But staff fear mercy rots the system. It could be a disastrous mistake. A comparison suggests itself here with observations on mistakes in another work setting:

> The ritual punctiliousness of nurses and pharmacists is a kind of built-in shock absorber against the possible mistakes of the physician . . . in dramatising their work these second-rank professions explicitly emphasise their role as saviours of both patient and physician from the error of the latter    (Hughes, 1951, p. 325).

Occasionally, middle-ranking staff take a senior's decision back to him before putting it into effect, and check that he realises its implications. The greatest fear is that a senior should unwittingly 'open the flood gates' – a generous decision might set a precedent which, the middle rank judges, prejudices the chances of others on the list. Especially unfortunate would be any decision which appears to reward the use of shock tactics – hysteria, suicide threats, abuse, the dumping of children in the department – for this would legitimate the use of such tactics and staff would undoubtedly have more hysteria, more abuse and more dumped children with which to deal. In addition, it would make a mockery of the system and of their own efforts. Those who abide by the system would suffer, and these are the applicants whom staff feel it is their duty to protect: 'It is left up to us to protect the weak and innocent, to protect them from being pushed down the list by those that come and shout at us . . .'

The Clearance section shares many of the interests of the Registration section, including the protection of the weak on the waiting list, but by a more indirect means. The chances of applicants on the list are reduced the greater the number to be rehoused from clearance areas. The danger is that by moving into clearance areas just before rehousing begins, households can jump the queue, gaining priority over all waiting-list cases. Thus the section's overriding concern is eligibility. Those who fail to

produce evidence of length of residence for the clearance visitor
to inspect are invited to bring such evidence to the Town Hall:
'Until you bring in some proof you'll not get anything from
us . . .' When evidence is produced its veracity must be assessed.
Staff must be on the alert for the telling of tales and the
fabrication of evidence. The risk of residents 'getting one over on
us' or 'pulling a fast one' is ever present. Seniors are felt to be too
generous. As for policy, staff were disgusted when, in 1972–4, the
corporation attempted to rehouse non-eligibles, albeit in hard-
to-let properties: this was allowing them to jump the queue.
When figures showed the increasing number of properties
allocated to non-eligibles, the director came to share the staff's
misgivings. The rules have been changed, denying non-eligibles
any chance of rehousing, unless families are still present when
demolition starts, in which case they count as homeless families.
This gives the section's vigilance greater point. A resident who
announced by phone that he had just moved into a clearance
area and so the corporation had to rehouse him, was told, smugly:
'Not any more, we don't!'

Lettings staff mutter among themselves about the rehousing of,
first, non-eligibles and then homeless families, both at the
expense of the waiting list. But the central preoccupation bred
by their work is very different from that of the Registration or
Clearance sections. It is with matching within time limits a stock
of properties and a pool of households. As staff constantly tell
residents: 'It is all a question of property availability.' The
absolute requirements are to rehouse the last few clearance-area
households in time to meet the scheduled date of demolition and
to prevent any property remaining unlet for long (since it is losing
revenue). Within these, the emphasis is on getting clearance-area
residents 'fixed up' and on getting rid of property which is
'sticking'. The available properties and the requests of the pool of
applicants never match exactly. But the quantities of each are not
flexible: stock changes over the months as new developments are
finished, and the pool can be enlarged by going further down the
waiting list or transfer list. The skill lies in fitting the people to the
stock by persuading them to consider areas they had not
requested. Selection officers can get the visitors to canvass for
them. They can assure applicants that areas are nicer than they
think: 'Yes, love, it *is* near the gas works, but there's a plan to do a

lot of environmental improvements' . . . They can offer to fix the desperate applicant up quickly on a less popular estate: 'We'll find a *nice* part of *Y*' . . . or warn a resident who insists on holding out for X estate that: 'Your prospects are not good. No, I'm *not* saying you *can't* have one, I'm saying that your prospects are not good . . .'

Clearly, Lettings deal with people. They share a front-line position with area office staff.

While Registration staff occasionally suspect that selection officers do not stick rigorously enough to the order of the waiting lists and selection officers think that visitors let residents believe they have been promised a house on the desired estate, area management staff accuse selection officers of not bothering where they put people. Good lettings practice, they tell you, is *not* to put a lad of twenty-one in a block of old-age pensioners' flats or a household with bugs in the middle of a maisonette block or a rowdy family on a quiet and desirable estate. It is area management which have to cope with the consequences.

Unlike other sections, area management's task is not part of a process through which the applicants pass, each officer doing his part and never seeing or hearing of the applicant again. The housing officer (H.O.) has a lasting relationship with the tenant. He will see the tenant every fortnight for a period of perhaps years. He will have to deal directly with the results of both the selection officer's work and his own, and indirectly with those of the architect and the various departments servicing the estates. With tenants already resident he has established some sort of relationship and has made some sort of judgement: he knows 'how things stand' and how to treat the tenant. Incoming tenants are an unknown and not very welcome quantity: he hopes they will not upset existing good tenants; he hopes they will be good tenants themselves, but fears the worst; he will judge once he has called for the rent a few times.

Arrears are the preoccupation of the office and bad tenants their most intractable problem. The housing officer is not bothered about the classification system or the rules of eligibility, neither of which he knows. He wants tenants who pay their rent, look after the properties and do not upset their neighbours. If Lettings could provide a steady supply of them he would not worry how they came to be selected for housing. For example, one H.O. could not see why a squatter in one of his properties could not be given the tenancy. He paid his rent, kept the place clean and was better than what Lettings would send them off the waiting list. Such an opinion would cause consternation indeed in the Town Hall. The question constantly posed in area offices is 'What sort of payer?' This compares with 'What class?' in Registration, 'Are they eligible?' in Clearance, and 'What clearance area?' (and hence what priority) in Lettings. These are the administrative distinctions which determine how each section proceeds and predetermines areas of conflict between them.

## Fairness

The prevailing theme of fairness runs through the accounts of each section. Registration insist it is unfair to applicants not to stick rigidly to the rules, Clearance feel it is unfair to them not to be strict about (area) eligibility, and there is comment in all sections against the injustice of housing the bad tenants among the good – this comment being loudest, naturally, in the area offices. H.O.s feel it is unfair that some good tenants have endured bad accommodation for years (faithfully paying their rent) while new tenants, regardless of standards, get new houses. They also object that good tenants pay their rent while others do not and 'get away with it'.

All these are grievances against policy-makers and management. The conviction prevails that seniors are swung by 'fuss', that they are too generous over eligibility and they may slightly change the order of clearance areas under pressure from a Member of Parliament. And, to recap, it is policy that the homeless and (1972–4) non-eligibles are housed in preference to the waiting list, that clearance-area residents get priority over waiting lists and transfers, that they get the pick of the available properties and that this applies to those with poor assessments too: they are not to be allocated only poor properties, nor are they segregated on the one estate.

Undeniably, staff disagree with 'top brass' on rehousing and management policies. Their definitions of the situation, the problem and the solution differ. They are, however, never asked.

These points of grievance are also the foci around which the various groups identity themselves.

## The Moral Community

While these differences are based on differing notions of justice and of the welfare state, they are best elaborated as traditional English moral values expressed within the constraints of a bureaucratic context. Together, they constitute the office perspective, which is conveyed as a continual effort to defend the office version of reality against any incursion from outside: the greatest threat coming from non-member clients. Certain values are central to the distinction between 'members' and 'non-members' (as Goffman, 1961, 1968). Among those most often articulated are the following:

*Work as such, is good; it is therefore better to do any work than to be idle ('The Work Ethic'). It is right and proper to provide for food, clothing and shelter before you spend on anything else ('There is no tenant who cannot pay the rent')* . . . *People should attempt to provide for themselves (with reference to housing in particular): if they cannot, the state should provide for those who are respectable (that is, deserve it), but these people should remember that they are being subsidised, that they are lucky* . . . *Everyone should know his place – particularly the tenants. They should not tug their forelocks, exactly, but neither should they claim things as of right, nor behave like customers instead of as beneficiaries of the council* . . . *Only the 'normal' family system is acceptable. Man and woman should be married, the relationship permanent, and concerned largely with the fulfilment of duties. Roles within the family are prescribed in detail: the man dominates, though his wife may nag. Families should be small, and a couple should not have children until they can afford them* . . . *Everyone is responsible for what he is and for what he does: explanations in terms of environment, deprivation or the like are not acceptable (although, inconsistently, it is sometimes conceded that children growing up on specified bad estates 'haven't a chance')* . . . *The bad should be punished because it is only fair to the good and as an example to all – particularly in the matter of rent arrears: evictions are a good thing, a moral victory* . . . *The law is right and should not be questioned (this conviction is firmest among elderly staff). Council policy, on the other hand, is too soft and is the root cause of many of the department's problems* . . . *Finally, it is not good to be extreme in any way, nor too 'political'. Although it is all right to have trade unions to guard people's interests, they should not get political . . .*

Officers approve of, like and occasionally favour ('put themselves out for') applicants/tenants to whom they impute the same beliefs. Observations made on the values of National Assistance Board officers are relevant here. One author, having warned that 'we must avoid laying too much emphasis on middle-class norms of respectability and contempt for those "unable to help themselves" since this would be to belittle NAB officers', writes:

> At one extreme there were those whose attitude to their clientele was one in which the safeguarding of public funds from the grasp of the poor was a primary consideration, whilst at the other extremes were some officers who readily recognised the inadequacy of the allowances they were empowered to grant and who were always on the lookout for their clients' needs. Perhaps the prevalent attitude was a combination of these two positions in which most officers sought to do as much as possible for the old and undeniably sick, but few had very much time for the long-term unemployed or for the women whose family life was of an unstable kind. In as much as these were the common attitudes it is unreasonable to represent the NAB officer as anything other than typical of the society from which he is drawn   (Hill, 1969, pp. 86–7).

Apart from these moral distinctions, officers dislike tenants who are unco-operative, impolite or unappreciative. While staff distance themselves from the corporation's failures, they identify with its successes: 'You'd think they'd be grateful when we're giving them a house' – 'we' means not just the corporation, but 'us', the people who man the system. Work satisfaction derives largely from gratitude for what 'we' have done: not only through the special efforts of the individual officer, but also, routinely, as the representative of the local authority. The impression is sometimes given that applicants are rehoused or properties repaired through the grace and favour of the officers.

Middle-aged and elderly tenants are more apt than are the young to show gratitude and deference towards the staff. Indeed, some old people appear to have so little notion of rights as to believe that rehousing/repairs are personal kindnesses.

Given the importance of gratitude, staff tend to be irked by those who talk about their rights to a house: this removes the grace and the favour. Staff become servants accused of failing to deliver a service. Rights are rarely mentioned unless they are contentious: the right of a non-eligible to be rehoused; the right of a waiting-list applicant to rehousing *now*; the right to a *house*; or to a *particular* estate.

The young are more likely to quote rights. Partly this is because the majority of non-eligibles and waiting-list applicants are young. More importantly, they are the children of the welfare state and the children of existing council tenants. Both of these circumstances incline them to see a council house as their right. In this they are encouraged by central government statements: '. . . a decent home for every family at a price within their means' (H.M.S.O., 1971, p. 1).

If they feel that their housing conditions are intolerable, they may resort to abuse, denying staff not only gratitude for their efforts, but even respect. A daily, probably hourly, occurrence, this has staff muttering in the back offices against the 'manners' of the young who have been 'given everything on a plate'. The plate, of course, is the welfare state. The cliché is delivered sometimes with great vehemence ('What a cheek . . . but of course these days . . .'), on other occasions with puzzlement to why some young tenants make such a mess of everything (when they've been handed everything on a plate). It is used by those who can remember a time before the welfare state. Whatever may be said in its favour, the welfare state is held responsible for a loss of moral fibre among the working class. This loss is indicated by the proclivities of the young to tell lies to get a house; to create overcrowding by having another baby or moving in with already crowded in-laws; to blame the council for their disintegrating marriage – and then, once they do have a place, to fall into arrears and then to demand a transfer. If they had the fibre of previous generations, and given that they have 'every opportunity', they would work to 'better themselves' by saving for a house. And there would be no babies until they had that house. They would be self-reliant, rather than shouting 'Gimme, gimme, gimme'! Staff can usually instance juniors in the office who *are* 'bettering themselves' in the proper way and support their case against those who are not.

**Dependence and Gratitude**

Staff in all sections are disparaging of the dependency of applicants and tenants, not merely over minor repairs, but also in the settlement of disputes with neighbours, how to get a separation etc. They never connect this with power – neither with the power of the corporation, nor the powerlessness of the tenant and the corporation's tendency to discourage initiative. There is never anything which the applicant/tenant can do: he should wait patiently on the list. The department will inform him when his turn comes. There is no point in his writing to the department unless he has a change of circumstances to report. He will be told when rehousing from his clearance area is starting . . . No, there is nothing he can do to ensure a house on X estate; it depends on the demand from the other forty clearance areas. Yes, he must wait in or leave the key with a neighbour; they cannot say when Direct Works will come. No, he cannot contact them himself. They have been given the order, it is just a matter of waiting . . . Waiting itself is a function of powerlessness.

The helplessness of the tenants and the fact that once they are tenants they expect the corporation to do everything for them, these are usually attributed to the decay of self-reliance. Occasionally, staff cite the tenants' desire to get their money's worth, having reluctantly become council tenants, and of high-rented property at that: 'The sort of thing that bothers them is draughts under the door. Before they became council tenants they'd just have bought a draught excluder, but now they have to have Direct Works come round in a van and spend an hour there – to feel they're getting their money's worth.'

In the staff view, tenants are mollycoddled. If they were owner-occupiers, like many of themselves, they could not just ring up an office about repairs and have everything done for them, regardless of expense. This rankles: 'Fancy expecting us to provide a new bit of rope for her pulley: she'll be wanting us to tie her shoelaces next'.

Tenants tend to see the department as all-powerful. Consequently, they are always being disappointed. The department – or at least many of its officers – are equally disappointed in the tenants, and disgusted at the lengths to which the corporation has to go on some of the estates just to make up for tenants' failings . . . 'Men have to be employed just to paint over the graffiti and to put their rubbish down the chute. They can't be bothered to do so themselves!'

That looking after tenants is perceived as a thankless task is not literally true: many tenants are grateful and their gratitude is a recognised reward for the job. But there are some ungrateful people and the effort put into trying to satisfy tenants (whether over 'offers' or over repairs) is generally frustrating.

Officers are all the more aggrieved because they see themselves and the department 'bending over backwards to help people'. For the same reason, they resent outsiders' calling the department inhumane: . . . 'The department is everybody's whipping boy'. 'The press always make out that the department is the villain and the applicant is getting a raw deal – what they *don't* say is that he hasn't got a leg to stand on.'

Some officers feel the department bends too far and would do better to adopt an upright position: this, of course, is the view of the systems' custodians in Registration and Clearance. Their disapproval of the department's moral gymnastics is the greater because most of those it strains to help are 'not worthy'. One commonly hears that government agencies (including the department) should help those who help themselves. Staff are suspicious of those who help the 'dead-legs'.

Social workers are derided on these grounds. They are 'trained to bend over backwards' and are always excusing the inexcusable, supporting those who ought to 'stand on their own feet'. And while they are helping the dead-legs, an endeavour neither justifiable nor profitable, they do not even get to know about the 'real hardship cases'. These are tenants who are too proud, too self-reliant to 'run to a social worker': old people, the chronically ill, the physically handicapped, families struggling on tiny incomes. But H.O.s do see them; *they* know where the deserving cases are.

Social workers appear to the department as the advocates of unmarried mothers, 'problem families', the potential battering parent, the 'mental' and the criminal. Their role is to press the corporation to rehouse these 'undesirables' and/or to foil their eviction. The conflict is explicit. One housing officer insisted: 'They're our enemy, the Welfare.'

In housing staffs' view, their own proper functions are to help old people and children, but to control the rest: 'The welfare ought to get him put away in a home,' said one H.O. of a difficult tenant. And of another: 'The Welfare ought to make her clean up her flat.'

Two other factors account for the dislike of social workers. One is their criticism of the department. The department, according to its staff, is 'the Welfare's' scapegoat: all clients' problems are the result of bad housing or of the inhumanity of the corporation landlord. The Welfare will, therefore, always take the side of the tenant against the department. Even though they are part of the corporation, they give no nod to the notion of inter-departmental co-operation: when an H.O. has a problem tenant who is obviously a case for social services, the social worker throws him back at the office, saying it is a housing matter.

The second contentious issue is the question of status. Social workers are better paid and generally better qualified than housing officials. They make claims to professional status which the latter cannot and would not make. Staff resent their status and their claims. In H.O.s' eyes: *These people expect to have everyone running round after them . . . They think themselves too good to work in a housing office, what with their grand salaries . . . Ridiculous to have people on £50 a week telling tenants on £15 how to live. What do they know about it? . . . 'We in the field', she says to me as if we've never been out of the Town Hall! She is telling me about one isolated old lady in a clearance area – I can show her hundreds . . .*

## Justice and Welfare

Social workers are the epitome of the welfare state. More exactly, they epitomise that part of it which has 'gone too far'. Few staff would argue for the abolition of the National Health Service or old-age pensions. But some would like to see the end of social workers, family allowances, supplementary benefits rights and housing rights.

'The welfare state' is held responsible for trouble at the office counter and for the state of the nation. The only other phenomenon of similar explanatory power (but used far less in the department) is immigration. This is tied up with the welfare state, since the latter allegedly acts as a magnet to 'the coloureds' and is stupid enough to support them. The black tenant who spoke of the D.H.S.S. as 'the free bank' is ample corroboration of their suspicions. Staff who have grown up with the welfare state are less damning. The extreme view is more common among older staff. Still there are exceptions who tend instead to describe the welfare state as the greatest victory of the working class. The case against it should be clear by now; by making self-help and mutual help unnecessary, it has eroded both self-reliance and community. Once dignified and independent members of the working class have been reduced to applicants, supplicants, claimants, clients and beneficiaries of the state. Self-interest and 'being out for all you can get' have replaced honesty and decency. Worse, the system is a great burden on the working population: it fails to discriminate sufficiently between people; it invites abuse.

These last two criticisms are made most fiercely by staff who generally support the welfare state. The assertion of failure to discriminate involves two issues of justice: the first, the tension between uniqueness and equity and between different equity goals; the second, the boundaries of the community to which the just rules apply. Writers on social administration have distinguished between *creative* justice – 'concerned with the uniqueness and therefore the differential need of individuals' – and *proportional* justice – 'fairness as between individuals in society' (Stevenson, 1972, pp. 25–6). The notion of fairness is much discussed in the department: fairness between different pairs of groups, fairness between claimants, fairness between claimants and similarly situated non-claimants, fairness between claimants and 'the tax-payer' (Bull, 1975).

The staff claim that the council favours tenants at the expense of other deserving groups: financially, at the expense of the tax-payer and the poor; and, by reluctance to evict the substandard, at the expense of waiting-list applicants. The questions of equity between applicants and between tenants relate to the second aspect of justice – its coverage.

There have been societies in which 'the people' means the slave-owners but not the slaves, the colonialists but not 'the natives', the bourgeoisie but not the proletariat. 'The people', in fact, are a moral community, and justifications are provided for the exclusion of others. Categories that are not wholly in-corporated into our society would include supplementary ben-efits claimants as readily as black and Asian settlers. Legally and politically citizens, socially they are not (Marshall, 1950). They may live in the same residential area and under the same conditions as 'us' – but they remain non-members nonetheless.

In the city at issue here, the tendency is for the local authority to take an increasingly universalistic approach to housing, while the staff remain firmly particularistic. They would like questions of equity to cover 'all of us' – which is to say 'all decent, honest people'. The boundary varies somewhat with circumstances. Those defined out would have no claim or a reduced claim to justice.

Staff do not ignore need. Many say, for example, that need should be the criterion of selection, but they are reluctant to accept among the needy those whose need is perceived as their own fault. Should justice extend to those who have no sense of obligation to society? If need is to be the sole criterion, the answer must be yes. But staff would like desert to have some weight. They would like the moral community to be recognised: the welfare state should be more discriminating. This is not an argument for more attention to the needs of individuals; their talk is of fairness and of disadvantage to particular groups. The differential needs of individuals are exactly that aspect of need which they think cannot be assessed, and should not be included in a classification system. Furthermore, if such need were officially recognised, this would most likely entail increased priority for those outside the moral community.

There are three ideas about the welfare state widely accepted among Housing Department staff and the English social strata from which they are drawn. All three are elaborators of authorised perspectives. The first is based on the points system. It is that moral credits and debits should be explicitly included in the calculations, as they are, implicitly, in some systems. Some applicants would have so many debits that they would always be at the back of the queue. Their claim to housing would, in theory, be reduced and, in practice, denied. Even more effective would be the exclusion of the deviant via the eligibility rules.

The second is inspired by National Insurance. Those who contribute regularly through taxes and rates are effectively putting down the deposit for a council house for themselves or their children. Those who have not so contributed must wait until they have 'saved up'. This, of course, would benefit those who worked (the tax-payers) and local people (the rate-payers) above ineligibles.

The third derives from the knowledge of finite limits on social services expenditure. This is interpreted concretely to mean, as one H.O. put it, that 'if too many coloureds draw Supplementary Benefits, there won't be any money left for my old-age pension'. Working people will be robbed of the money in their National Insurance piggy banks.

None of these ideas is given any credence in the 'professional' view of welfare, in which need, rather than means or desert, is the criterion of service provision. Justice, in this view, takes from each according to his means and gives to each according to his needs. Problems of equity would be dissolved by a far more generous provision of resources and a minimum wage set at a decent level. Hidden needs replace abuse as the preoccupation.

The alternative, more traditional and surely prevalent view sees state provision as a last resort, and certainly not a right – apart from education and those services provided on an insurance basis. Justice is limited to the moral community, queuing is a just way of distributing services among members of this community, though exceptional need can be taken into account. Equity is only achieved if swift action is taken against those falling below standard or abusing the system. Such people are ineligible and can only have been included in the moral community by mistake.

## Conclusion

Of these two views of the deviant minority, the 'professional' view is increasingly dominant in the Housing Department. As a consequence, traditionally-minded staff are obliged to ignore what they perceive to be the moral boundary.

Staff have always related well to tenants with whom they can identify and/or sympathise. They recognise in them a shared set of values – the sense of 'us' that can be called ethnicity. They will 'put themselves out' for these tenants when they can, but they regret that they cannot do very much. The bureaucratic structures of the department limit the scope for individual discretion in worthy cases, and the tenets of the welfare state preclude the exclusion of the unworthy.

The latest 'professional' innovation is a tenant-oriented approach in estate management – a policy of being nice to all the tenants. Staff are not disgruntled by the essence of the policy, only by its undiscriminating coverage. Perhaps because their work does not allow them to make any material distinction between 'us' and 'them'. In such a context, the elaboration and use of notions of Englishness serve to mark the moral boundary very effectively.

# 7

It is said that 'race' reduces the mobility of non-white labour, and/but becomes less significant to mobility as economic activity increases. This detailed economic analysis of the movement of Europeans, Maoris and Islanders up and/or through a large, multiple-activity New Zealand company shows these correlations to be misleading on three counts.

One, there is a distinction to be made between vertical job mobility (in which the individual moves up a well-defined promotion ladder 'with a view to economic advancement'), and horizontal job mobility (in which he or she drifts out of one job into another without necessarily changing status).

Two, whatever the constraints of the various labour markets there is some scope for choice of work; and however similar the economic position of non-white 'racial' minority groups, they (may) have different options and objectives and they (may) make different decisions or decisions with different effect.

Three, there is competition for workers between firms and between sectors in the economy; and ('informal') non-economic (sometimes ethnic) systems of organisation can be used to place or move individuals in or across the ('formal') industrial structure.

# Maoris, Islanders and Europeans

# Labour mobility in New Zealand industry

John Macrae

This paper deals with the question of what determines worker mobility at the firm level using data from a New Zealand case study. Particular attention is paid to the significance of 'ethnicity', taken here to mean the co-existence of a majority (European) and two separate minority 'racial' groups: an indigenous Maori minority and an immigrant islander minority which is drawn from the small South Pacific islands of Western Samoa, Cook Islands, Tonga etc., under New Zealand's economic influence. Work in the United States has suggested that 'race' both reduces labour mobility and becomes a less important determinant of it as economic activity rises (Stoikov and Raimon, 1968). But it is not clear why the significance of 'race' reduces mobility, nor why it fades over the cycle. This paper takes up the first point in more detail, using data on monthly termination rates and a survey of reasons for termination drawn from a large multiple-activity New Zealand company which employs substantial numbers from each 'racial' group.

Decisions about changing employment may be understood in terms of the range of 'inputs' which are held to determine these decisions. Some of the most important of these are isolated in Section 1, which provides a general framework for interpreting the data on labour turnover. An important distinction made is between vertical and horizontal mobility. This distinction is closely paralleled by that made in dual labour market theory between primary and secondary labour markets. Vertical mobility is likely to be much more common in a primary labour market. In this sort of market, job mobility is often up well-defined promotion ladders, relatively isolated from direct outside competition.

Section 2 considers the ways in which ethnicity may influence observed patterns of labour mobility. Discrimination against minority groups will limit labour mobility to the extent that it reduces the gains from moving to a new job relative to those from staying in the present job. Ethnic and kinship networks affect the type and amount of information which is fed into the decision – closer links being likely to correlate with more efficient information flows. These links also influence an individual's placement in the job queue: it is commonly noted that minority groups aim to pre-empt vacancies arising in their firm or team for members of their own family. Alternatively, hostility between members of different minority groups who are economic substitutes and so in competition with each other, will be a force making for ethnic job or team specialisation. In various ways, therefore, ethnicity can be expected to influence worker mobility.

Section 3 analyses the comparative patterns of labour mobility by ethnic group in New Zealand. It is found that (vertical) mobility (interpreted as responsiveness to changes in economic opportunities) is greater for the majority European group and that, as between the two minority groups, the pattern of the immigrant Islander group is the more dynamic. These findings are corroborated by the results of a survey of reasons for termination, although various caveats of interpretation are in order.

The conclusion of the study is that internal labour market systems contribute to greater labour stability, particularly among minority groups. They can also help to minimise the possibility of discrimination by enabling attention to fix solely on the crucial entry points on the promotion ladder. External labour market discrimination is more diffuse and so more difficult to identify or police.

## Section 1 – The Measurement of Employment Mobility

The movement of labour resources between jobs is essential to the optimal use of scarce resources. It enables individuals to find jobs for which they are best suited; it permits the stock of labour to improve as older workers retire and are replaced by younger, better educated ones; it encourages the accretion and consolidation of skills; and it enables the economy to adapt to bottlenecks appearing in different sectors at different points of time. In this frame, the study of 'quits' has various advantages over the study of 'discharges' if we want to cut right down to an analysis of individual decision-making. Observing quit behaviour is as near as we can come to identifying individual free market marginal decisions. Nor does it involve study of collective organisations such as unions (Freeman, 1976).

We shall begin by distinguishing two types of labour mobility – horizontal and vertical. Vertical mobility is undertaken primarily with a view to economic advancement, movement up a career structure or to a higher paying job. Horizontal mobility, on the other hand, is mobility of a random or autonomous nature. Many workers leave jobs to 'drift on' to others, with little economic ambition or betterment involved, others shift horizontally from one kind of job into another or out of the job market altogether. *A priori*, horizontal mobility could be expected to occur at a greater rate than vertical mobility, and the latter to be more significant to 'development' or 'equality'.

The distinction between the two types of mobility relates to the dual labour market classification which divides the labour market into a primary and a secondary sector (Doeringer and Piore, 1971). The former offers good wages and other conditions and, on account of its institutional structure, encourages worker stability. The secondary sector does not offer these advantages and does not require, in fact may even discourage, stable work habits (Gordon, 1972). In addition, the primary sector is usually characterised by a structured internal labour market, whereas the secondary sector is not. An internal labour market occurs within a firm or a department of a large firm or between very similar firms and is largely isolated from outside competition. It is characterised by a pattern of different jobs which are hierarchically arranged on a promotion ladder. Entry into the 'market' is limited to one or to a few points at the bottom of the ladder, all other new opportunities being filled by the transfer or promotion of workers already positioned on the ladder. Examples of internal labour markets have been cited for the United Kingdom

(Atkinson, 1975, ch. 6) and for the New Zealand job context from which the data in this paper are drawn (Macrae, 1975, ch. 6).

Internal labour markets have evolved with increasing job specialisation and are a means of minimising the costs of on-the-job training for the employer. Employers' adjustment costs of labour turnover, particularly for replacement at higher levels of the promotion ladder, tend to be lower when replacement comes from within the same general work environment. Movement within an internal labour market is a clear case of vertical job mobility. Since, however, it does not normally involve changing job location, it is difficult to monitor efficiently.

While some amount of horizontal labour mobility must occur in the primary sector, we hypothesise that this movement is more characteristic of secondary-sector employment. This sector, therefore, works more to the pattern of an external labour market.

The determinants of horizontal mobility will be different from those of vertical mobility. Within the secondary sector, the risk of termination varies from job to job as a result of various random or autonomous factors. Turnover risk seems to be higher for jobs of a less pleasant nature and/or those in isolated places. It is higher also for younger workers and for more recently hired bachelors with low specific or general skill endowments. In the secondary sector there is little skill accretion and poor promotion prospects. Jobs are mainly, though not exclusively, filled by members of minority groups, women and youths (M. Reich, 1973). Consequently, these groups tend to be stereotyped as less dependable workers and will suffer from it in their job-search experience, whatever the realities of the case. The New Zealand Maori has, for instance, been described as relatively unreliable, preferring variable routines to any continuous, monotonous work pattern (Ritchie, 1968). And yet another study reported no difference in dependability and little in termination rates between Maori and European bus-drivers within a given work context (Pierce, 1969). (It should be noted that important variables such as age, skill and marital status were not controlled.)

Whereas variables such as age, race or skill may be significantly associated with horizontal labour mobility in the manner suggested, a full explanation of labour mobility must encompass the analysis of vertical labour mobility which is the economically more important form. Not all less-skilled workers nor all members of minority groups display high turnover or unstable employment performances. In New Zealand as in other countries, empirical studies confirm that minority groups and unskilled workers are in some respects a *more* stable element of the workforce. In some cases, unskilled workers have, in later life, such stable work habits that their presence inhibits the proper functioning of the labour market by blocking the turnover of labour stocks and the replacement of older by younger workers. This has been documented in a recent study of the effects of a policy of high urban wages on labour turnover and employment in Kenya: 'Older, generally unskilled workers tend to stay longer at their jobs, keeping out the better educated and potentially more productive younger people' (Nigam and Singer, 1974). (It is suggested, in consequence, that in these circumstances a policy of encouraged early retirement would improve the quality of the labour force and so raise productivity.) Such relatively unexpected behaviour patterns can be explained if the distinction between types of labour markets and types of mobility is made. Thus, if an 'unskilled' worker is operating within a small internal labour market with limits on both horizontal and vertical mobility as the top of the ladder is reached, this stable employment pattern is readily understood.

Before we consider, in the next section, the significance of ethnicity on labour mobility, the factors determining labour turnover may be summarised under the following three headings:

(i) Autonomous factors: Factors such as age, location, marital status, and so on may be treated as having an independent and separable influence.

(ii) Information and search costs: Time and complementary (mainly financial) resources must be invested in the search for new opportunities which may or may not be realised. Information available to the individual determines the set of opportunities from which choices are made. The gathering of information is more or less costly according to how this information is produced and relayed. The lower these search costs, the greater the likelihood of (successful) job mobility (Morgenstern, 1970; Stigler, 1962).

(iii) Economic returns: It may be expected that a move will be made if it results in a net monetary gain. A leading question is how will changes in the nature of a person's work experience affect his/her lifetime income profile?

In recent years there have been several articles dealing with the importance of the returns to job 'experience' understood as a form of investment in 'skilling'. These returns contribute significantly to the explanation of differences in incomes between individuals, and between races and regions (Thurlow, 1968; Weiss and Williamson, 1972; Link, 1975; Welch, 1973). Analysis usually distinguishes between two types of past experience – schooling and past work experience. To relate this approach to job mobility we shall here make a distinction between past (job) and present (job) experiences, measured in terms of years. An individual's income $(Y)$ may thus be represented as the sum of the returns to these two types of experience – that is,

$$Y = r_1 E_1 + r_2 E_2$$

where 1 and 2 refer to present and past, the $r$s are (variable) rates of return, and the $E$s are amounts of experience.

It is obvious that as soon as a worker moves, his present experience becomes past experience, it will be added to previous past experience if he has already changed jobs. In considering his move he will therefore compare the return $(r_1)$ to carrying on his present job relative to changing jobs – converting this experience to past experience $(r_2)$. The rates of return to experience are assumed to show diminishing returns, more rapidly for past than for present experience. These assumptions have been verified by empirical analysis in New Zealand (Macrae, 1975, ch. 6; see also Welch, 1973, table 1). The situation is portrayed in Figure 1.

Consider the case of a worker who has not moved before and has $E_1$ years of present experience. Since the marginal return to $E_1$ is greater for present $(r_1)$ than past $(r_2)$ experience (namely, point 2 is north of point 1) then he will not move. Conversely, at $E_2$ there will be a force for job mobility (point 4 is north of 3) since returns to past experience are greater in this case. In an internal labour market, the worker is less likely to have moved already (he may be an immigrant minority group member), and the sort of situation described above may be expected to operate – that is, a

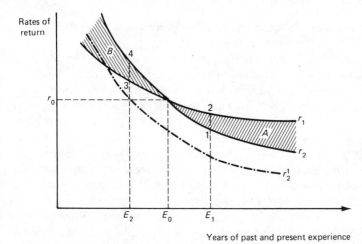

FIGURE I

'locking in' effect at high levels of age and experience, reducing labour mobility.

In the case of a 'pure' internal labour market where experience and skills gained in a present job are entirely firm specific, returns for moving will be zero and there will be no stimulus for moving at all. In the terms of Figure 1, for the case of a worker considering his first move, any factors affecting the shape and position of the $r_1$ and $r_2$ schedules, which serve to raise the size of shaded area $A$, to the right of point $r_0 E_0$, and reduce shaded area $B$, will definitely reduce employment mobility. The actual or observed rate of turnover will therefore depend on the distribution of the labour force according to years of past and present experience, and on the structure of experience returns which individuals face at a given point in time.

The type of labour mobility analysed here is vertical mobility, although horizontal mobility may be interpreted as a special case where returns to the present job $(r_1)$ and returns to a past job or jobs held $(r_2)$ coincide and, in the case of a totally unskilled worker, coincide at a zero level of returns. Using this framework, we may now turn to consider the influence of 'ethnicity' on employment mobility.

## Section 2 – Ethnicity and Employment Mobility

The inclusion of 'ethnicity' complicates the analysis by adding an extra dimension and requiring a model which can highlight the importance of ethnic differences. There are two limiting approaches which one may adopt. Either one assumes, *a priori*, no differences in 'subjective' factors, that is job preferences (of either employer, employee or co-worker), and attempts to analyse differences in terms of 'objective' factors such as prices, incomes, information flows and so on; or else one starts from an assumption of subjective differences and analyses ethnic contrasts in the light of this assumption. One may label these approaches respectively in the traditions of the economist and the anthropologist. However, in recent years, the two disciplines have tended to move towards each other. Economists, for example, have attempted to integrate a subjective factor in the form of discriminatory tastes into their analysis (Becker, 1971). This has not been an easy task because it can lead to predictions which conflict with the overlying competitive model used by the economist (Arrow, 1972). Market forces ought in the long run to erode price or wage differences based on differences in tastes; if not, and there is collusion among employers, then differences may still be broken down if the costs of policing any 'agreement' are high (Sowell, 1975, ch. 6). For present purposes, we shall consider how ethnicity may be expected to affect employment mobility as defined in Section 1, that is, how it affects the sets of variables (i), (ii) and (iii). We are interested in only two aspects of ethnicity – discrimination by employer, foreman or fellow worker; and the role of kinship and ethnic resources.

The first of the three sets of variables of Section 1 are autonomous ones and as such are not themselves influenced by ethnicity. However, as we have already indicated, if many minority members arrive with no recognised skills or capital and fall disproportionately into those objective categories which are highly horizontally mobile, then a greater amount of minority-group mobility can be explained or factored out via these variables than is the case for majority groups. Relatively less mobility is the upward mobility which may be analysed in terms of shifts in economic opportunities and returns (see (iii) above).

In the New Zealand case study to be given in Section 3, relatively little of the mobility recorded was in fact dynamic vertical mobility in response to changes in economic opportunities.

Turning to the influence of discrimination by employers on the second set of mobility determinants, we may use again Figure 1. Discrimination often takes the form of misplacing minority workers, or of not taking into account hiring decisions, previous experience or qualifications. In New Zealand, discrimination in the form of failure to recognise non-New Zealand qualifications is often complained of in the nursing and teaching professions. Less skilled immigrants may suffer to the extent that employers will not credit them with any valid past experience at all. This form of discrimination obviously reduces the returns to past experience (reflected in Figure 1 as a drop in $r_2$) and so serves to reduce labour mobility. On-the-job discrimination, as on the part of the foreman, instead reduces the returns to present experience $(r_1)$. Other things being equal, this will be a force making for greater mobility. It is unlikely, however, to be as strong as the 'opposite' force of employer discrimination since there is a greater chance that the minority-group member will be under a foreman from his own ethnic group. (We are ignoring here the possibility of discrimination *within* ethnic groups themselves; that is against members of another island group or tribe, or even against one's own 'kin' (see Wallman, 1974).) Finally, discrimination in the quality of past experience supplied, for example, in the quality of schooling received by minority groups, will also tend to reduce mobility (Welch, 1973).

In general, therefore, we may expect vertical mobility to be less for minority groups. They will be likely to see their opportunities much more narrowly in terms of promotion within an internal labour market, even though the ladder may have only a few steps. They will be more likely to develop firm-specific skills and firm loyalties than to engage in general skilling, such as trade training, the product of which is more transferable between firms. So, also on account of the nature of their skill accretion, will the minority group be likely to be less upwardly mobile and less responsive to changing economic opportunities.

One of the best known pieces of research into variations in turnover rates tests for the significance of various determinants of the 'quit rates' of fifty-two industries in the United States

(Stoikov and Raimon, 1968). Racial intensities (Negro percentage in each industry) are included and a negative sign posited and verified between it and the quit rate. Interestingly the analysis finds that this variable fades in significance as general business activity improves. We shall return to this later.

Let us now consider the influence of co-worker discrimination or aversion on employment mobility. Of the two possible types of co-worker aversion – between complementary and between substitute workers – co-substitute workers aversion seems likely to be more pervasive. In this terminology, complementary worker relationships are foreman/supervisory–floor worker relationships; substitute workers are competitive or interchangeable workers (see Arrow, 1972). The nature of this competition is summarised in a recent work: 'A certain benign contempt may exist toward a group that is clearly on the bottom and showing no signs of rising. But once they reach the stage of becoming threats to others' jobs or status, a much more active and intense hatred may develop' (Sowell, 1975, p. 162). However, the same work cites the experience of American Jews and negroes, to show that the economic advancement of groups suffering from this hostility does not have to wait for the elimination of this form of discrimination.

Two effects of co-worker (substitute) aversion may be noted here. First, it will be a force contributing to ethnic occupational specialisation. Group collusion will act to reserve available jobs for members of the same ethnic group. Such specialisation may extend to entire internal job markets. In New Zealand it has been recorded in particular departments or sets of occupations within firms (Macrae, 1975, ch. 6). But full specialisation along ethnic lines, even for a given occupational group, is limited by the nature of job organisation. For instance, if shift rather than normal day-working occurs, then job specialisation can be limited by the number of shifts, that is, there is ethnic specialisation in different shifts – but not in different jobs. Full occupational specialisation along ethnic lines is rarely observed (cf. Brooks and Singh, in this volume).

Second, co-worker aversion can affect employment mobility by influencing the range of jobs for which, or locations at which, a worker will queue. Given that hostility is greater between competing ethnic groups, then this type of discrimination may be expected, *cet. par.*, to reduce mobility of minority groups below that of majority groups. In the latter case, the worker will be prepared to place himself in a larger number of queues, hence improving his general mobility. In terms of the framework of Section 1, discrimination of this sort reduces employment mobility of minorities by raising their search costs (cf. Kosmin, in this volume).

We turn now to the influence of kinship and ethnic group resources on search and information costs. A general hypothesis would be that effective use of these resources can considerably reduce both search and information costs involved in employment mobility. It is often remarked how members of a minority group attempt to reserve a place in the job queue for their relatives. In New Zealand, recommendations to employers or foremen that relatives of existing workers should fill any vacant spot are often said to come from members of the islander group. Kinsmen also help to pay the air travel and accommodation expenses of new immigrants from the islands and we may expect similar subsidies to be available for internal transfers of islander workers between jobs. To the extent that information about jobs flows through informal channels – as seems often to be the case in New Zealand (Hohepa, 1964; Chapple, 1970) – then better developed social ties will enable more efficient provision of information about job openings, so reducing search costs and enabling greater employment mobility. On this reasoning, we may offer the simple (but cf. Wallman, 1974) prediction that more recently urbanised minority groups will have better kinship networks and hence be better able to respond to changes in opportunities that are offered.

This section has offered a number of predictions concerning the likely influence of ethnicity on labour mobility. We may summarise these by saying that (i) for various reasons we expect employment mobility to be *less* for minority groups generally, and (ii) that between minority groups themselves, mobility is likely to be *greater* for more recently arrived groups – using recency of arrival as a proxy for the use of kinship and ethnic resources in job-search activity (cf. Saifullah Khan in this volume).

We now present some empirical evidence to test these hypotheses.

## Section 3 – The New Zealand Case

The data used to test for differences in ethnic employment
mobility are taken from a survey of the labour force of a larger
New Zealand company. The skill and ethnic composition of this
labour force, amounting in total to 3396 wage-earners, is given in
Table 1.

TABLE 1

| | Percentage of existing labour force in | | Percentage of total labour force |
|---|---|---|---|
| | *Skilled occupations* | *Unskilled occupations* | |
| *European* | 54 | 46 | 68 |
| *Maori* | 34 | 66 | 19 |
| *Islander* | 28 | 72 | 13 |
| *Total labour force* | 47 | 53 | – |

Total labour force 3396
SOURCE Macrae (1975, ch. 5)

The over-representation of the majority European group in
skilled occupations is, although evident, perhaps not as great as
might have been expected. This is accounted for by the inclusion,
in this category, of jobs where skill embodied by experience is
valued equally with formal training. The embodiment-of-skills
effect explains instead the relative inferiority of the more recently
arrived Islander minority which is clearly reflected in these
figures. The gap between the minority groups is, however,
markedly less than that between them and the majority group.

To test whether the various influences of skill accretion,
discrimination and information flows, analysed in the last
section, operate as suggested, it is necessary to have data on the
turnover of this labour force by race and date of termination,
together with an index of general business activity as a proxy for
changes in job opportunities. We had information on monthly
terminations by race, job classification, date and so on, for the
period March 1973 to March 1974. We used as an index of
changes in job openings an index of overtime hours worked by

the total workforce of the company, which may be taken to reflect both the growth in aggregate demand from outside and the emergence of new opportunities in other departments of the company itself. (Internal transfers were officially recorded as terminations.) This index of changes rose from a base of 1000 in May 1973 to 1145 in July, then fell to 1086 in December and rose again to 1136 in March, so that the observations cover two periods of short-run upswing.

The model used was a simple linear function, fitted by the method of least squares regression. Thus: $P(T) = a + bE$ where $P(T)$ is the probability of termination for each ethnic group and $E$ is the index of economic activity reflecting new opportunities.

This is, admittedly, a limited formulation. For example, it would be desirable to add a variable which reflects more accurately short-run movements in the demand for labour in the economy as a whole. However, the most suitable index for this (monthly job vacancies less registered unemployment) displayed such strong correlation with $E (r = 0.78)$ that it was excluded from the equation to be tested.

The prediction is that $b$ is positive for the European regression, and that it is more positive than for either of the minority groups. Between the minority groups, we have suggested that the Islander data will show greater responsiveness than the Maori data. The results of fitting the equation to the data are shown in Table 2.

TABLE 2

| | Termination regressions (t-values in parentheses) | | $R^2$ | F-ratio |
|---|---|---|---|---|
| European | −14.305 (−1.88) | +0.017E (2.42) | 0.42 | 6.52 |
| Maori | 4.715 (0.85) | −0.001E (−0.26) | 0.008 | 0.09 |
| Islander | −8.712 (−1.77) | +0.009E (2.18) | 0.37 | 5.28 |

d.f. = 8
SOURCE Macrae (1975, ch. 6)

The Maori regression signifies no statistically important relationship between Maori turnover and the short-run index of economic activity (the *F*-ratio is less than the 5 per cent critical value). This contrasts with the Islander regression (a significant *F*-ratio and the positive *b*-coefficient not quite significant at the 5 per cent level). These latter results are much more akin to the European ones where turnover is found to vary significantly (that is, at the 5 per cent level) with shifts in demand. These results support the prediction that the degree of actual mobility, chosen or otherwise, is generally less for minority groups and among minorities; that it is least amongst Maoris. The findings are also consistent with a conclusion that the islander benefits from better kinship information networks and lower search costs than does the Maori.

However, the evidence is based on a relatively small number of observations. If Europeans do show superior vertical mobility, this ought to be reflected in the reasons which workers give for termination. The company had made a survey of 'official' reasons for termination of its workforce during the months April to August 1973, and made the results of this survey available to us. These are shown in Table 3.

Vertical mobility or movement into better jobs (Table 3: reasons 7 and 8) accounted for almost 40 per cent of European terminations, but only 22 per cent of Maori and 27 per cent of islander terminations. It is interesting that between six and eight out of every ten observed terminations did not explicitly reflect vertical mobility. The picture emerges of a 'disciplined', highly stable Islander workforce perceiving their opportunities for advancement *within* the firm rather than elsewhere and of their doing so notably more than the Maori (Table 3: reason 8). The important role played by the internal labour market in generating vertical employment mobility among islanders is also illustrated by these findings. The complete absence of recorded Islander discharges contrasts sharply with the ratio of almost one out of every four Maori terminations.

But this latter figure must be viewed in relation to the high proportion of Maoris leaving for reasons 'not known'. Maori workers told us that their co-workers would often walk out rather than accept, as Islanders were prepared to, aspects of work procedure which they found disagreeable. Strictly speaking, they were leaving for 'unknown' reasons. But if at the last moment the foreman or supervisor 'fires' a Maori worker, knowing he was

TABLE 3

Reasons for termination
(percentage of total terminations for each group recorded during survey period)

| | (1) Retired/ deceased | (2) Discharged | (3) Working conditions | (4) Job dissatisfaction | (5) Community dissatisfaction | (6) Family/ personal | (7) Better job elsewhere | (8) Transfer within firm | (9) Temporary worker | (10) Not known | Total |
|---|---|---|---|---|---|---|---|---|---|---|---|
| European | 4.4 | 6.8 | 5.2 | 1.2 | 1.3 | 16.3 | 25.0 | 13.3 | 3.6 | 24.0 | 100 |
| Maori | 2.9 | 23.4 | 2.9 | 0 | 0 | 22.0 | 20.6 | 1.5 | 1.5 | 25.0 | 100 |
| Islander | 6.0 | 0 | 0 | 0 | 12.0 | 51.5 | 12.1 | 15.1 | 0 | 3.0 | 100 |

Totals do not add up because of rounding
SOURCE Macrae (1975, ch. 6)

going to walk out anyway, the reason for termination will be recorded as 'discharge'. The *real* reasons for termination may therefore differ greatly from the *official* ones given in Table 3. For example, if some of the 51.5 per cent of Islander terminations for family/personal reasons (official reason 6) were in fact moves to better jobs, this would help explain the greater sensitivity of Islander turnover to shifts in demand. This discussion serves to underline the point that it is extremely difficult to get reliable information on exit behaviour of the labour force (Meyers and Pigors, 1973, p. 222).

Lastly, it is important to note what these results are *not* saying. They are not saying that improvement in the employment mobility of minorities does not follow improvements in economic conditions. We have already noted that racial aggregation loses its significant effect on quit rates as business conditions improve (Stoikov and Raimon, 1968). It would be quite incorrect to infer that the condition of minority groups in New Zealand did not greatly improve in the phase of almost continuous full employment after the Second World War. What the results *do* indicate is that the rate of response to changes in opportunities is likely to be less for minority groups.

## Conclusions

The results of the empirical investigation have tended to support the general predictions of Section 2: minority groups display less vertical mobility than majority groups, and/but the efficient use of kinship and ethnic resources can help to reduce the costs of job search. In New Zealand, the two minority groups have become more and more integrated into internal labour market structures. This seems likely to have improved their prospects for advancement, but at the expense of their general mobility even to equivalent jobs within their own internal labour market.

Internal labour markets cannot eliminate discrimination by employers. This may still operate at the point of selection into the market, usually at the bottom rung. But the existence of internal labour markets will reduce the costs of correcting discrimination to the extent that it allows corrective attention to be focused on these entry points only. In an external labour market, by contrast, discrimination is likely to be more diffusely spread and more difficult to record. Internal labour markets also provide a means of bypassing the problem of co-worker (substitute) aversion and the competition between ethnic groups that it entails. Within such a market, workers of different background may be 'separated' into non-competing, or rather less-competing, sectors. The long-run economic costs of discrimination will be reduced as ethnic groups adapt themselves to their particular occupational niche. But if particular job capabilities are not and do not become the special reserve of different minority groups, then the economic costs of this type of discrimination will not be eliminated. There will instead be pressure to break-down the young monopolies over different segments of the labour market. Technological change which alters the structure of the workplace and the nature of jobs; public policy – such as employment quotas – and the pressure of public opinion may all contribute to a reduction in ethnic specialisation, and even to the elimination of ethnic differences in employment mobility of the kind discussed in this paper.

# 8

*The title of this essay signals a change in perspective. While the previous papers have been concerned to show the play of ethnic identity and ethnic organisation in particular contexts of work, the last three put the emphasis instead on ('formal' and 'informal') factors which limit or enhance the scope of ethnicity. These papers are not, therefore, dealing with particular ethnic groups, but with spheres of organisation in which ethnic resources have little or no value.*

*The point made remains the same: the value of ethnicity is dependent on the total dynamic of the system in which it operates; and it will vary according to the options and objectives of particular situations.*

*This paper reviews the evidence which associates entrepreneurial talent or activity with particular cultural or ethnic populations as such. By reference to a wide range of examples, it demonstrates that group-specific effort or success in business enterprise is closely linked to the way in which political power and economic resources are distributed throughout the social system, and to the group's opportunity for access to those in control.*

# Politics and Business Enterprise

# Limits on the scope of ethnicity

## David Clark

It is readily observed that certain ethnic groups have been unusually successful in business enterprise. The observation has led some to explain business success in terms of the particular ideological or cultural orientation of a particular ethnic group. Such explanations have generally neglected the political and economic context in which business enterprises developed.

## The Social and Political Mobility Model

Two attempts have been made to link in a very direct manner the ideological orientation of entrepreneurial groups with their social and political environment. The first argued that economic development and, explicitly, the development of modern business enterprise, was rooted in the social and structural foundations of any given society (Geertz, 1963). Innovative entrepreneurs arose in certain social and political situations and were recruited from some groups rather than others. Such entrepreneurs were able to harness traditional methods of social organisation for non-traditional ends. Of crucial importance to this argument was the fact that the motivation for innovative entrepreneurship was not to be found in the profit motive as such, but rather in the search for a social position in accordance with ideological notions of a person's true worth in society.

In the Javanese town of Modjokuto, an ambitious shopkeeper class provided the main entrepreneurial group. This group was set apart from the rest of the townsmen by their social origins as

strangers and outsiders to the traditional court-orientated In-
donesian social structure. This distinctiveness was reinforced by
adherence to an intense and reformist Islamic movement. It was
this group which consciously tried to carve out an innovative
entrepreneurial role which would gain it recognition.

In the Balinese town of Tabanan, on the other hand, the very
core of the traditionalist element was at the forefront of
innovations. In the post-colonial situation, the traditional court-
ly rulers came to see themselves as a displaced and threatened
group. They, therefore, sought to harness their traditional
resources, both in terms of wealth and in terms of control over
people, to create modern business enterprises. By this means they
hoped to maintain their position as cultural, social and political
leaders.

Thus it was not the cultural values themselves which determined the existence of innovative enterprise; reformist or
conservative values could be equally effective in channelling
business initiative. It is the social and political aspirations of those
engaged in business enterprise which are more revealing.

This second theme was central to a study of Kenyan businessmen (Marris and Somerset, 1971). Its focus was a group who had
applied for loans to the Industrial and Commercial Development
Corporation, a Kenyan government agency which had been set
up specifically to help and encourage African business enterprise.
These African businessmen did not seem to belong to any
particular minority group, whether religious, ethnic or otherwise. Yet the occupational careers of the businessmen themselves
were very distinctive by comparison to the rest of the labour
force. Most of them had travelled widely and, in their occupation
immediately prior to the launching of a business enterprise, they
were much more likely to be in paid employment than were the
rest of the adult male population, and to be employed at skill
levels higher than the national average. As a group, the
businessmen supported by I.C.D.C. loans stood out
as men who had been relatively successful in employment, but
who had seldom achieved positions of importance. Yet these
businessmen for the most part lacked sufficient formal education
for them to be promoted up the occupational structure. Three-
quarters of them had never gone beyond primary schooling, and
half of the rest had not completed secondary schooling. They

were thus excluded from careers which would give them satisfying and influential positions in their own eyes. The authors, therefore, suggest that it is the frustrated occupational ambitions of these businessmen which led them to seek alternative means of gaining influence and status.

A different explanation for the emergence of an entreprene-urial group is given in a study of achievement motivation in Nigeria (Le Vine, 1966; see also McClelland, 1961, 1971). It is concerned to explain why one Nigerian ethnic group, the Ibo, were on the whole very successful in commercial enterprises, even outside Iboland, while another Nigerian ethnic group, the Hausa, had been far less enterprising in such ventures. Other studies had shown that Edo, Yoruba and Ibo businessmen were over-represented in industries in comparison with their pro-portion in the total population; while Efik, Ijaw and Hausa were under-represented (Harris, 1970). This one argues that the difference in participation of Ibo and Hausa in the new occupations can be traced to differences in their social institutions and social structure. Among the Hausa there is a strong hierarchical system of authority, based on ascriptive criteria such as descent which give little opportunity for upward social mobility and so tend to maintain the *status quo* and to discourage innovation. The Ibo, on the other hand, have a more in-dividualistic social structure in which status is determined by achievement – and one way of achieving status is through the accumulation of wealth. Hence the Ibo are more inclined to engage in commercial activities and to seek advancement through education. The achievement and motivation levels that will be most appropriate to the type of status mobility system in any society are communicated to the child in the process of socialisation. This explains whey there is higher achievement motivation levels among the Ibo than among the Hausa (Le Vine, 1966).

Thus, in the 1960s, two types of explanations were offered to account for the rise of entrepreneurial skills within a certain section of the population. One explanation focused attention on the dynamics of advancement within the wider society and on the social and political aspirations of particular individuals. Such individuals were either previously on the margins of society or of the power structure and sought novel means to advance their status and wealth and to gain social recognition which was more in line with their aspirations. Or such individuals could belong to an elite whose power base was being threatened by recent events and who sought to maintain their position by rechannelling their resources towards more profitable business enterprises. The other type of explanation focused on the internal dynamics of advancement within the ethnic group. The argument suggested that, in a strongly hierarchical social system in which power positions were ascribed rather than achieved, there would be few possibilities for social advancement and hence few incentives for innovative enterprise. In a more egalitarian and decentralised social system, the opportunities for social advancement would be that much greater and hence a much larger number of people would be willing to take the risks involved in business enterprise. Both types of explanation linked the rise of entrepreneurial skills to aspirations towards social and political advancement, yet both explanations can be criticised for laying too much emphasis on the normative elements in the equation.

## The Power Relationship Model

Ethnicity is relevant to a discussion of entrepreneurial activity only to the extent that it provides a medium for the expression and transmission of power relationships. Two aspects of power relationships are relevant here. First, the divisions of power within the city-state, the colonial-state or the nation-state, which are *external* to ethnic or business organisation, are crucial to an understanding of the resources available to the entrepreneurial sector. In some cases, ethnicity is an important criterion in the allocation of power, while in others it is not. Second, the *internal* organisation of the business enterprise may be based on the model of power relationships which are traditional to the cultural or to the kinship system of that particular group, in which case ethnicity will be stressed within the business organisation itself. Where the internal distribution of power within the business organisation is modelled on that of other institutions within the wider society, ethnicity will be irrelevant and so de-emphasised within the work situation (cf. Wallman, 1974).

# The Politics of Ethnicity

The distribution of power within the city-state or nation-state is important in determining the allocation of resources. Certain advantages or privileges which are granted by the state may lead to quasi-monopolistic situations. In other cases, the state can reinforce an advantage gained by a particular group in the economic field. Whenever an ethnic group has been able to establish a competitive advantage for itself in a particular economic sphere, it may seek to maintain this advantage by legitimising its position in terms of the distribution of power in other spheres. If the balance of power legitimises their position in the economic field, then, and only then, will the rhetoric of ethnicity be used in an explicit manner by the businessmen themselves in their dealings with the wider society.

The implications of an initial competitive advantage gained by an ethnic group can be illustrated by the history of the Indians in East and Central Africa, where they first came to settle at the beginning of this century. The Indians had certain advantages. They came mostly from castes of small landowners or craftsmen in which the cash basis of the economy was already well established. Some of them, though by no means all, had some prior experience in business in India (Dotson and Dotson, 1968). They had the basic skills required for business, including literacy skills which many East and Central Africans lacked at the time. The Indians even had some competitive advantages over Europeans in Africa. They were willing to start their businesses with little capital, and expected small returns for a period of several years. This willingness to defer gratification and to live austerely over long periods of time was simply not tolerable for most European immigrants whose ambitions were, in any case, on a much grander scale. As the Indians came to establish and run most of the retail and wholesale trade, they became entrenched in their economic position and received the support of the colonial administration in maintaining it. They in fact established a near monopoly in retail and wholesale trades; a monopoly held by people who formed a distinct ethnic group. The colonial government was concerned that the Indians should not enter activities which the Europeans considered to be their

particular spheres of interest; in return, the Indians were allowed
to maintain their position as middlemen in commerce. Thus the
Indians owed their commercial success to an initial competitive
advantage which was subsequently maintained and given impetus through the power of the colonial administration.

The Hausa in Nigeria provide an even more striking example
of a group obtaining an initial competitive advantage – all the
more striking in view of the contrary findings of the achievement
motivation study (Le Vine, 1966). A number of Hausa communities were established outside of the Northern Region, the
Hausa homeland. The main economic base of such communities
was the long-distance trade in cattle, which were transported
southwards, and in Kola nuts, which were sent to the north
(Cohen, 1969). The Hausa traders were able to establish a virtual
monopoly in the long-distance trade of cattle and kola nuts by the
fact that they were uniquely placed to capitalise on the cattle
trade. This trade involved buying cattle from the nomadic Fulani
tribes who lived in an area controlled by the Hausa. The Hausa
traders were able to use the Hausa domination of the Northern
Region to exclude other traders from dealing directly with the
Fulani. At the same time they could use traditional reciprocal ties
between Hausa and Fulani to ensure a steady supply of cattle for
the market. The position of the Hausa traders was further
enhanced by the colonial government's explicit policy of indirect
rule. This entrenched the power of the Hausa rulers in the north.
It also had the effect of legitimising Hausa control and monopoly
of the cattle trade, since they controlled the areas in which the
cattle were raised. Again, an initial competitive advantage was
converted into a quasi-monopolistic situation.

In these two situations, colonial administrations were willing
to legitimise the economic gains made by certain sections of the
population insofar as they fitted into their schemes. In East and
Central Africa, the colonial administrations sought to safeguard
the economic dominance of the white population in the more
lucrative parts of the cash economy. They were thus quite willing
to see Indian businessmen take control of the retail and wholesale
markets, seeing this as less of a threat than the potential rise of an
African entrepreneurial group. In Nigeria, on the other hand,
the colonial administration established a measure of indirect rule
for the sake of maintaining overall control over the country. This

favoured the development of Hausa business enterprise in Nigeria and in other parts of West Africa. African business enterprise, in fact, predates the arrival of European colonisers by at least a millennium, but here the point is that the colonial administration in effect supported the business interests of one ethnic group against another at a particular point in time. The enforcement of indirect rule led to a tightening of the control that the Hausa traders had established over the cattle trade. In such a situation, it was obviously useful for a potential cattle trader to be able to claim that he was Hausa.

A more complex situation arose in Jamaica. The Chinese established control over the retail trade in Kingston towards the second half of the nineteenth century. They subsequently expanded into the rest of the island and into the wholesale trade (O. Patterson, 1975). The Chinese were successful in this sector of the economy not so much because they had any particular economic advantage, but simply because they faced no competition whatsoever. Those members of Jamaican society who had the skills and resources necessary to develop the retail trade – that is, the mixed-race population and the white middle and upper classes – were not interested in engaging in such trade. The mixed-race population sought to emulate the white ruling class in every respect and so avoided all occupations which might be considered to lower their social status. The same considerations applied to the white middle classes and to all those aspiring to social recognition by the ruling class. The black population remained too poor to launch a successful attempt in the business sphere.

The Chinese, however, launched themselves into the retail trade in Jamaica on a highly individualistic basis and not as an organised ethnic group. Only *after* they had established a firm and viable economic base for themselves did they begin to organise themselves on an ethnic basis. Economic success enabled the Chinese to set up voluntary and charitable organisations; it enabled the Chinese to devote some of their wealth to the foundation of a Chinese school and to the emphasis of some aspects of their culture. Increasingly, they sent their sons to China for a part of their education. Yet economic success also encouraged the growth of Chinese ethnicity because it was good for business. Increased ethnic contact facilitated trade by extending the network of communications available to the individual trader.

The distribution of power within Jamaican colonial society had facilitated the growth and expansion of the Chinese retail trade by diverting the interests of whites and coloureds towards more socially acceptable roles. As a result of their economic success, the Chinese in Jamaica were able to strengthen and consolidate their ethnic consciousness. Yet with the demise of the colonial regime and the advent of nationalism after the Second World War, the Chinese found that they had to redefine their position in both economic and social terms. A self-conscious, separate ethnic identity could not be sustained in the face of the new nationalist mood, nor could a tight control on the retail and wholesale trade be legitimised within the context of a national policy. In the economic sphere, the Chinese moved away from retailing and wholesaling; they established supermarkets and moved into the import–export business; they even began to move into the professions and towards managerial and clerical occupations. It is important that the Chinese were able to move into these new sectors of the economy only on the strength of the wealth and position they had previously gained in the retail and wholesale trade. In the social sphere, the Chinese began to de-emphasise their ethnic solidarity. This was apparent not only in their life style, but also in their residential pattern. Many Chinese have moved out of Chinatown, out of the Chinese quarters and into the suburbs. For some, the traditional values of Chinese family life remain an important aspect of their lives, yet for most Chinese businessmen, being 'Chinese' is no longer essential to success.

## Non-Ethnic Power Relationships

It is conceivable that group-specific business enterprise could, in the course of time, emerge in a setting in which no particular group has a prior advantage over other groups. In Zambia, for instance, economic enterprise among Africans is such a new phenomenon, having been repressed even more firmly by the colonial administration than in Kenya, that no one group has yet emerged with a clear-cut competitive advantage. A recent study reports that African businessmen in Zambia were found not to belong to any specific social stratum or to be drawn from any particular ethnic or religious group. They did not share any particular features in their educational or occupational careers, nor did they share any common values or political orientation (Oberschall and Beveridge, 1972). It is arguable that it is only a question of time until institutional channels and networks are created which will eventually favour one set of businessmen over another, but that these will not necessarily be ethnic specific.

Business enterprise is dependent to some extent on the distribution of power within any given society. Where ethnicity is not relevant to amassing the necessary resources or to mobilising political support, other means may be employed. Apart from corruption and bribery (which are used in highly industrial societies no less than elsewhere), participation in the wider political process is generally considered to be an acceptable alternative to ethnic politics. The business lobby has been institutionalised in American politics and is an established feature of national politics in other countries as well. While this aspect of business involvement in politics is undoubtedly important, we are concerned here with the possibility of direct involvement in politics by businessmen themselves.

A link between business enterprise and political participation has been noted in a study of businessmen in Kenya, although this feature was not given any particular prominence. The authors (Marris and Somerset, 1971) report that half the I.C.D.C.-supported businessmen who were Kikuyu, or who belonged to other tribes subjected to Emergency Regulations in the 1950s, had actually been detained as Mau Mau sympathisers by the colonial administration. Many of the businessmen interviewed had maintained an active interest in politics even after independence. One-tenth of them were either town councillors or county councillors at the time of the interview, and a further 14 per cent had withdrawn from active politics only because they wished to devote all their energies to business enterprise. As many as one-quarter of the businessmen stated that they had used their political contacts in order to facilitate the award of an I.C.D.C. loan and claimed that this strategy had helped them to obtain a loan more quickly.

It appears, therefore, that businessmen with an active political record must have an initial advantage, vis-à-vis other businessmen, in securing loans from a government agency. This certainly seemed to be the case in Kenya and may well prove to be the case in Zambia. But the relationship between business enterprise and political participation is not so simple. Political activism is only one means of many by which an entrepreneur might seek to establish an advantage over his competitors. Yet at the grassroots level, a very strong link between business enterprise and participation in local party organisations has been widely documented. This aspect is discussed in more detail towards the end of this paper.

Where direct involvement in the political process does not seem possible or advisable, businessmen will seek to influence the decisions of governments, whether central or local, by forging links with officials and office-holders in government. This can be achieved through existing communication channels within the social structure, such as kinship ties linking businessmen to the ruling class, kinship ties linking princely families to the royal family, or ethnic ties which are strengthened and reinforced by the creation of ethnic voluntary associations and ethnic pressure groups. In other cases, such channels of communication are established and legitimised purely in the sphere of business enterprise itself as, for instance, by the development of such institutions as the Chamber of Commerce or the more diffuse, but equally powerful, 'business lobby'. Any of these channels of communication can be lubricated by the careful use of bribes in cash or kind. Thus, although the relationship of a particular entrepreneurial group to power in a given society can sometimes be usefully analysed in terms of the ethnic balance of power in that society, it should be remembered that the power structure itself may contain channels of communication open to an individual businessman whatever his ethnic affiliation. Direct involvement in party political organisation would serve this function. It would be useful to have better cross-cultural understanding of its potential.

## Power Relationships Within the Business Organisation

The other sphere in which ethnicity may be a useful concept in the analysis of business enterprise is in the *internal* division of power within the business organisation itself.

Perhaps it is within a strongly hierarchical society that business enterprises develop in a most structured manner. Innovations and business enterprise are not discouraged so much as controlled within the confines of the hierarchical system. The Hausa case is said to be one in which enterprise would be discouraged (Le Vine, 1966), but here the patron–client model of business development seems quite appropriate. The process has been observed in great detail among the Hausa of Ibadan: 'The principal business function of the landlord is that of mediation between dealers from the North and from the South, against the receipt of a special commission, widely known by the Hausa term, *lada*. For the purpose of fulfilling this function of mediation, the landlord has a number of clients who work for him as commission agents' (Cohen, 1969, p. 74). The Hausa 'landlord' in Ibadan is the nodal point of an intricate network of social relations which allows goods to flow back and forth between northern and southern Nigeria. The network of 'clients' who act on the landlord's behalf helps the landlord to expand his business enterprise and to accept more commissions; the element of risk-taking is divided and sub-divided and spread over as many people as possible (contrast Brooks and Singh, in this volume).

The essence of such a system of patron–client relationships is that social ties which are inherent in the structure of a given society are mobilised and exploited in a way that facilitates trade and allows individual firms and enterprises to grow and expand. Traditional elements are used to create patron–client ties and to maintain such ties once these are established. Among the Hausa, the recruitment of clients is largely through kinship ties, and is generally of kin who are in a subordinate position to the 'landlord'. The system of fostering children is another means of recruitment such that the client stands in a filial position to the landlord and may eventually marry into the landlord's family. The contractual nature of the patron–client relationship does not itself ensure the smooth performance of mutual obligations. The landlord will often, therefore, assert the moral and normative elements of the relationship in an effort to control the activities of his clients. This is achieved by stressing kinship links and by creating additional ties and obligations: a client may marry the foster daughter of the landlord's wife; the landlord may provide the client with the marriage payment; or the client's children may be fostered by the landlord. As the relationship is strengthened over time, the landlord will entrust more and more financial responsibilities to the client (Cohen, 1969).

Other studies of entrepreneurial activity in hierarchical societies document a similar use of patron–client relationship overlaid with moral and normative elements. Business enterprise in the Balinese town of Tabanan is described in this way. The traditional allegiance owed the nobility and the overriding loyalty invested in the *Seka* working groups enabled the noble families to convert moral obligations into patron–client relationships (Geertz, 1963). In Mexico, the *compadrazzo* (godparenthood) system has sometimes been used by rural peasants and traders to establish ties with richer townsmen. Such townsmen can then be called upon to provide the necessary urban contacts for the sale of the rural person's goods (Foster, 1967, pp. 81–5).

The pattern of Indian business in East and Central Africa would seem to confirm this relationship between a hierarchical social structure and the use of patron–client relationships in business enterprise. Such businesses have been studied in Zambia, Rhodesia and Malawi (Dotson and Dotson, 1968); in Kenya (Marris and Somerset, 1971); and in Uganda (Desai, 1964). Typically, an Indian business was started by an original settler at the beginning of the century with very little initial capital, which was either brought along from India or else earned in Africa as an employed craftsman. If after several years of relatively low returns the business was successful, then the original owner might sponsor a junior relative to come over from India and join him as a junior partner. The junior partner would be given room and board but would be expected to work for practically no wages and be treated at first more like a junior employee than like a partner. If the business was expanding and the junior partner had established his trustworthiness he might be put in charge of a second shop or of another branch of the business on behalf of the senior partner. In this manner, Indian businessmen were able to expand their enterprises and set up various branches in different parts of the town and even in different towns. The typical path of expansion was the setting up of chain stores. After a number of years of service the junior partner could either be given a lump sum of money so that he could leave and set up business on his own account, or else he could decide to stay on and become a more active partner in the business. Thus superordinate/subordinate relationships within the Indian family system and the Indian social structure could be converted into moral obligations whereby a businessman was provided with a trustworthy labour force and trustworthy supervisory personnel which would make relatively few demands on his resources. With this help, the Indian businessman was able to set up shop and expand his business (cf. the case described by Herman, in this volume).

## Other Styles of Power Relationships within Business Organisations

The significance of patron–client relationships in the growth and expansion of businesses will become clearer by reference to a situation in which they were absent. The managerial problems facing Kenyan businessmen have been discussed in terms of the lack of necessary and competent personnel in supervisory positions and the lack of sufficient technical skills (Marris and Somerset, 1971). In the industrial enterprises studied, the businesses were typically partnerships, or private companies with no more than twenty shareholders. The partners or directors were all of the same generation and the commonest ties between business associates were not kinship ties, but rather those established by working together or by having attended the same school. Thus business associates were generally of the same social status. The entrepreneur could not rely on moral sanctions based on superordinate/subordinate social roles in order to place his business associates in subordinate managerial roles. Neither was this solely a question of the delegation of managerial duties; the same problem presented itself in relation to the supervision of the workforce. Pilfering was common unless and until the work could be organised in such a manner as to reduce the need to rely on the trustworthiness of the workers. The businessmen's ideal of labour relations seemed to be modelled on that of the classroom with its own internal rewards and punishments. The workers were to be closely supervised like schoolchildren, and the employers, like schoolmasters, had to urge them to identify their own interests with the tasks set before them. The weakness of such business enterprises was the over-dependence on close personal supervision by the owner-manager of all aspects of his business. This led most businessmen to proliferate small-scale organisations compatible with proprietary style of management: 90 per cent of the businessmen interviewed were involved in the management of other business enterprises in addition to the one for which they had received a government loan. Yet, as their business concerns grew and multiplied, personal supervision became increasingly difficult until the inability to delegate actually inhibited further expansion and development.

These are the problems that face enterprises in a more egalitarian society without hierarchical, asymmetrical relations that might be converted into patron–client relationships. Partnerships tend to be among equals as against the senior/junior partnerships described for Hausa and Indian enterprises. There is no ready-made authority structure which can be exploited by the managers in order to delegate responsibilities, nor can they exploit traditional obligations and allegiances to ensure the loyalty of their workers. This is not to say that patron–client relationships are essential to business development, but to stress that institutional relationships must be established in business management. In a hierarchical society, patron–client relationships serve as a means of institutionalising relationships among business associates and between workers and employees; in non-hierarchical societies, other means must be found to institutionalise such relationships.

Grassroots involvement in politics does seem to provide the opportunity for the development and creation of an authoritarian role relationship which businessmen may convert into the sphere of work. The creation of such an authoritarian relationship is most likely to be crucial to business enterprise in egalitarian societies which lack a tradition of authoritarian leadership. Successful competition for local government office confers on the incumbent an aura of authority which could be channelled towards a greater degree of control over business associates and employees. Whereas the Hausa 'landlord' might seek to extend his control over his clients by bringing them more

closely into the web of kinship ties and obligations, the entrepreneur in a more egalitarian society seeks to tighten his
control in the work situation by seeking a leadership role in the
party political system, and in the context of the nationalist
movement.

The Kenya study referred to specifically mentions that a
number of businessmen interviewed were not only actively
involved in local-level politics, but also explicitly associated their
businesses with the goals, aims and methods of the senior civil
service. These businessmen explicitly emphasised their contributions to national development and nation-building, to modernisation, and to the growth of knowledge and skills in Kenya
(Marris and Somerset, 1971).

Even those who were not successful in obtaining office in local
government found the competition for such office itself advan-
tageous. They could in any case seek out leadership positions
within the local party hierarchy. A study of two housing estates in
Kampala mentions that bar-owners in the area were particularly
keen to compete for local government positions since this was
likely to enhance their popularity and so enable them to attract
more customers (Parkin, 1969). In a more recent study of a
residential area in Nairobi, which was divided into thirteen sub-
divisions of the local KANU branch (Kenya African National
Union), all the chairmen and office-holders of the KANU sub-
area branches were either Sudanese landlords who first settled in
the area or else non-Sudanese businessmen who were resident in
the area (Clark, 1972, ch. 4). In the period from 1969 till 1971, all
those non-Sudanese residents who had competed for office as city
councillor were businessmen, and virtually all candidates for the
parliamentary seat (which covered a wider area than the locality
of the study) were involved in one type of business enterprise or
another.

The competition for local government or for local party office
is not simply a gimmick to attract customers. In the first place,
the competition for office may be an extension of economic
competition between rival businessmen into the political arena.
The aim of the businessman may be limited to transferring the
political allegiances of the public towards his person and, by
extension, towards his business enterprise. In the second place,
the businessman may utilise his leadership role to strengthen his

own position within the business enterprise. He may feel the need to tinge his relationship with business associates and employees with a normative element which will justify and strengthen his leadership role. Again, this is probably more likely in an egalitarian society in which ascriptive or kinship roles cannot be used in a hierarchical asymmetrical fashion.

Finally, the involvement of businessmen within the local and national political system or in party politics can contribute to their economic well-being. This applies equally to egalitarian and to hierarchical social systems. Central governments can legitimise monopolistic or quasi-monopolistic situations, either by the selective granting of trade licences to some groups to the exclusion of others, as was typical of colonial administrations, or else by the granting of specific franchises. In this way the economic viability of the business enterprises of princely families in the Balinese town of Tabanan was partly based on their ability to secure government franchises for their businesses (Geertz, 1963). The provision of loans and other resources was equally important and, in many cases, political considerations were far from irrelevant in determining who got what.

## Conclusion

The rise of entrepreneurial skills within a particular ethnic group cannot be accounted for simply by reference to the cultural orientation of that group, or by reference to the social and political aspirations of individuals within it. The nature of power relationships within a society directly affects the manner in which a particular section of the population may seek to enhance its economic position, and they are crucial to an understanding of the manner in which an entrepreneur is likely to conduct his business.

In some cases the balance of power within a particular society may be based on ethnic distinctions. This was particularly true of colonial situations in which colonial powers sought to 'divide and rule'. Generally speaking, however, entrepreneurial groups had to achieve a working relationship and alliance with the ruling class. These might be established through the manipulation of kinship ties which linked the entrepreneur directly to elite

families, but the entrepreneurial group was generally forced into
a more explicit alliance with the dominant ruling class, either in
economic or in political terms.

In the economic sphere, the state might accord privileges and
quasi-monopolistic rights to a particular entrepreneurial group
in a particular economic sector as long as they contributed to the
power of the state ruling class. This economic contribution could
constitute a more or less tacit undertaking not to interfere in the
more lucrative enterprises controlled by the dominant class or,
more directly, it could entail the performance of economic
services such as brokerage roles, or the provision of loans and
financial assistance. Bribery and corruption are also examples of
economic assistance provided to the ruling class. Such examples
underline the varieties of economic interdependence linking
those in control of the state machinery with those belonging to a
successful entrepreneurial group.

Sometimes alliances between entrepreneurs and the ruling
elite are established in the political arena. The participation of
businessmen in party political organisation, in national politics
and in competition for office in central and local government, is
one means by which they may establish links with the powers-
that-be. Participation in pressure groups is a less direct means to
the same end. These may be based on regional or ethnic
groupings, on business institutions such as the Chamber of
Commerce or the 'business lobby', or on associations such as the
Rotary Club or the Lions' Club which have a middle-class or
professional bias.

The need to get economic privileges and advantages from the
state, to legitimise gains made in the economic sphere and to
ensure their preservation and consolidation, all involve the
successful businessman in some form of alliance with the
dominant ruling class. Where the divisions of power follow
ethnic lines, businessmen may seek to make the boundaries of
competition ethnic boundaries, and so to demarcate areas of
economic influence for particular ethnic groups. Where ethnicity
is not a relevant criterion in the distribution of power within a
given society, or where the legitimacy of ethnic power relationships is being challenged, the businessmen are likely to
establish working relationships with the powers-that-be on a
totally different basis. In such circumstances the entrepreneurial

group will probably offer economic or political support to the ruling class in return for the legitimisation of their own new economic role.

Within the internal organisation of business enterprises, ethnicity will be emphasised only if the entrepreneur is able to exploit authority role relationships which are already well established within the social structure of his ethnic group. The superordinate/subordinate role relationships characteristic of hierarchical social systems are most readily transposed to the work situation. In other situations, the entrepreneur may have to create an authoritarian role for himself in order to justify and legitimise his authority over business associates and employees. Where bureaucratic or technocratic means of ordering relationships at work are not yet institutionalised, and where hierarchical asymmetrical role relationships do not exist or cannot easily be adapted to the work situation, then participation in party political organisation may be the best means to authority that the entrepreneur can then convert for use in the sphere of business enterprise.

Ethnic business enterprise cannot be studied in isolation from the whole range of economic and political relationships in which it operates. Business enterprise is, under certain kinds of circumstances, organised on ethnic lines. Yet the same businessmen are at the same time engaged in a multiplicity of other relationships in which ethnicity is not, and should not be assumed to be, a relevant dimension.

# 9

*This paper deals with casual labouring in Toronto as a sphere of work in which ethnic resources have only very limited value as principles of organisation or identification.*

*This is not to say that there are no ('informal') cracks in the ('formal') structure. Casual labour is described here as integral to the structure of industrial capitalism. This form of organisation must ensure for itself a reservoir of cheap and transitory workers who can be hired and fired 'casually' – that is, in response to fluctuations in the demand for unskilled labour caused by seasonal or cyclical variations in industrial productivity.*

*Nor is it suggested that there are no bonds of solidarity and loyalty between casual labourers. On the contrary, the generally appalling conditions of casual manual employment are mitigated by 'local' systems of organisation and communication, focused not on the work site, but on the sphere of work itself. Although outside or official observations of it invariably note (at least in the Canadian setting) the 'ethnic affiliations' of casual labourers and the 'ethnic mix' of the workforce, ethnicity is rarely relevant in this context to the options and objectives of individual workers.*

# Controlling the Job

## Levels of organisation in casual labour[1]

David Stymeist

A traditional sociological analysis of ethnicity in casual labour might begin with a discussion of the different 'ethnic groups' represented, proceed to an examination of the inter-relationships between members of those 'groups', and conclude with some historical speculations. If such a study were done in Toronto in the winter of 1975, it might note, as points of interest, that Chinese, Japanese and North American Indians were not represented at the *calls*; that most casual labourers were of central and southern European extraction, former inhabitants of the British Isles, East (Asian) and West Indians, or native Canadians; and that maritimers were considered by themselves and others as a distinct ethnic category. Statistical analysis would have generated statements about the ethnic origins of casual labourers: $x$ per cent Irish, $y$ per cent East Indian, and so on (as Pilcher, 1972). The study might also have noted that members of each major ethnic category occasionally associated with one another, that joking occurred between members of certain ethnic categories, but that between members of other categories it did not.

Such analysis, however thoroughly done, would neglect the salient characteristic of casual labour. Despite possible appearances to the contrary, casual labour is externally very constrained by the overall economic structure, and it is internally highly organised. The hypothetical analysis described would ignore the intrinsic organisation of the institution and would be blind to the levels of organisation within it. If ethnicity is made the focal point of research, the mere existence of ethnic heterogeneity gives prior importance to the ethnic dimension. In this way, ethnicity is made the crucial factor, the variable over other variables, even when its general relevance is not confirmed by experience (cf. Wallman, 1974).

It may well be true in certain situations and/or in other times and places that:

> . . . regarded as a status, ethnic identity is superordinate to most other statuses, and defines the permissible constellations of statuses or social personalities which an individual with that identity may assume. In this respect, ethnic identity is similar to sex and rank in that it constrains the incumbent in all his activities, not only in some defined social situations. One might also say that it is *imperative*, in that it cannot be disregarded and temporarily set aside by other definitions of the situation   (Barth, 1969, p. 17).

However, the case of casual labour presents other impressions. Within the world of the casual labourer, ethnicity is not an immutable fact of life but a tool wielded to achieve practical goals. Ethnic identities exist among a repertoire of identities and one's ethnicity is more a role to be assumed and discarded than a fixed and unchanging social identity.

The notion of levels of organisation allows recognition of the distinction between *external* and *local* (or informal) organisation in the sphere of casual labour. This distinction pertains both to ethnicity as a dimension of identity and interaction, and to casual labour as an economic institution and way of life. Both levels of organisation co-exist in each dimension in the day-to-day lives of casual labourers. External organisation is, however, shaped and modified by local organisation and it is that process that will be considered here. Although external systems of ethnic identity and casual employment were 'givens' for casual labourers, the workers themselves created parallel systems to achieve pragmatic goals. Such creativity is most significant: despite their relative powerlessness, casual labourers are not simply actors in a drama scripted by others. They were active in organising the meagre materials at their disposal towards the achievement of distinct – if sometimes contradictory – goals. It is the interface of these

systems of local organisation with the various external systems
that forms the subject of this paper.

## External Systems of Casual Labour

Casual labourers are workers whose importance to society is
equalled only by the anathema that society places on them. They
are essentially hired bodies without minds or wills attached –
rented slaves, whose task in life is heavy menial labour for a bare
subsistence. Numbers of casual labourers work in every city of
any size each day. Much of their work is injurious to the health,
and some of it is highly dangerous. Their existence is taken for
granted by employers and ignored by the rest of society. They are
paid a minimum wage only for the hours that they work. They
work only if needed by an employer and, generally, only if
selected by a middleman patron.[2] For most, no other alternatives
exist and 'casualism' has become a way of life.

One acquaintance, for example, worked a ten-hour shift with a
broken nose and a possibly fractured jaw sustained in a mugging
the previous evening. His attitude to the injury was fatalistic and,
although occasionally in severe pain, he was motivated to work
for as long as possible hoping thereby (as he stated) to buy time to
seek medical attention. This man's ethnic identity or identities
pertained very little to his immediate situation. His ethnicity did
not cause his injury nor was he able to use his ethnic identity to
obtain succour. His predicament was simply one of pressing
financial need. No context except that of casual labour was able
to fulfil that need.

Casual labour is only one part of a greater, pre-existing
economic structure. It is apparently essential to the maintenance
of any industrial economy. In a circumstance in which goods are
produced in one locale and sold in another, their movement
depends on human hands and backs which load and unload
cargo. In any manufacturing or merchandising enterprise where
labour demand fluctuates seasonally or sporadically, additional
labour is necessary during peak periods. In Canada in 1975,
casual labourers fulfilled both needs. Accordingly, most of their
work involved loading and unloading goods, assembly line or
production work, moving furniture and equipment, delivering

advertising circulars, and removing snow and debris. The menial nature of casual labour continues to be its singular characteristic despite technological change. Certain technological advances such as the containerisation of goods have only served to shift the locale of casual labour from, for example, ship docks to the loading and unloading docks of warehouses (Wilson, 1972). Containerisation was, in part, a response to higher loading and unloading costs incurred through the unionisation of dock-workers: casual labourers are not so organised. The nature of their work has remained much the same.

Casual labourers are recruited in a variety of ways. Processes of industrial capitalism continually produce men unable to find employment in any other sphere. Age, ethnic and racial prejudices in the wider society deny appropriate positions to the otherwise qualified, and social service agencies, particularly welfare offices, immediately refer the able-bodied unemployed to casual labour. At any given point in time the number of casual labourers greatly exceeds available jobs. A recent study of longshoremen refers to the much earlier work of Beveridge (1930):

> In his detailed study of the problem of unemployment, Beveridge refers to casual employment as an employment system in which rapid and irregular fluctuations of work at a number of different centers are met by engaging irregular hands for short periods – these hands being taken on, at least in part, by chance, as they present themselves. Casual employ-ment, he explains further, tends to involve a quite un-necessarily large number of individual workers; it also runs throughout the industrial system. Nearly every industry at times takes on casual labourers, thereby attracting a more or less steady group of unskilled workers and gradually making them unfit for other work    (Morewedge, 1970, p. 14).

The final assertion is questionable: it is not that the workers are 'unfit' for other work but that employers are reluctant to hire a man with a history of casual labour as a permanent employee (cf. Macrae, in this volume). Many casual labourers recognise this and have, in informal conversation with me, expressed extreme pessimism regarding their chances of ever obtaining secure employment.

The work day of a casual labourer normally begins at five o'clock in the morning and ends twelve to fifteen hours later. He travels from home to a casual labour office by bus, aiming to arrive there between 6.00 and 6.30 a.m. Those who arrive later than this seldom get work for the day; in the jargon of casual labour, they do not 'get out'. Once at the labour office, the men try individually to make their presence known to the dispatcher who controls available jobs. It is the dispatcher who decides who will and who will not work that day. Some give him books and magazines; others fetch coffee or newspapers, shovel the snow on the sidewalk, or run various errands. If the dispatcher is in an especially good mood, some may engage him in conversation, laugh at his jokes, or attempt to humour him in other ways. If the dispatcher is not, these attempts may recoil into verbal or physical violence.

Following these preliminaries, the men sit and talk together, forming temporary clusters, participating in serial conversations and exchanging basic information and cigarettes. The content of these exchanges will be taken up later in this discussion. At this point it is important to note only that conversation is restrained. The men are under the constant surveillance of the dispatcher who dislikes a loud atmosphere because of the nature of his own work. Some men may try to sleep during this period of time, but these are not usually selected for work. If more than one or two fall asleep, moreover, the dispatcher rudely wakens them by shouting or shock noise. One dispatcher, for example, occasionally fires a .22 blank cartridge in a toy cannon kept in open display on his desk. Reading, too, is generally frowned on.

Employers begin calling the casual labour office between 7.00 and 7.30 a.m. Between 7.30 and 8.00 a.m. the dispatcher signals selected men to his desk, prepares a time sheet for them, gives them instructions for getting to the job site, admonishes them against misbehaviour by threatening dismissal, and pays out an advance if it is requested. One by one or in groups of two to five, the men leave for work – again by bus or streetcar. Those who are still in the office after 8.30 a.m. will not likely work that day. A few linger silently for an hour or two, but most are gone by noon. Invariably, labour supply exceeds demand and every day some number of men are not selected for work.

These circumstances are apparently characteristic of casual

labour. A report on London dockworkers before the First World War is indicative:

> In January 1912, a busy month in a busy year, 27,200 attended the calls per day, but the largest number taken on was 19,861 and the average was nearer 15,000. No one was getting more than four days work a week with any regularity: 70.2 per cent of the men got between three and four days' work; 12.4 per cent between two and three; 5.4 per cent between one and two; and 11.9 per cent less than one day   (Wilson, 1972, p. 68; see also Jensen, 1971; Liverpool Univ., Dept. Soc. Sci., 1954; Morewedge, 1970; Simey, 1956).

In the casual labour office, the men are clearly in the power of the dispatcher, and anyone who incurs his displeasure will not get work for a number of days. If a major breach occurs, he will not work from that office again. Various workers reported once working out of a certain office, but because of a disagreement with the dispatcher were unable to continue there and had moved on. A few had virtually exhausted opportunities in Toronto and were contemplating relocating in another urban area. Some had recently moved to Toronto for similar reasons.

Once on the job, the casual labourers report to a foreman, a permanent employee of the workplace, who shows them what is to be done and, if necessary, how to do it. They work under greater or lesser surveillance and pressure from that time on, taking breaks for food and coffee only when and if allowed to do so by their foreman. They work until dismissed, but most must then return to the casual labour office. There, another advance is paid, and the workers return home. The cycle is repeated the following day.

Pay is low. A casual labour office charges employers $4.50 to $5.00 an hour for each employee; a minimum of four hours is charged. However, the workers receive $2.75 an hour, the minimum wage, and from this income tax and Unemployment Insurance deductions are subtracted. The evening advance is calculated at $2.00 an hour with the morning advance, if requested, subtracted from that amount. The balance of earnings is paid Friday the week following. Bus fare costs between $1.60 and $2.00 per day and lunch from 2 to 3 dollars. A forty-hour week would net a casual labourer $108.00, but such weeks are rare at best. Most are able to work between three and four days a week, and their earnings barely cover basic expenses. (The weekly budgets of one casual labourer are given in the Appendix at the end of this chapter.)

Although the locale of their work changes from day to day and from week to week, casual labourers are, if anything, less free than the permanent employees of an economic institution. Their activities and options are severely constrained by the nature of their employment. Most are chronically short of funds. If they do not get work on a given day, they may find themselves with little to eat and nothing to spend on entertainment or diversions. If they do work, however, they may be so exhausted that sleep itself is a luxury. Orwell's description of the Parisian *plongeur* is immediately reminiscent of the dulling, repetitive cycle of meaningless and strenuous work characteristic of casual labour:

> For nothing could be simpler than the life of a *plongeur*. He lives in a rhythm between work and sleep, without time to think, hardly conscious of the external world; his Paris has shrunk to the hotel, the Metro, a few bistros and his bed. If he goes afield it is only a few streets away, on a trip with some servant-girl who sits on his knee swallowing oysters and beer. On his free day he lies in bed till noon, puts on a clean shirt, throws dice for drinks, and after lunch goes back to bed again. Nothing is quite real to him but the *boulot*, drinks, and sleep; and of these sleep is the most important   (Orwell, 1933, p. 123).

## Local Organisation of Casual Labour

Work looms large in the lives and minds of casual labourers. When a man works casual labour, he thinks continually about casual labour; about opportunities; about the weather and how it will affect job opportunities; about the state of his finances, and whether or not there will be work on the following day and the amount of money that can be spent if work is not forthcoming. If there is work, he wonders if it will be more or less exhausting than the previous day's work, how the latest injury is healing, or about the deteriorating condition of his work clothes. The life of a casual labourer is largely his work. Few friends exist outside the ranks of casual labour and relatives are either estranged or far away.

Accordingly, interaction between casual labourers is based on work and work experiences. When the men are waiting in line for the casual labour office to open, sitting in the office waiting to 'get out', eating lunch or drinking a beer after work, conversation – although periodically touching upon other subjects – most often focuses on casual labour itself. In such settings, the activities of previous days are minutely examined. The highlights of reminiscence fit into a table of experiences which are shared and relished. These conversations have, therefore, certain recurring themes. The men talk about how difficult specific employers are and how unpleasant a particular workplace is or, in contrast, how decently they were treated by this or that foreman and how in some workplaces the workers can take turns resting behind a pile of boxes or sleeping in a vacant office. They share information about various dispatchers and consider closely observed features of their personalities, weighing possible advantage. Occasionally, they talk about each other and express opinions on who is 'good to work with', who is untrustworthy, who drinks on the job and so forth. Finally, information and access to other casual labour opportunities is sometimes presented. One casual labourer told a group of four fellow workers:

*You can get $5.00 an hour plus vacation pay added in every time it snows. You go to the Department of Streets, 143 Old Weston Road. Got to get there about 5.00 or 5.30 a.m. and they'll let you in. Got to wait till about 6.00 a.m. or so for the office people to get there, but there's a guy working there all night and he'll let you in and you can sit in the lunch room.*

*They give you a number on a card that you can use over and over again. All you need is your social insurance number. That's all they ask for . . . so, you have to get there early, particularly on the weekends when all the school kids are out because they come there a lot. But on weekdays you're probably all right to get there between 5.30 and a quarter to six.*

*Now the work is mostly real easy. All you do is go out in a truck with a bunch of guys and they let you and this other guy off on a street corner and tell you to shovel off all the corners and the bus stops from wherever they let you off back to some other place.*

*When I did this last week, we finished half the job by 11.00 a.m. and spent two hours in a bar for lunch and another couple of hours in a coffee shop in the afternoon. You just show up where you're supposed to be at about 4.30 p.m. and they let you go home. All the regular guys work for the city so they don't really care.*

*The only thing is that it has to snow a lot – between two and five inches but at least two inches – or else they don't hire nobody. And its Old Weston Road, not Weston Road, a couple of blocks up from St Clair, just east of St Clair and Keele.*

This was all precise information to be used as circumstances allowed. As it was offered, the men sat fully attentive and appreciative of what was being given. Some would reciprocate with similar items at a later date.

This work-focused interaction fulfils a variety of practical functions. The sharing of similar experiences may serve to knit together a disparate collection of persons into something more substantial. More immediately, such conversations provide a form of mutual aid insofar as they supply information of potential benefit to participants. The experiences of other casual labourers are valuable, not just as lessons, but as the accumulated knowledge of different workplaces and employers. This knowledge is likely to be of eventual importance to any individual casual labourer. A newcomer listening to these conversations learns the expectations of both employers and other casual labourers and is introduced to strategies to maximise income:

*A lot of new guys think that they can steal things on the job. Well, this is a pretty big mistake. Sometimes I guess that you can get away with it but mostly these people [permanent employees] keep a pretty close watch on what goes in and out of a truck. They watch you pretty close even if you think that they don't.*

*Last week some guys decided to boost some coats out of Marks– Spencer. The foreman didn't see them, and they got away with it – or so they thought. But the store [receiving the goods] found out that they were short two coats so they called the warehouse and the warehouse called John [the dispatcher]. That's when the shit hit the fan. John found the guys playing pool in their new coats! He got the coats back, but those guys are through here forever . . . lucky not to end up charged!*

*I've found that the best way to get a tip is to ask the guy [foreman] if you can buy some of that stuff. He usually doesn't want to hassle with selling it, but if you work good and get along with him, he'll probably just give you something at the end of the day.*

Informal interaction also introduces the newcomer to the principal values of the group. The generalised reciprocity and mutual aid so highly valued by casual labourers are exemplified and reinforced by the exchange throughout these conversations of cigarettes, chewing gum and small items of food. The same ethos can be expressed in joking:

There was a big Scotsman, Bill something or other, on the Ballentyne Pier. He was a dock foreman. A bunch of us were waiting there for a Blue Funnel to dock one morning. He pulled out a pack of cigarettes and lit one and folded up the pack. As he folded it I called him a tight so-and-so and all that sort of thing and grabbed the pack out of his hand and passed them around and insisted that everybody have one. When I got through there were two left in the package and I passed them back to him and he said, 'What the hell are you giving me those for?' I said, 'Why?' He said, 'I took them out of your pocket.' That was one of the best ones ever pulled on me   (quoted from 'Roy Mason, a Vancouver longshoreman', in I.L.W.U. Local 500 Pensioners, 1975, p. 59).

Local organisation as it is revealed in informal interaction is also shown in the work performed by casual labourers. On the job, a multitude of decisions involving the division of labour and the pace of work have to be made. These decisions need to be both spontaneous and consensual. No one casual labourer can be in a position of authority over another, but all will be blamed for the failing of any one of them. Similarly, however, all will benefit if the hours of their employment can be artificially extended.

The circumstances of casual labour engender a flexible organisation of work in which responsibility to fellow workers is important (cf. Pilcher, 1972, p. 99). More difficult tasks are interchanged and the members of a crew may rotate their positions periodically. If supervision is light, workers will take turns 'hiding', that is finding an inconspicuous place to rest. Even if supervision is strict, periodic and extended visits to the washroom are in order and the members of a crew will generally attempt to conceal or explain away the absence of one of their number. Persons who have previously worked at a particular establishment can provide valuable information to those who have not, and together they can structure the pace of work so as to make a job last for as long as practically possible.

In one instance, four casual labourers were assigned to unload a boxcar filled with boxes of paper towels. The boxes were light and bulky, and it appeared to one experienced in such matters that if the men worked quickly the boxcar could be unloaded in four hours. Various devices were initiated to extend the hours of employment and the job eventually lasted $7\frac{1}{2}$ hours. At one point the men stood in a circle and passed a box from one to another. The foreman worked in another part of the warehouse and from his vantage point it must have appeared that the men were working – even while they accomplished nothing for their employer.

Although spontaneous, this agreement was not unique. It is reported also in a situation involving dockers:

> In the boom following the First World War there was another spate of unofficial disputes; Bristol employers reeled off a list of stoppages to Lord Shaw, where the men demanded larger gangs for bushelling grain, and £1 again for one and a quarter hours' work on manganese ore; when extra payments were refused on another ship, the men contrived to spin out the discharge of 122 bags – half an hour's normal work – from 4.30 p.m. on a Friday through a half-day on Saturday and into Monday morning (Wilson, 1972, p. 55).

In these ways, the organisation of work and interaction can provide tangible benefits to participants. It is considered essential that the men 'get along' – not just for the psychological reward of a modicum of enjoyment in their toil that sociability brings, but also so that maximum earnings could be obtained for each worker. Competition between casual labourers once on a job would clearly be destructive. It would advance employers and, by implication, the casual labour office, but would do nothing for the workers themselves. This fact is fully recognised.

## External Systems of Ethnicity

Casual labourers are of diverse ethnic backgrounds. Their ethnicity is, to some extent, 'real' – an intimate part of their personalities inculcated by socialisation experiences – and, to some extent, putative – supposedly accruing to them as the inheritance of the ethnic identities of their forebears. It nevertheless remains the case that casual labourers, like other members of Canadian society, recognise a list of ethnic categories and hold ideas about the characteristics associated with those categories. Each has ideas about 'ethnic' collectivities and understands something of the historical relationships between different ethnic populations. Such systematic information can be considered external to their present situation: it was learned by them prior to the work site.

Such external systems intermesh, however imperfectly, with present or historical reality. They relate both to the organisation of persons in communities, regions and states, and to certain assumptions not encompassed by any one personal experience. Some thought, for example, that the Irish were 'closer' to the English than were West Indians and that East Indians (that is, people from the Indian sub-continent) were 'closer' to West Indians than to Newfoundlanders. Others did not share these perceptions and defined 'difference and identity' quite differently. The ethnic dimension in casual labour, therefore, reflects a welter of impressions about ethnicity. These impressions are learned in various social settings other than that of casual labour. Each labourer has ideas about his own ethnicity and the ethnicity of fellow workers but these ideas were not the same for all casual labourers. In addition, members of many different ethnic categories are routinely jumbled together in one small office or as workers at a particular job site on which they must cooperate.

## Local Organisation of Ethnicity

Against this background of diverse identities and conceptions, the local organisation of ethnicity can be discerned. Particular agreements are occasionally reached by members of a single ethnic category. Men of the same or similar ethnic affiliation occasionally associate during lunch and coffee breaks and while waiting for the morning call or, more rarely, while working together on the job. Although they do not often analyse their ethnic affiliations or discuss (at least not in public) the ethnic credentials of others, they do talk about their place of origin, its food, drink, entertainments and social life. They also consider politics and religion in a general sense and find or create in them some common ground.

This 'ethnic' interaction is not confined to the ranks of casual labourers. It is extended when possible to include the permanent employees of a workplace. Although any contact of this sort is necessarily temporary, the casual labourer will make every effort to forge useful ethnic links. If he did this seeking any preferential treatment short of a permanent position, the effort would be highly detrimental to his standing among other casual labourers. He will, therefore, forge those ethnic links which are, or which may be, to the mutual advantage of all the casual labourers on the job site. It is, for example, occasionally the case that a casual labourer of the same or similar ethnic background to the foreman will select himself or be selected as the one to request coffee breaks or extended lunch periods, and generally to negotiate conditions of work. Ethnicity is not the only element involved in the creation of links between permanent and casual employees, but it is used where appropriate and if no other strategy is deemed to have a greater chance of success.

The historical past provided the subject matter for joking relationships between certain ethnic categories. These possibilities were utilised to create fellow feeling and to foster contact and communication. Thus Bob Evans, a 'Welshman', and Richard Toombs, an 'Englishman', while working together unloading a 40-foot container of food imported from the United Kingdom, established a joking relationship based upon their ethnic labels. That relationship was active and useful insofar as it made the drudgery of their labour more bearable, but it was also 'ethnic' because it was centred on presumed ideas of who each was in relation to his past and his biological stock. Neither participants or spectators, however, believed that any real animosity existed between them.

Toombs played 'straight-man' to Evans' deprecatory comments on the monarchy, defending it with examples drawn from English history, a subject he once taught in London. Evans played a Welsh nationalist, countering Toombs' 'Englishness' with family wisdom and memories of his childhood in Wales. Neither was serious about their respective positions. Toombs was a monarchist only in pretence, describing himself once as a 'backsliding communist'. Evans, although potentially committed to his position in a serious encounter, seemed purposefully to exaggerate his points to enliven the banter. Both fully recognised that they were in Canada and trapped in the same confining situation. Although their backgrounds differed, their reality was much the same. Neither was a member of a corporate block of persons labelled respectively 'Welsh' or 'English'. Like much of their presented ethnicity, their joking relationship was traditional. One sensed that they assumed a joking relationship, not because of any real tension between them, but because it was possible to assume such a relationship; their self-identification as Welsh and English created a chance for such communication. That chance was seized by both.

## Bridging Devices

Between members of other categories, however, joking possibilities are minimal and various bridging devices used instead. These figure also in both previously mentioned strategies (same ethnicity and joking relationship) but are of particular importance in establishing channels of communication between persons who cannot easily be linked together by reference to external systems such as ethnicity.

Communication can sometimes be established on the basis of personal interest. One newly-arrived worker talked consecutively to a number of persons until he found one interested and knowledgeable about motorcycles. A long, technical conversation ensued, and on following mornings the newcomer attempted to sit beside his acquaintance and to continue discussion of the same subject. In other cases, links were established by reference to drugs and alcohol, racehorses or literary pursuits, religion or politics. The ethnic identities of persons so communicating did not enter directly into these conversations at all.

Finally, a generalised, ritualistic sexism provides a common ground in circumstances where, apparently, no other exists. While waiting for the casual labour office to open, the men verbally accost women passing on the street. This is invariably followed by jokes and laughter among the men. While waiting in the office for the morning call, copies of the *Toronto Sun* (a morning tabloid) are passed around and some men make comments on the 'SUNshine girl', a feature of cheesecake photography printed in each issue. They brag of their prowess and tell stories generally deprecatory of women. All of this interaction establishes a definition of the situation in which men are sharply contrasted to women. Such emphasis creates a common ground on which assumptions of male superiority can be reiterated and shared. Ethnicity is not relevant to these exchanges.

## Ethnicity in Casual Labour

In essence, each casual labourer attempts to establish multiple, cross-cutting links with as many other casual labourers as possible. These links are built on diverse principles; ethnicity being but one such principle. Each casual labourer has an ethnic dimension which may be stressed in communication with one of the same or similar background or in joking relationships with those of different but historically linked background. Alternatively, the ethnic dimension can be suppressed and suspended in interaction with others of distinctly different and not closely inter-related ethnic identities. In these circumstances, other realms of communication become important. This can be visualised as a two-way movement: one towards ethnicity as a dimension of interaction and another away from ethnicity into other domains. Each casual labourer has a network of acquaintances, some based on ethnicity, others not. Ethnicity is, in this sense, assumed and discarded from one situation to another. Ethnic identities and idioms are considered important where they are useful. Where they are not they are rejected for identities more germane to the context.

Thus, although systems of ethnic identity are externally defined, local organisation makes of them a tool for the creation of multiple, cross-cutting linkages with other individuals. These links are part of the spontaneous, reticular (cf. Gerlach and Hine, 1970) organisation of casual labour which is necessary to the economic survival and physical wellbeing of each casual labourer.

## Conclusion

The external organisation of the institution of casual labour demands a certain response from casual labourers. The self-interest of each casual labourer more or less automatically leads him to associate and communicate with his fellow workers. The effective local organisation of casual labour produces tangible benefits for the workers, and ethnicity is best understood as a tool utilised for its improvement. This context is clearly different from one in which ethnicity itself has economic importance for the members of an ethnic category; or one in which the sub-ordination of one ethnic category furthers the economic advantage of another. In both of these circumstances, ethnicity and class are socially synonymous. In the situation of casual labour, however, diverse ethnic identities are underscored by a common class membership that is more salient than those identities. Casual labourers recognise the diversity of their origins but realise the commonality of their class position. And although class antagonism was of potential benefit to them ('Let's rip off the big shots'), they could not afford the luxury of ethnic conflict.

All of this is somewhat contrary to established anthropological opinion, and those who hold dearly to established opinion may dismiss casual labour as an isolated, atypical case. Barth's view (1969) is echoed here:

Anthropologists who directed or undertook fieldwork during the 1950s and early 1960s found that they could not ignore or neglect the processes of change or resistance to change, whose concrete expressions were all around them. Many of these anthropologists worked in plural societies, characterised by ethnic diversity, sharp economic inequalities between ethnic groups, religious differences, political and legal hetero-geneity – in short, major asymmetrics of sociocultural scale and complexity between their ethnic constituents (Swartz, Turner and Tuden, 1966, p. 3).

It may be that such background has coloured our understanding of ethnicity and given a greater rigidity to the ethnic dimension than it has in specific social situations.

Recent work on kinship has illustrated that far from being an inflexible social charter, systems of relatedness can provide but one field of possible interaction for the members of a society – one field, paralleled by others (cf. Schwimmer, 1974), in which persons align themselves not so much by order of strict rules, but through exchange and negotiation. It is said for a Ceylonese group that:

Since all members of the *variga* are relatives, any two of them can always represent themselves as being of the same 'ideal' *pavula* by making an appropriate choice of common ancestor (Leach, 1961, p. 112).

And, more generally:

. . . kin ties are nowhere consistently used since they are social resources whose existence will be exploited, ignored, or denied as each situation warrants (Wallman, 1974, p. 105).

Something similar can be said about 'ethnic' situations in poly-ethnic societies. Casual labour may not, therefore, be atypical but representative of a class of circumstances in which the relevance of ethnicity varies with the constraints of reality.

One further point remains. It concerns the highly defamatory language generally used to describe casual labourers. Booth (1893) is quoted (in Simey, 1956, pp. 1–2) describing casual labourers as, '. . . parasites eating the life out of the working class, demoralising and discrediting it'. He continues: 'Why should we suffer the evil of a system of employment which discourages honest and persistent work and favours the growth of a demoralised and demoralising class of bad workers and evil livers?' Mayhew describes casual laborers as, '. . . a striking instance of mere brute force with brute appetite, as unskilled as the force of the hurricane' (Quennell, 1949, p. 543).

A textbook from the 1920s claims:

> Men who are unfitted for other occupations seem to drift into dockwork as naturally as the drainage system of the country finds its way to the lowest level   (Cunningham, 1926, p. 104).

More recently, outright defamation has yielded to insinuation:

> Among the men, the conditions of casualness produced defensive and self-serving reactions and attitudes which created fixed customs and practices   (Jensen, 1971, p. 2).

Within the perspective of this study, however, such 'defensive and self-serving reactions' are an adaptive response made both possible and necessary by the local organisation of casual labourers and directed towards some, albeit marginal, improvement of their lot.

The following passage appears in the novel *The Factory Ship*:

> The company was always very careful about the fishermen they signed up. They hired model youths selected by the village heads or the police chiefs of the areas canvassed. Among workers they chose those who had no interest in labour unions and who did as they were told. Shrewdly they saw to it that the cards were stacked in their favour. But now the situation aboard the factory ship was shaping up in ways that they had not foreseen: the workers were uniting and organising. Even the shrewdest among the capitalists were unaware of this strange turn of events. Ironically, it was as if they had gone to all the trouble of assembling the unorganised and unrehabilitable drunkards and were now teaching them how to unite   (Takiji Kobayashi, 1973, pp. 67–8).

Although based upon an actual incident, this account is

fictional and is probably coloured by the political orientation of the author. But the spontaneous organisation of workers in response to external pressure is very similar to the informal organisation of casual labourers. Unlike the workers on *The Factory Ship*, however, their being organised has not resulted in overt political action, nor in class confrontation as such. But it has fostered the solidarity of men who have in common no more than an occupational niche – the constraints of getting, keeping and surviving a job.

In the circumstances described, non-work contacts are neither useful nor negotiable. The strength and flexibility of informal local organisation among casual labourers makes the conditions of their work more nearly tolerable and may even allow the occasional covert sabotage of formal industrial operations. But because it is the shared experience of casual labourers in casual labour which dominates their lives, they identify more often and more cogently as an under-class work group than they do with ethnic loyalties which would cross-cut that group. Given the exigencies of survival in this context, notions of ethnicity are not often useful.

## Appendix: Weekly Budgets of One Casual Labourer

WEEK 1

**Earnings**

| Period ending | Hours | Rate | Total earnings |
|---|---|---|---|
| 1 Feb 76 | 18½ | $2.75 | $50.87 |

**Deductions**

| Federal income tax* | Canada pension | U.I.C. | Advance |
|---|---|---|---|
| — | $0.64 | $0.84 | $37.00 |

**Net**
$12.39

**Expenses**

| Rent | Bus fare | Lunch | Food | Total expenses |
|---|---|---|---|---|
| $20.00 | $6.40 | $6.00 (approx.) | $18.00 (approx.) | $50.40 |

**Surplus**
$0.47

WEEK 2
**Earnings**

| Period ending | Hours | Rate | Total earnings |
|---|---|---|---|
| 15 Feb 76 | 27 | $2.75 | $74.25 |

**Deductions**

| Federal income tax* | Canada pension | U.I.C. | Advance |
|---|---|---|---|
| — | $1.06 | $1.23 | $54.00 |

**Net**
$17.96

**Expenses**

| Rent | Bus fare | Lunch | Food | Total expenses |
|---|---|---|---|---|
| $20.00 | $7.20 | $9.00 (approx.) | $25.00 (approx.) | $61.20 |

**Surplus**
$13.05

* No federal income tax was deducted for this worker as he purposefully neglected to fill out the appropriate forms.

# 10

The last essay reviews models of economic structure and process, and takes up issues raised by treating each sector or sphere of the economy as an autonomous system. While the author addresses the wider problems of urban poverty and development and argues the necessary interdependence of all the many systems of work which make up the modern economy, his analysis in effect sets out the context in which any ethnic system of work must be operating. Just as 'formal' and 'informal' sectors are integrated and complementary to each other, so the work niches occupied by particular categories or groups of people are structured by 'others' at every level.

It is only in this systematic sense that the ethnic organisation of work can be appreciated. It flourishes in opportunity-spaces – in chinks within the economic structure – and its scope is necessarily limited by the constraints of that structure. The ethnic system is never more than a sub-set of the wider economy. It will thrive insofar as its success is functional to the larger system, and it will succeed to the extent that it takes advantage of changes occurring in other sectors or at other levels. For this reason, even radical change in the allocation of work or patterns of specialisation at the level of ethnic groups or population categories may leave national and international economic structures entirely unaffected. In sum, it is important that the part should not be mistaken for the whole.

# Circuits of Work

# Interdependencies in the urban economy[1]

## Milton Santos

The combination of rapid economic and demographic growth in many Third World cities has resulted in concentrations of wealth and poverty within them (Santos, 1971a, 1971b). It was once thought that industrialisation would cure the situation of social crisis which was generated as a consequence. The current state of many long-established industrial cities testifies to the contrary: economic divisions within the urban system persist in the face of official efforts to improve conditions of housing, education and, most recently, of work.[2]

It is the purpose of this paper to review the models of urban economy which attempt to explain these divisions, and to indicate that they fail to do so because they stress the independence of each sector rather than the interdependencies between them. We argue that the work of all city-dwellers forms part of a single system. While each category of workers may be analysed apart, each sector of work constitutes a sub-system of the whole. 'Formal' and 'informal' sectors are only *conceptually* separable.

## Studies of Urban Poverty

The economy of the poor living in cities used to be known as the tertiary sector. It was generally considered parasitic and archaic. Although the approach to it remained either sectorial or unilateral, the dynamics behind it were implicit. It was only towards the end of the 1960s that the first explicit studies appeared.[3]

Three recent analyses of urban poverty are germane to the present paper. The first (McGee, 1974) focused on the reasons for the permanence of the activities of the poor in cities; and on the way the elasticity of the labour market came about as the population increased – despite the fact that there was no expansion of permanent employment. The study of the activity of hawkers lent itself to this investigation.

These reflections suggested a new category within the usual division of social classes: the protoproletariat (McGee, 1974, p. 18). The protoproletariat has three economic dimensions. First, it is possible to identify it by the fact that its activities occur primarily in only one of the two sectors identified in the 'dualistic model' of urban economic organisation; that is, the lower circuit. Second, the protoproletariat can be defined structurally as basic to the mode of production in which it is participating. Third, it is characterised by a particular set of job or income opportunities and a predominance of self-employment and household enterprises. Small-scale manufacturing, trading, street-vending, repairs and services can be included in these categories of work. So can prostitution and other so-called 'anti-social' or typically illegal activities.

The second study (Quijano, 1972) focused on the formation of classes and segments of classes within the framework of post-war urbanisation, and in situations of dependent economic development. From this angle, the study of social classes involves the analysis of concrete modes of production and the position of each group within the society in relation to those modes.

In this analysis, the process of exclusion and the formation of 'marginals' as it occurred in the past is differentiated from the present restructuring of urban social classes. The present marginal population is much larger and comprises three distinct groups. The marginal petty-bourgeoisie includes those who have been made marginal by the change or diminution of their role in the system. Craftsmen, small-scale suppliers of services and small-scale traders are part of this group to the extent that their position in society is different from that of the average worker in the wage-earning sector. They are marginal from a social rather than an occupational standpoint. A second group is formed by those who have either given up rural activities or have never been employed, and who indulge in a wage-earning activity only marginally. These are the marginal wage-earners, an extension of the industrial urban proletariat. A third group is designated the marginal proletariat. It originates from the same marginalisation of petty bourgeois occupations and the degradation of the conditions of marginal wage-earners, but members of the two categories converge in the third which tends to be numerically the largest. The basic trend of all these 'marginals' is towards concentration in two kinds of occupation: the petty bourgeoisie and the marginal proletariat.

The starting point of the third study (Santos, 1970b) was different, and its focus was another element of the urban network: the dimension of inter-urban relations. The city is not an aggregate structure, but consists of two economic sectors. Inter-urban relations do not take place in the same manner within the two sectors. We therefore undertook a detailed study of these sectors, regarding them as two genuine sub-systems of the urban system, interdependent and complementary, but nevertheless graded against each other. We then defined their structures within totalities at different geographic levels: city, country, world. The analysis is discussed in the following sections.

## The Two Circuits of Urban Economy

Where Geertz (1963) has spoken of firm-centred economy and of bazaar economy for the sake of taking into account the variety of situations in the cities of the Third World, we prefer to speak of two circuits of urban economy: the upper circuit and the lower circuit (Santos, 1971b). We had previously called these 'modern' and 'traditional' circuits (Santos, 1970a), but now recognise that the terms modern and traditional are misleading. The activities of the upper circuit are defined less by their historic age relative to similar activities in the countries of the core than by their mode of organisation and behaviour. As for those of the lower circuit, the word 'traditional' is inappropriate because they are now structurally subordinated to processes of modernisation. This sector feeds itself partly by modernisation and is involved in a permanent process of transformation and adaptation to it.[4]

We thus arrived at the following characteristics of the two circuits (Santos, 1975b):[5]

|  | Upper circuit | Lower circuit |
|---|---|---|
| Technology | capital-intensive | labour-intensive |
| Organisation | bureaucratic | primitive |
| Capital | abundant | scarce |
| Work | limited | abundant |
| Regular wages | normal | not required |
| Inventories | large quantities and/or high quality | small quantities and/or poor quality |
| Prices | generally fixed | generally negotiable between buyer and seller |
| Credit | from banks and other institutions | personal, non-institutional |
| Benefits | reduced to unity, but important due to the volume of business | raised to unity, but small in relation to the volume of business |
| Relations with clientele | impersonal and/or through documents | direct, personal |
| Fixed costs | important | negligible |
| Publicity | necessary | none |
| Re-use of goods | none | frequent |
| Overhead capital | indispensable | dispensable |
| Government aid | important | none or almost none |
| Direct dependence on foreign countries | extensive outward-oriented activity | small or none |

The notion of circuits is essential, for circuit is 'a word which better denotes the internal flows existing within the sub-systems. This model accepts the sub-systems as part of an interlocking, overall city economic structure' (McGee, 1973, p. 138).[6]

In other words, within each circuit, the characteristics are mutually explanatory: they are part of a system. Taken in isolation, each characteristic of a circuit is the reverse of the corresponding characteristic of the other circuit. Hence it constitutes an opposition – a dialectical opposition since the characteristics of the lower circuit are explained by the whole economy in which the upper circuit is in a dominant position. The two circuits are both opposed and complementary. This complementarity is a complementarity with domination, which is the mark of structures and systems of structures. Urban economy taken as a whole is a system of structures and not a system of simple elements. Hence it is impossible to study either circuit in isolation.[7]

Alongside these studies, another trend is discernible. Its preference goes to the study of one side of urban economy, the informal sector. Let us recall that the designations upper circuit and lower circuit were put forward to draw attention to the fact that urban economy, being a totality, should be analysed as a structure *à dominante* (L. Althusser, 1965). Complementarity is secured at the cost of the dependence of the lower circuit upon the upper, both being subordinated to the general laws of capitalist development. The same is true at the level of occupation. Marx wrote of small-scale manufacturers and traders that: 'In the capacity of owner of the means of production, he is a capitalist. In another capacity, he is his own hired worker. Thus as capitalist, he pays himself wages and extracts profit from his capital, i.e. he exploits himself as a hired worker and, in the form of surplus value, pays himself that tribute that labour must pay to the capitalist . . .' Of the current historical period in underdeveloped countries, it is said that 'under the conditions of a dominant capitalist structure, small-scale production becomes one of the forms of capitalist production, and the craftsman, even though he does not resort to hired labour, is a capitalist in certain sense' (Kus'min, 1969, p. 5).

A small producer seldom accumulates from his investment. Nevertheless, those who employ people do reconstitute capital with hired labour. Certainly craftsmen and small traders participate at various levels in the general process of capitalist economy.

What then are we to make of the designations 'formal sector' and 'informal sector'?

## The Informal Sector

The expression 'informal sector' is variously attributed to Tina Wallace (1973), to Weeks (1973, p. 11) and to Keith Hart (1973) (compare Worsley, 1972, p. 228; Remy and Weeks, 1973, p. 11). The expression 'Bazaar economy' used to refer to forms of small-scale trade once characteristic of the Orient, has practically disappeared from the relevant literature. So have the terms 'non-structured sector' and 'transition sector' (in transition towards what?) (Lerner, 1958). Other designations have suffered the same fate. Against this, however, the use of the analogous notions of 'formal' and 'informal' sector has increased. Here, we may actually witness a case of word fetishism. When important institutions such as the World Bank and the Institute of Development Studies of the University of Sussex (1973) decide, for different reasons, to sponsor a word, official research and individual researchers have a tendency to follow suit: '. . . it is curious that whilst heuristic concepts of formal and informal organisations have virtually been exhausted by students of organisational behaviours, the dichotomy is making a comeback in the field of development studies' (Henley, 1973, p. 568). But for our present purposes, the popularity of the terms is less important than the meaning ascribed to them. What is implied by 'informality'?

## Informality as Irrationality

The notion of informal as opposed to formal organisation draws its origin chiefly from the concept of rationality introduced by Max Weber. In this connection, only formal organisation is effective, having at its disposal 'clear rules and roles, systematic procedures for selection, training and promotion, the right span of control . . . needed for the best use of the resources which are available to you, in pursuit of the ends you desire' (Lipton, 1972, p. 45). Similarly: 'Formal organisation generally refers to the organisational pattern designed by management . . . the rules and regulations about wages, fines, quality control etc. Informal organisation refers either to the social relations that develop among the staff or workers beyond the formal one determined by the organisation (e.g. they not only work as a team on the same machine but are also friends), or to the actual organisational relations as they evolved as a consequence of the interaction between the organisational design and the pressures of interpersonal relations among the participants.' In formal organisation, scientific management is crucial; in informal organisation, the stress is on human relations (Etzioni, 1964, p. 40).

Dualists, when referring to underdeveloped countries, make an opposition between a developed sector, which is a coherent whole of rational, efficient actions, and a non-developed sector, which is by contrast an inarticulate set of irrational, inefficient and archaic actions. An irrational action would be one for which there is no rational economic 'cause or effect'. By this definition, an action which effectively bridged the gap between one economic system and another must be rational. What, then, about workers who participate alternatively in the activities of both circuits without changing their socio-economic status?

The narrow notion of rationality is not simply a poor yardstick by which to measure other than industrial bureaucratic forms of organisation: it smacks of cultural arrogance. The fact is that 'if someone in another society makes different decisions from ours, it probably indicates that he has a different hierarchy of values and priorities, not that his behaviour is irrational or mistaken' (Wilkinson, 1973, p. 198). Which is only to say that there is not *one* economic rationality but *several* (Godelier, 1972, p. 298).

## The Poor Economy, 'Formality', Alienation

But does this allow the claim that there is an informal sector in contrast to and separate from the formal?

Some have proposed that industrial urbanism was the only rational model of thought and work (Anderson, 1964, p. 57). Others link rationality to modernisation, modernisation to scientism (Gutkind, 1967). At least one influential writer states that the 'tertiary' sector is economically as unproductive as it is irrational (Morse, 1964).

Others, on the contrary, have shown the underlying rationality of the poor economy of Third World cities (for example, Geertz, 1963, p. 43; Saylor, 1967, p. 99; Hill, 1970, p. 4), thus: If irrationality is closely linked with impulsiveness and irrational action is provoked more by blind psychological forces than by deliberate calculation, then there is no irrationality in the behaviour of the inhabitants of Latin American shanty towns (Poetes, 1972, pp. 269–70). Detailed studies in Hong Kong and other cities of the Far East show the activities of the 'informal sector' to operate most effectively (McGee, 1974, p. 40). Even street-vendors are efficient in supplying the poor population with work and cheap commodities. On the other hand, the members of the Katwe co-operative in Kampala (Uganda) operate in a fashion that could be regarded as 'informal' despite their typically formal legal status (Shepard, 1955). Formal classifications of status are therefore irrelevant (Halpenny, 1972). The real significance of the so-called informal sector lies in the relative flexibility and fluidity of its operation.

A human action is irrational only insofar as it neither achieves objectives nor leads to behaviour stable enough to give rise to consistent rules. But in the lower circuit of the urban economy there are certain relationships which recur everywhere and all the time, between agents, between agents and clients, in the execution of the activity itself, and in its overall significance within the society (Santos, 1971a; 1971b; 1975a). For example, operational costs are consistently lower in the lower circuit. Even dependence relationships with the upper circuit are governed by a consistent logic. Each civilisation or class regarded as superior attributes logic only to its own actions. This does not alter the fact that the poor economy operates in a logical and therefore rational fashion.

The lower circuit of urban economy constitutes a permanent mechanism of integration, supplying a maximum number of job opportunities with a minimum amount of capital. It responds directly to general conditions of employment, to the availability of capital and to the consumption needs of an important fraction of the population. Its functioning is governed by laws: the same effects follow in response to recurring causes. The characteristics which identify it as 'informal' are precisely the marks of its rationality: a hand-to-mouth existence with uneven expenditure over any pay period; flexibility of consumption units; and proliferation of credit in all commodities (Hart, 1973, p. 5) – these are economically rational and adaptive behaviours. In effect, the lower circuit too is governed by the mechanisms and processes of the capitalist economy whose effect appears consistently, but under different forms, in each sub-system. The lower circuit constitutes a sub-system within the larger urban system, and the urban system is itself a sub-system of the national system.

If the notion of informality or irrationality is applied to one of the two economic sectors of any one society, the implication must be that this very society does not operate in an overall manner. This view obviously supports a dualistic approach in which the two circuits are regarded as parallel, and which ignores the problem of the dependence of one circuit upon the other.

The Weberian notion of rationality or rational reckoning is based on 'the conformity of the action with the logic of a system of values' (Kende, 1971, p. 63) – necessarily, in this case, the capitalist system of values in which Weberian rationality is prerequisite to expansion. For a production machinery based on exchange value and surplus value to be successful, a total rationalisation of the way in which the various factors are used becomes necessary – rationality having here the meaning of mutation from quality to quantity, of the pre-eminence of abstract systems over concrete ones – of, in other words, alienation.

There is a parallel between this Weberian notion of rationality and the Marxist notion of reification. Each is 'a species within the genus alienation' (Lukacs, 1959). Capitalist expansion is accompanied by a reified objectivity (Riu, 1968, p. 24), and by the progressive elimination of the worker's human and individual qualities.

It is those who constitute the lower circuit (the 'informal sector') who suffer least the alienation which characterises the working world in modern societies. They are still able to identify themselves with the product of their labour. Moreover, to the extent that participation in one's work is perhaps the most conscious political feeling (Halpenny, 1972, p. 16), the activities of the 'informal sector' allow a greater sense of political involvement.

A discussion on the validity of a term as such may bring us no nearer understanding what it is supposed to designate. Originally, the designation 'informal sector' was restricted to the situation of income employment. Two types of urban economic activity were distinguished: formal income activities and informal income activities, the latter being sub-divided into legitimate and illegitimate forms (Hart, 1973, p. 69). But income employment does not operate alone. The notion became a means of defining a whole sector of the economy, and the definition of the 'informal sector' entailed the recognition of its opposition to the 'formal sector' (Sethuraman, 1974a, p. 6).

But the use of arbitrary criteria to identify the enterprises of the 'informal sector' detracts from the scientific validity of the approach. Because much of this economic research was directly oriented towards the needs of planning, the tendency has been to start from premises to be demonstrated or from ideas to be justified; to seek to quantify; and to take into account only a single criterion: the productivity of labour. The planning objective also led to the pursuit of a clear distinction between rational/formal and irrational/informal. The cut-off is impossible to demarcate in reality unless both the qualitative aspects of work and the complementarity of productive systems are, *a priori*, set aside. It is simply not correct to infer that to make the 'informal' sector 'formal' (that is, the 'lower' circuit 'upper'), it would suffice to inject greater productivity into the former, so making it more capitalistic. This would obscure the fact that the operation of the lower circuit is directly responsive to the operation of the upper circuit at local, national and international levels.

## Circuits of Asymmetrical Exchange

It has been said that poor urban economy (the lower circuit) is exploited by the other sector (the upper circuit) through terms of trade which limit the ability of small-scale manufacturers to grow over extended periods (Bienefeld, 1975, p. 4). But we must go further: the possibly essential function of the lower circuit is to diffuse the capitalist mode of production into the poor population through consumption; and to suck household savings and surplus value generated by small firms into the upper circuit via the financial mechanisms of production and consumption. Transmission channels are various, both formal and informal. Bank agencies, co-operatives, residential building companies and the state itself, through the double channel of taxation and unequal distribution of resources, are all instruments pumping surplus value into banks and powerful national and foreign firms. The same function is achieved, often even more effectively, by all types of middlemen, wholesalers, truck-drivers and traders on temporary markets – all of whom are characterised by remarkable flexibility of behaviour (Santos, 1975a; 1975b).

Any lessening in the imbalance of exchange will therefore mean very little if the flows of surplus value continue to impoverish some and to enrich others. It is utterly misleading to say that 'the informal sector, both urban and rural, represents a vital part of the economy, and its existence reflects a necessary and on the whole beneficial adjustment to the constraints imposed by the prevailing economic situation' (Singer and Jolly, 1973). An adjustment necessary and beneficial to whom? To admit the statement is to imply a literal interpretation of Joan Robinson (1962, p. 45): 'The misery of being exploited by capitalists is nothing compared to the misery of not being exploited at all.' To adopt such a view in the planning of the lower circuit is, to say the least, short-sighted. The setting and even the achievement of sectorial objectives frequently enhances the modern sector of the economy without creating employment opportunities or reducing poverty.

The elimination of the dominance of the upper circuit over the lower and the dependence of the lower circuit upon the upper can only come about as an effect of structural change. Ideally, no doubt, the lower circuit should become less low. But, given the relation between them, this could only happen if the upper circuit became less high. Studies focusing on the informal sector as such cannot be of any help since they break up reality before looking at the interdependencies within it.

## Conclusion

The lower circuit can be defined as a single system (Santos, 1971b). But we must recognise that the division of reality into separate levels of organisation or scale is a conceptual device by which we divide up the totality to get a better grasp of its complexity. There cannot, in reality, be a separate informal sector within an overall formal society. The entire thing is governed by the same set of rules. The lower circuit is dynamic, but its dynamism is conditioned and constrained by other elements in the overall economic system. It cannot be the object of planning or even of analysis which does not take into account the dynamism of the other circuit and fails to recognise that both operate within an economy which is itself dependent on higher and wider processes.

# Notes and References

## Introduction

1. This introduction makes direct reference only to the body of the volume. Theoretical background and bibliography to the main themes may be found in a small number of core references. The notion of *ethnicity as a resource* is elaborated from Wallman (1974), in which the model is applied to the analysis of kinship. See also Lyman and Douglass (1973), Wallman (1977b). On *boundaries*, see Douglas (1970), Leach (1976) and Wallman (1978). The classic statements on *spheres* of exchange, etc., are in Barth (1963 and 1967) and are taken up in Leyton (1970). On the relation between *structure and perception*, see variously Goffman (1975), Firth (1972) and Wallman (1977a). Each of the contributors makes full reference to the literature appropriate to his/her chapter. All the references are listed together in the Bibliography at the end of the volume.

## Chapter 1

1. Field data are based on twelve months' participant observation on camps in southern England between 1970 and 1972 and in three months in 1974 as well as on regular communications and visits. I was engaged in a research project at the Centre for Environmental Studies (London) and sponsored by the Rowntree Memorial Trust, and awarded a pre-doctoral research grant from the S.S.R.C. in 1973. Quotations in the text not otherwise credited are from the author's field notes.
2. Neither are they so formalised by Gypsies. They are

generalisations made by an anthropologist on the basis of observation and analysis of field data.

3. Personal communication – M. Kaminsky of the Social Anthropology Institute, Goteborg, Sweden.

## Chapter 4

1. The research on which this paper is based was carried out when both authors were on the staff of the Social Science Research Council's Industrial Relations Research Unit (I.R.R.U.) at the University of Warwick, 1970–4 and 1971–5 respectively. The findings reported here constitute one aspect of a wider study, to be published for the I.R.R.U. We are indebted to the Leverhulme Trust for financing the project, and to the I.R.R.U. for housing it. We are grateful to those workers – both black and white – who answered our many questions with such patience; and to managers, supervisors and trade-union activists in the seven plants studied.

The interpretations and opinions presented here are, of course, ours, and do not necessarily represent those of the I.R.R.U. or of our present employers.

2. Evidence of black recruitment in response to labour shortages and, by implication, to the 'least desirable' jobs, is to be found in all the relevant literature. See Brooks (1975a; 1975b); Commission on Industrial Relations (1970, p. 19); Davison (1964, p. 34); Department of Employment (1972, pp. 27, 37, 57); K. Jones and A. D. Smith (1970); Patterson (1963, 1968, pp. 229–33); Peach (1968); P.E.P. (1967, pp. 40–2); Rimmer (1972, p. 10); Wright (1968, pp. 41–50);

3. The three names refer in order to the region of origin, religion, and (agricultural) caste. Our evidence is primarily from, and concerning, Punjabis, but may be generalised for other groups of Asian origins.

4. The exact relationship to Gurdial Singh is signified in brackets. Punjabi kinship terminology is much more comprehensive than is the English and it is necessary to differentiate between, for example, two kinds of brothers-in-law.

5. The term *ilaqa* refers to the villages in the immediate vicinity of one village.

6. A *patti* is a localised sub-area of each village. In many villages it is assumed that traditionally all the families (of the same caste) in the *patti* are descended from a common ancestor.

7. The term 'broker' is commonly used by anthropologists referring to mediating individuals who command resources and their distribution. While a more specific term would be desirable, the function of a broker in the control and allocation of resources covers the essential features of Punjabis emerging at the interface with the foundry industry.

8. See Mayer (1966, pp. 97–8): '. . . (quasi groups) are ego-centred, in the sense of depending for their very existence on a specific person as a central organising focus . . .'

## Chapter 5

1. These terms refer to the same activity, but from opposite perspectives. From the employer's point of view, an employee who works outside the factory is an 'outworker'. From the employee's point of view, someone who works at home for an outside employer is a 'home-worker'. The latter term is used throughout this paper.

2. In Britain, the official tally of the unemployed includes only those registered as unemployed during the week of the count. Those not entitled to unemployment benefit or not wishing to use official channels for job-seeking – both of which characteristics apply to anyone working or seeking work outside the 'formal' sector – would have no reason to report themselves for the official count. Unemployment benefit is not the same thing as Supplementary Benefit or 'the dole'. These are allocated on the basis of money need rather than work need and would be claimed by a different economic category.

## Chapter 9

1. This essay is based upon fieldwork initiated in Toronto, Ontario, during the winter of 1975, during which the author lived and worked as a casual labourer for four months. Anthropological interest was initially superseded by financial

considerations: upon the completion of a doctorate, other employment opportunities were not immediately forthcoming. Something of a total immersion in the life of casual labour ensued and the author's indentity as an anthropologist was never revealed to other labourers.

2. The Department of Manpower and Immigration has established casual labour offices in the major Canadian urban centres. In these offices, men are employed directly by employers and are selected for work in the order in which they appear at the office. However, the government's policy is to avoid competition with private enterprise and the existence of its offices is not openly advertised. Private casual labour offices employ salesmen to make their services known to prospective employers and engage in various forms of advertising. Most casual labour opportunities are channelled to privately-owned casual labour offices; the few jobs that do come through the government casual labour offices tend to be extremely dirty and/or hazardous. Most casual labourers work for a privately-owned firm and are under the jurisdiction and control of that firm's permanent employees.

## Chapter 10

1. This paper was originally translated from the French by Marie-Francoise Eze.

2. Studies carried out in the I.L.O.'s research program on Urbanization and Employment relating to the problem of the two circuits of urban economy include: Sethuraman (1974a, 1974b); Bose (1974); Schaefer and Spindel (1974); Lubell (1974); *Planungsgruppe Ritter* (1974); Joshi, Lubell and Mouly (1974); Gerry (1974). Relevant studies sponsored by the I.L.O.'s World Employment Program include: Lecaillon and Germidis (1974); Hsia and Chau (1975); Oberai (1975); Villanueva (1975).

3. D. C. Lambert (1965) analysed the consequences of import substitution coupled with a high-rate demography in Latin America. They have led to a tertiary urbanisation structurally different from the one in developed countries. In underdeveloped countries, he calls it *tertiaire refuge*.

Armstrong and McGee (1968), using for the city the notion of involution created by Geertz (1963) for the rural world, introduce the notion of auto-inflationary economy. Santos (1968) analyses the functioning of the lower circuit, in search of an explanation for the subsistence of so many poor in Third World cities. All these articles have, as it happens, been published by the journal *Civilisations*.

4. Among the authors still using the dichotomy 'modern sector – traditional sector', we find C. R. Frank (1968, p. 251). The former term has been used differently by Mortimore (1972) in his study of Kano: the modern sector is the area outside the city's walls. The old city, the *birni*, is characterised by traditional activities.

5. New themes of research involve repetitions and convergences, and language itself is a strong handicap to the diffusion of research findings. Thus, Sethuraman (1974a, pp. 1– 5) admits that urban economy is divided into two sectors, but complains that their characteristics have never been clearly defined.

6. Among the empirical works using this theory are: Albertini *et al.* (1969); Chollet *et al.* (1969); Erdens (1969); H. Lamicq (1969); Valladares (1969); Motti (1970); Charleux (1970); Lejars (1971); Loupy (1971); Champseix *et al.* (1972); Mataillet *et al.* (1973); Couvreur-Laraichi (1973); Coutsinas (1974); Missen and Logan (1975). All these works are also indebted to McGee's theoretical contribution.

7. Some recent works complement the synthesis we have been attempting (Santos, 1971b, 1975b). Remy and Weeks (1973) use the term 'informal' but, unlike Hart, they prefer to give it a political meaning. Weeks (ibid.) insists particularly on the role of the state which persecutes the *lower circuit* and protects the *upper circuit*. Gerry (1974, pp. 79–82) emphasises the same point using the example of Dakar. Remy and Weeks have also considered the linkages between the two circuits. Their rich study of Zaira (Nigeria) underlines the importance of studying the lower circuit in rural areas. Storgaard (1973) and Mortimore (1972) also made studies from this last standpoint. G. Coutsinas (1974) shows the behaviour of the two circuits in the planned economy of Algeria. His remarks have a general theoretical value. Missen and Logan (1975) considered the two circuits in the frame of the urban network in Kelantan, West Malaysia.

# Bibliography

ABRAMOVITCH, H. (1943) 'Rural Jewish Occupations in Lithuania', *Yivo Bleter*, vol. XXII, pp. 205–21.

ADAMS, B., OKELY, J., MORGAN, D., and SMITH D. (1975) *Gypsies and Government Policy in England* (London: Heinemann).

ALBERTINI, P., AMILCAR, V., DE ALEXANDER, J., BURDEINICK, M., and ALVAREZ, L. M. (1969) *Estudio Regional de Calabozo, Doc. de Trabajo, Projecto Venezuela II de las Naciones Unidas*, (Maracay, mimeo).

ALEXANDER, S. (1976) 'Women's Work in Nineteenth-Century London: a study of the years 1820–50', in Juliet Mitchell and Ann Oakley (eds), *The Rights and Wrongs of Women* (Harmondsworth: Penguin).

ALLEN, S. (1971) *New Minorities, Old Conflicts* (New York: Random House).

ALTHUSSER, L. (1965) *Lire le Capital* (Paris: Editions Maspero).

ANDERSON, N. (1964) 'Aspects of urbanism and urbanization', in Nels Anderson (ed.), *Urbanism and Urbanization* (Leiden: E. J. Brill).

ANNIVERSARY BOOKLET OF THE BENEFIT SOCIETY OF OŠČIMA (1957) (Toronto).

ARDENER, S. (ed.) (1975) *Perceiving Women* (London: Malaby).

ARMSTRONG, W. R., and McGEE, T. G. (1968) 'Revolutionary Change and the Third World City', *Civilisations XVIII*, no. 3, pp. 353–77.

ARROW, K. J. (1972) 'Models of Job Discrimination', in Pascal (ed.), *Racial Discrimination in Economic Life* (Lexington, Mass.: Heath).

ATKINSON, A. B. (1975) *The Economics of Inequality* (Oxford: Clarendon Press).

AURORA, G. S. (1967) *The New Frontiersmen* (Bombay: Popular Prakashan).

AVIMERI, S. (1968) *The Social and Political Thought of Karl Marx* (Cambridge University Press).

BANTON, M. (ed.) (1966) *The Social Anthropology of Complex Societies* (London: Tavistock).

BAROU, N. (1945) *The Jews in Work and Trade* (London: Trades Advisory Council).

BARTH, F. (1955) 'The Social Organisation of a Parian Group in Norway' *Norveg*, reprinted in F. Rehfisch, (1975) op. cit.

—— (1963) *The Role of the Entrepreneur in Northern Norway* (Oslo: Scan. Univ. Books).

—— (1967) 'Economic Spheres in Darfur', in Firth (ed.), *Themes in Economic Anthropology* (London: Tavistock).

—— (1969) *Ethnic Groups and Boundaries* (Boston: Little Brown and Company).

BECKER, G. (1971) *The Economics of Discrimination*, 2nd ed. (Chicago University Press).

BEFU, H. (1966–7) 'Gift-Giving and Social Reciprocity in Japan', *France-Asia*, no. 188.

BEVERIDGE, W. (1930) *Unemployment, a Problem of Industry* (London: Longman).

BIENEFELD, M. (1975) *The Informal Sector and Peripheral Capitalism, The Case of Tanzania* (mimeo, 17 pp.).

BLAUG, M. (1974) *L'Education et le Problème de L'Emploi dans les Pays en voie de Development* (Geneva: B.I.T.–I.L.O.).

BLISHEN, B. R. (1973) 'Social Class and Opportunity in Canada', in J. E. Curtis and W. G. Scott (eds) *Social Stratification: Canada* (Scarborough, Canada: Prentice-Hall).

BÖHNING, W. R. (1972) *The Migration of Workers in the United Kingdom and the European Community* (London: Oxford University Press for the Institute of Race Relations).

BOISSEVAIN, J. (1974) *Friends of Friends* ( Oxford: Blackwell).

BOLTON, B. (1975) *An end to homeworking?*, Fabian Tract 436 (London: Fabian Society).

BOOTH, C. (1893) *Inquiry into Life and Labour of the People of London* (London: Macmillan).

BOSE, A. N. (1974) *The Informal Sector in the Calcutta Metropolitan*

234  *Bibliography*

*Economy* (W.E.P./U.E.R.P., I.L.O. Geneva).

BRODY, D. (1960/9) *Steelworkers in America: the non-union era* (Harvard University Press, 1960, and New York: Harper and Row, 1969).

BROOKS, D. (1975a) *Race and Labour in London Transport* (London: Oxford University Press for the Institute of Race Relations and the Acton Society Trust).

—— (1975b) *Black Employment in the Black Country: a Study of Walsall* (London: Runnymede).

BROOKS, D., and Singh, K. (1972) 'Does Unemployment Breed Racism?' *Race Today*, vol. 4, no. 7, July.

BROWN, M. (1974) *Sweated Labour: A Study of Homework*, Low Pay Pamphlet no. 1 (Low Pay Unit, London).

BULL, D. G. (1975) 'Equity and Justice in Supplementary Benefits', unpublished teaching material in the Department of Social Administration, Bristol University.

BUNT, S. (1975) *Jewish Youth Work in Britain* (London: Bedford Square).

CAKOLOV, G., LJABOVA, I., and STANKOV, Z. (1961) *Bulgarsko-Angliski Recnik* (Sofija: *Drzavno izdatelstvo 'Nonko i Izkustro'*).

CANADIAN FAMILY TREE, CANADIAN CITIZENSHIP BRANCH, DEPARTMENT OF THE SECRETARY OF STATE (1967) Published in co-operation with the Centennial Commission, Ottawa.

CANADIAN MACEDONIAN CALENDAR AND COMMERCIAL DIRECTORY (1961) (Toronto: Ivkov N. P.).

CHAMPSEIX, G., GUIBERT, J. J., LAZZARI, CH., and MIGNON, J. M. (1972) *Contribution aux Methodes d'Analyse Regionale: le cas de la ville de Saida* (Institut d'Etudes du Developpement Economique et Social, Université de Paris).

CHAPPLE, D. (1970) *Forest and Village*, M.A. thesis, social anthropology (University of Auckland, New Zealand).

CHARLEUX, J. L. (1970) *Etude sur Tindivanam, dans l'Inde du Sud* (Institut de Geographie, Université de Paris, mimeo).

CHOLLET, J., SANCHEZ, G., BOLIVAR, M., RODRIGUEZ, J., and DA COSTA, J. R. (1969) *Estudio Regional de Coro y Punto Fijo* (Doctor de Trabajo, Proveto Venezuela 11, Caracas).

CIVIC TRUST (1968) *Disposal of Unwanted Vehicles and Bulky Refuse* (London: Graphic Press).

CLARK, D. (1972) 'Social Dynamics in a low-income Neighbourhood in Nairobi' unpublished M.A. thesis (Department of

Sociology, Makerere University, Uganda).

COHEN, ABNER (1969) *Custom and Politics in Urban Africa* (London: Routledge and Kegan Paul).

COHEN, A. (1971) *Everyman's Talmud* (London: Dent).

COMMISSION ON INDUSTRIAL RELATIONS (C.I.R.) (1970) *Report No. 4* (on the Birmid-Qualcast Group) Cmnd. 4264 (London: H.M.S.O.).

COUTSINAS, G. (1974) *A propos des Deux Circuits de l'Economie Urbaine: un Example Algerien Communication presentée lors du Seminaire Espace Maghrebin* (Alger, 18–24 Fevrier).

COUVREUR-LARAICHI (1973) *Beni-Mellal, une Ville Marocaine* (Université de Strasbourg).

CRVENKOWSKI, D., and GRUIK, B. (1965) *A Little Macedonian-English Dictionary* (Skopje: Prosvetno Delo).

CUNNINGHAM, B. (1926) *Port Economics* (London: Pitman's Transport Library).

CVIJIC, J. (1966) *Balkansko Poluostrovo i Juznoslovenski Zemlje* (Osnovi Antropogeografie) (Beograd: Zavod za izdavanje udbenika, Socikalisticke Republik Srbije).

DAHYA, B. U. (1973) 'Pakistanis in Britain: Transients or Settlers?' *Race* vol. XIV, no. 3, January.

DAVISON R. B. (1964) *Commonwealth Immigrants* (London: Oxford University Press for Institute of Race Relations).

DEPARTMENT OF EMPLOYMENT (1972) *Take 7* (London: H.M.S.O.).

DESAI, R. H. (1964) 'The Family and Business Enterprise among the Asians in East Africa', paper presented to the Conference of the East African Institute of Social Research (Makerere University College).

DOERINGER, D. B., and PIORE, M. (1971) *Internal Labour Markets and Manpower Analysis* (Lexington, Mass.: Heath).

DOKLESTIC, L. (1964) *Kroz Historiju Makedonije* (Zagreb: Skolska Knjiga).

DOTSON, F., and DOTSON, L. (1968) *The Indian Minority in Zambia, Rhodesia and Malawi* (Yale University Press).

DOUGLAS, M. (1970) *Purity and Danger* (Harmondsworth: Penguin).

ERDENS, A. D. (1969) *A Conurbacao Barcelona-Puerto La Cruz e sua Regiao* (Caracas, mimeo, 45 pp).

ETZIONI, A. (1964) *Modern Organizations* (Englewood Cliffs,

N. J.: Prentice-Hall).

FIELD, F. (1976) *70 Years On: a new report on Homeworking, Low Pay Bulletin*, August–October 10/11.

FIRTH, R. (1972) 'The Sceptical Anthropologist?: Social Anthropology and Marxist Views on Society' in *Proceedings of the British Academy LVIII* (Oxford University Press).

FOSTER, G. M. (1967) *Tzintzuntzan: Mexican Peasants in a Changing World* (Boston: Little Brown).

FRANK, C. R. (1968) *Urban Unemployment and Economic Growth in Africa*, Oxford Economic Papers, July.

FREEDMAN, M. (ed.) (1955) *A Minority in Britain* (London: Valentine, Mitchell).

FREEMAN, R. B. (1976) 'Individual Mobility and Union Voice in the Labour Market', Papers and Proceedings of the American Economic Association, *American Economic Review*, vol. 66.

FURNIVAL, J. S. (1939) *Netherlands India: A study of Plural Economy* (Cambridge University Press).

GARTNER, L. P. (1973) *The Jewish Immigrant in England*, 2nd edn. (London: Simon Publications).

GEERTZ, C. (1963) *Peddlers and Princes* (Chicago University Press).

GEORGANO, G. N. (1971) *A History of the London Taxi Cab* (Newton Abbot: David and Charles).

GERLACH, L., and HINE, V. (1970) *People, Power, Change: Movements of Social Transformation* (Indianapolis: Bobbs-Merrill).

GERRY, C. (1974) *Petty Producers and the Urban Economy: a case study of Dakar* (Geneva: W.E.P./U.E.R.P., I.L.O.) September.

GODELIER, M., (1972) *Rationality and Irrationality in Economics* (London: New Left Books).

GOFFMAN, E. (1961) *Asylums* (New York: Doubleday Anchor).

—— (1968) *Stigma: notes on the management of spoiled identity* (Harmondsworth: Penguin).

—— (1975) *Frame Analysis* (Harmondsworth: Penguin).

GORDON, D. M. (1972) *Theories of Poverty and Unemployment* (Lexington, Mass.: Heath).

GOULD, S. J., and ESH, S. (eds) (1964) *Jewish Life in Modern Britain* (London: Routledge and Kegan Paul).

GOULET, D., and WALSHOK, M. (1971) 'Values among underdeveloped Marginals: the case of Spanish Gypsies' *Comparative*

*Studies in Society and History*, vol. 13, no. 4.

GUTKIND, P. C. W. (1967) 'The Energy of Despair: social organisation of the unemployed in two African cities', *Civilisations*, vol. XVII, nos 3 and 4.

HAALAND, G. (1969) 'Economic Determinants in Ethnic Process' in F. Barth (ed.), *Ethnic Groups and Boundaries* (Boston: Little, Brown).

HALL, D. (1973) 'The Canadian Division of Labour Revisited' in J. E. Curtis and W. G. Scott (eds), *Social Stratification: Canada* (Scarborough, Canada: Prentice-Hall).

HALPENNY, P. (1972) 'Getting rich by being "unemployed", some political implications of "informal" economic activities in urban areas not usually represented in official indices', unpublished paper delivered to Universities Social Sciences Conferences, Nairobi.

HALPERN, D. B. (1956) *Changes in the Structure of Jewish Industrial and Commercial Life in Britain* (London: Trades Advisory Council).

HARRIS, J. (1970) 'Nigerian Entrepreneurship in Industry', in K. Eicher and C. Liedholm (eds), *Growth and Development of the Nigerian Economy* (Michigan State University Press).

HART, K. (1973) 'Informal income opportunities and urban employment in Ghana', *The Journal of Modern African Studies*, vol. 1, no. 73, pp. 61–89.

HEGEL, G. (1942) *Philosophy of Right*, 1821, trans. T. M. Knox (Oxford University Press).

HENLEY, J. S. (1973) 'Employment relationship and economic development – the Kenyan experience', *The Journal of Modern African Studies*, vol. II, no. 4, pp. 559–89.

HILL, M. J. (1969) 'The Exercise of discretion in the National Assistance Board', *Public Administration*, no. 47.

—— (1972) *The Sociology of Public Administration* (London: Weidenfeld and Nicolson).

HILL, P. (1970) *Studies in Rural Capitalism in West Africa* (Cambridge University Press).

H.M.S.O. (1971) 'Fair Deal for Housing', Cmnd. 4728 (London: H.M.S.O.).

HOHEPA, P. (1964) *A Maori Community in Northland* (Wellington, N. Z.: (Reed Publishing).

HOPE, E., KENNEDY, M., and DE WINTER, A. (1976) 'Homewor-

238    *Bibliography*

kers in North London', in Diana Leonard Barker and Sheila Allen (eds), *Dependence and Exploitation in Work and Marriage* (London: Longmans).

HOYLAND, J. (1816) *An Historical Survey of the Customs, Habits and Present State of the Gypsies* (London).

HSIA, R., and CHAU, L. C. (1975) *Income Distribution and Employment Characteristics: Hong Kong 1971* (Geneva: W.E.P./I.D.E.P., I.L.O.).

HUDSON, K. (1970) *Working to Rule* (Bath: Adams and Dart).

HUGHES, E. C. (1949) 'Queries Concerning Industry and Society Growing out of the Study of Ethnic Relations in industry', *American Sociological Review* vol. XIV, no. 12, April.

—— (1951) 'Mistakes at Work', *Canadian Journal of Economics and Political Science*, August.

HUGHES, E. C., and HUGHES, H. M. (1952) *Where People Meet: Racial and Ethnic Frontiers* (Glencoe: Free Press).

I.L.W.U. LOCAL 500 PENSIONERS (1975) *Man along the Shore: The Story of the Vancouver Waterfront as Told by Longshoremen Themselves 1960–1975* (Vancouver: College Printers).

Institute of Development Studies (1973) 'Informal Sector?', *J.D.S.*, vol. V, no. 213, October.

ISTORIA NA MAKEDONSKIOT NAROD (1972) (Skopje: Provento Delo).

JENSEN, V. (1971) *Decasualization and Modernization of Dock Work in London* (Ithaca: New York State School of Industrial and Labour Relations, Cornell University).

JOHN, D. (1969) *Indian Workers' Association in Britain* (London: Oxford University Press for the Institute of Race Relations).

JONES, K., and SMITH, A. D. (1970) *The Economic Impact of Commonwealth Immigration* (London: Cambridge University Press for National Institute of Economic and Social Research).

JOSHI, H., LUBELL, H., and MOULY, J. (1974) *Urban Development and Employment in Abidjan* (Geneva: W.E.P./U.E.R.P., I.L.O.) October.

KENDE, P. (1971) *L'Abondance est-elle possible?* (Paris: Gallimard).

KOBAYASHI, T. (1973) *The Factory Ship and the Absentee Landlord* (University of Tokyo Press).

KOSMIN, B. A., and GRIZZARD, N. (1975) *Jews in an Inner London Borough* (London: Research Unit, Board of Deputies of British Jews).

KOSMIN, B. A., BAUER, M., and GRIZZARD, N. (1976) *Steel City Jews* (London: Research Unit, Board of Deputies of British Jews).

KRAUSZ, E. (1962) 'Occupation and Social Advancement in Anglo-Jewry', *The Jewish Journal of Sociology*, vol. iv, no. 1.

—— (1969) 'The Edgware Survey: Occupation and Social Class', *The Jewish Journal of Sociology*, vol. xi, no. 1.

KUMAR, K. (1976) 'The Salariat', *New Society*, vol. x, no. 21, 1976.

KUS'MIN, S. A. (1969) *The Developing Countries, Employment and Capital Investment* (White Plains, New York: International Arts and Sciences Press).

LAMBERT, D. (1965) 'L'urbanisation accelerée de l'Amerique Latine et la formation d'un secteur tertiaire refuge', *Civilisations*, vol. xv.

LAMBERT, R. D. (1963) *Workers, Factories and Social Change in India* (Princeton University Press).

LAMICQ, H. (1969) *Realite et limites du role de la ville de Maturin dans l'organisation de l'espace de l'Etat Monagas (Venezuela)* (Université de Paris, mimeo 136 pp.).

LEACH, E. (1961) *Pul Eliya* (Cambridge University Press).

—— (1964) *Political Systems of Highland Burma* (London School of Economics and Political Science).

—— (1976) 'Social Anthropology: a Natural Science of Society?' in *Proceedings of the British Academy LXII* (Oxford University Press).

LECAILLON, J., and GERMIDIS, D. (1974) *Les disparités de revenus entre salaries et travailleurs independants dans les secteurs non agricoles au Senegal Madagascar et Coté d'Ivoire* (Geneva: W.E.P./I.D.E.P., I.L.O.).

LEJARS, J. (1971) *Contribution a la connaissance de la situation industrielle de Vientiane (Laos)* (Université de Paris, Institut de Geographie, mimeo, 145 pp.).

LERNER, D. (1958) *The Passing of Traditional Society* (New York: Free Press).

LEVINE, R. (1966) *Dreams and Deeds: Achievement Motivation in Nigeria* (Chicago University Press).

LEWIS, O. (1958) *Village Life in Northern India: Studies in a Delhi Village* (Urbana: University of Illinois).

LEYTON, E. (1965) 'Composite Descent Groups in Canada', *Man*, vol. LXV, no. 98.

—— (1970) 'Spheres of Inheritance in Aughnaboy', *American Anthropologist*, no. 72, pp. 1378–88.

LINK, C. (1975) 'Black Education, Earnings and Interregional Migration – a Comment and some New Evidence', *American Economic Review*, vol. 65.

LIPMAN, V. D. (1960) *Social History of the Jews in England 1850–1950* (London: Watts).

—— (1960) 'Trends in Anglo-Jewish Occupations' *The Jewish Journal of Sociology*, vol. II, no. 2.

LIPSET, S. M., and BENDIX, R. (1967) *Social Mobility in Industrial Society* (Berkeley and Los Angeles: University of California Press).

LIPTON, T. (1972) *Management and the Social Sciences* (Harmondsworth: Penguin).

LIVERPOOL UNIVERSITY DEPARTMENT OF SOCIAL SCIENCE (1954) *The Dockworker; an analysis of the conditions of employment in the port of Manchester* (University Press of Liverpool).

LOUPY, E. (1971) *Problemes posés par le ravitaillement des marchés de Vientiane* (Université de Paris IV, mimeo, 86 pp.).

LUBELL, H. (1974) *Calcutta, its urban development and employment prospects* (Geneva: I.L.O.).

—— (1974) *Urbanisation and Employment, insights from a series of case studies of Third World metropolitan cities* (Geneva: W.E.P./ U.E.R.P., I.L.O.) November.

LUKACS, G. (1959) *El Asalto a la Razon* (Mexico: Fundo de Cultura Economica) (translation of *Die Zerstorung der Bernunft*).

—— (1960) *Histoire et Conscience de Classe* (Paris: Minuit).

LYMAN, S. M., and DOUGLASS, W. A. (1973) 'Ethnicity: strategies of collective and individual impression management', *Social Research*, vol. 40, no. 2, pp. 344–65.

MACRAE, J. T. (1975) *A Study in the Application of Economic Analysis to Social Issues: the Maori and the New Zealand Economy*, unpublished Ph.D. thesis, University of London.

MARRIS, P., and SOMERSET, A. (1971) *African Businessmen: a Study of Entrepreneurship and Development in Kenya* (London: Routledge and Kegan Paul).

MARSH, P. (1967) *The Anatomy of a Strike: Unions, Employers and*

*Punjabi Workers in a Southall Factory* (London: Institute of Race Relations, Special Series).

MARSHALL, T. H. (1950) *Citizenship and Social Class* (Cambridge University Press).

MATAILLET, D., ROMAIN, D., and URDANETA, G. (1973) *Essai d'analyse d'une economic urbaine: le cas de Tlemcen (Algerie)* (Memoire IEDES, Université de Paris).

MAUSS, M. (1960) *The Gift* (London: Cohen and West).

MAYER, A. C. (1966) 'The Significance of Quasi-Groups in the Study of Complex Societies' in M. Banton (ed.), op. cit. (1966).

McCLELLAND, D. (1961) *The Achieving Society* (New York: Van Nostrand).

—— (1971) *Motivational Trends in Society* (New York: General Learning Press).

McGEE, T. G. (1973) 'Peasants in the cities: a paradox, a paradox, a most ingenious paradox', *Human Organisation*, vol. 32, no. 2, pp. 135–42.

—— (1974) *The Persistence of the Protoproletariat: occupational structures and planning of the future world cities* (Australian National University, Research School of Pacific Studies, Department of Human Geography, mimeo, 60 pp.).

McLUHAN, M. (1967) *The Medium is the Message* (New York: Bantam Books).

MEYERS, C., and PIGORS, P. (1973) *Personnel Administration* (New York: McGraw-Hill).

MINISTRY of HOUSING and LOCAL GOVERNMENT (1967) *Gypsies and Other Travellers* (London: H.M.S.O.).

MISSEN, G. J., and LOGAN, M. L. (1975) *National and Local Distribution System and Regional Development: the case of Kelantan* (presented at the symposium Alternatives for Development Strategies in Asia and the Pacific, Canberra).

MOREWEDGE, H. (1970) *The Economics of Casual Labor: a study of the Longshore Industry* (Berne: H. Lang).

MORGENSTERN, D. T. (1973) 'A Theory of Wage and Employment Dynamics' in E. S. Phelps (ed.), *Microeconomic Foundations of Employment and Inflation Theory* (New York: Norton).

MORSE, R. (1964) 'Latin American cities: aspects of function and structure', in J. Friedman and W. Alonso (eds), *Regional Development and Planning* (Cambridge, Mass.: M.I.T. Press, reprinted from *Comparative Studies in Society and History*, vol. 4, July 1962).

MORTIMORE, M.J. (1972) 'Some aspects of rural–urban relations in Kano, Nigeria', *La Croissance Urbaine en Afrique et à Madagascar* (Paris: C.N.R.S.).

MOTTI, P. (1970) *Mecanismes commerciaux et organisation de l'espace dans un pays sou-developpe: les foires de la region de Salvador Bahia (Bresil)* (Université de Toulouse, Institut de Geographie mimeo., 143 pp.)

NIGAM, S. B. L., and SINGER, H. W. (1974) 'Labour Turnover and Employment: Some Evidence from Kenya', *International Labour Review*, vol. 110.

OBERAI, A. S. (1975) *An Analysis of Migration to Greater Khartoum (Sudan)* (Geneva: W.E.P./P.E./19, I.L.O.).

OBERSCHALL, A., and BEVERIDGE, A. (1972) 'African Businessmen in Zambia' paper presented at the Meeting of the Eastern Sociological Society at Boston, Massachusetts.

OKELY, J. (1975a) 'Gypsy Identity' ch. 2, in B. Adams, J. Okely *et al* (1975) op. cit.

—— (1975b) 'Work and Travel', ch. 5, in B. Adams, J. Okely *et al.* (1975) op. cit.

—— (1975c) 'Gypsy Women: Models in Conflict', in S. Ardener, S. (1975) op. cit.

—— (1976) 'Ritual Boundaries among English Gypsies', paper given at the British Association for the Advancement of Science, Lancaster.

ORWELL, G. (1933) *Down and Out in Paris and London* (London: Gollancz).

PARKIN, D. (1969) *Neighbours and Nationals in a City Ward* (London: Routledge and Kegan Paul).

PATTERSON, O. (1975) 'Context and Choice in Ethnic Allegiance: a theoretical framework and Caribbean case study', in N. Glazer and D. P. Moynihan (eds), *Ethnicity: Theory and Experience* (Cambridge, Mass.: Harvard University Press).

PATTERSON, S. (1963) *Dark Strangers* (London: Tavistock).

—— (1968) *Immigrants in Industry* (London: Oxford University Press for Institute of Race Relations).

PEACH, C. (1968) *West Indian Migration to Britain* (London: Oxford University Press for Institute of Race Relations).

PIERCE, B. (1969) *Maoris and Industrial Technology*, unpublished

Ph.D. thesis, University of Auckland, New Zealand.

PILCHER, W. W. (1972) *The Portland Longshoremen: a dispersed urban community.* (New York: Holt, Rinehart and Winston).

PLANUNGSGRUPPE RITTER (1974) *Report on the two Surveys (in Ghana)* (Geneva: W.E.P./U.E.R.P., I.L.O.) September.

PLOWDEN REPORT (1967) *Children in their Primary Schools* (London: H.M.S.O.).

POETES, A. (1972) 'Rationality in the slum: an essay of interpretive sociology', *Comparative Studies in Society and History*, vol. 14, no. 3, pp. 268–86.

POLITICAL and ECONOMIC PLANNING (P.E.P.) (1967) *Racial Discrimination* (London: P.E.P.).

PORTER, J. (1965) *The Vertical Mosaic* (University of Toronto Press).

QUENNELL, P. (ed.) (1949) *Mayhew's London* (London: Pilot Press).

QUIJANO, A. (1972) 'La constitucion del mundo de la marginalidad urbana', *EURE*, vol. III, no. 5, July, pp. 89–106.

REHFISCH, F. (1975) *Gypsies, Tinkers and Other Travellers* (London: Academic Press).

REICH, M. *et al.* (1973) 'A Theory of Labour Market Segmentation', *American Economic Review*, vol. 63.

REMY, D., and WEEKS, J. (1973) 'Employment, occupation and inequality in a non-industrial city', in R. Wohlmuth (ed.), *Employment Creation in Developing Societies* (New York: Praeger).

RICHMOND, A. H. (1964) 'Social Mobility of Immigrants in Canada', in B. Blishen (ed.), *Canadian Society* (Toronto: Macmillan).

RIMMER, M. (1972) *Race and Industrial Conflict* (London: Heinemann).

RITCHIE, J. E. (1968) 'Workers', in E. Schwimmer (ed.), *The Maori People in the Nineteen-Sixties* (Auckland).

RIU, F. (1968) *Historia y Totalidad: el concepto de reification in Lukacs* (Caracas: Monte Avila Editore).

ROBINSON, J. (1962) *Economic Philosophy* (London: Watts).

ROMANOV' POCKET RUSSIAN–ENGLISH, ENGLISH–RUSSIAN DICTIONARY (1964) (New York: Washington Square Press).

SADNIK, L., and AITZETMULLER, R. (1955) *Handwörterbuch zu der Altkirchenslavishen Texten* (Heidelberg: Carl Winter Universitätsverlag).

SAHLINS, M. D. (1965) 'On the Sociology of Primitive Exchange' in Michael Banton (ed.), *The Relevance of Models for Social Anthropology* (London: Tavistock).

SAIFULLAH KHAN, V. (1975) 'Asian Women in Britain. Strategies of Adjustment of Indian and Pakistani Migrants', in *Women in Contemporary India* (Delhi: Manohar).

—— (1976a) 'Purdah in the British Situation', in Diana Leonard Barker and Sheila Allen (eds), *Dependence and Exploitation in Work and Marriage* (London: Longmans).

—— (1976b) 'Pakistani Women in Britain', *New Community*, vol. v, no. 1–2, Summer.

—— (1976c) 'Perceptions of a Population: Pakistanis in Britain', *New Community*, vol. v, Autumn.

SANTOS, M. (1970a) 'Le role moteur du tertiaire primitif dans les villes du Tiers Monde', *Civilisations*, vol. XVIII, no. 2, 1968 – idem in M. Santos, *Dix Essais sur les Villes des Pays Sous-Developpés* (Paris: Editions Ophrys).

—— (1970b) 'Une nouvelle dimension des reseaux urbains dans les pays sous-developpés', *Annales de Geographie*, no. 434, Juillet-Aout, pp. 425–45.

—— (1971a) *Les Villes du Tiers Monde* (Paris: Editions M.Th. Genin-Librairies Techniques).

—— (1971b) 'L'economie pauvre des villes des pays sous-developpés', *Les Cahiers d'Outre-Mer*, vol. XXIV, no. 94, pp. 105–22.

—— (1975a) 'The periphery in the pole, the case of Lima, Peru', in Harold Rose and Gary Gappert (eds), *The Social Economy of Cities*, vol. IX (Urban Affairs Annual Reviews) (London: Sage Publications).

—— (1975b) *L'Espace Partage: Les deux circuits de l'economie urbaine en pays sous-developpés et leurs repercussions spatiales* (Paris: Editions M.Th. Genin).

SAYLOR, R. G. (1967) *The Economic System of Sierra Leone* (Durham, N. C.: Duke University).

SCHAEFER, K., and SPINDEL, C. (1974) *Urban Development and Employment in Sao Paulo: a preliminary summary of a case study* (Geneva: W.E.P. 2–19, I.L.O.) August.

SCHUTZ, A. (1967) *The Phenomenology of the Social World* (Chicago: Northwestern University Press).

SCHWIMMER, E. (1974) 'Friendship and Kinship: an attempt to

relate two anthropological concepts', in E. Leyton (ed.), *The Compact: Selected Dimensions of Friendship* (St John's Newfoundland: Institute of Social and Economic Research, Memorial University of Newfoundland).

SETHURAMAN, S. V. (1974a) 'Towards a definition of the informal sector', draft for comment (Geneva: W.E.P. 2–19, I.L.O.) January.

—— (1974b) *Urbanisation and Employment in Jakarta: summary and conclusions of a case study* (Geneva: W.E.P., I.L.O.) May.

SHAH, SAMIR (1975) *Immigrants and Employment in the Clothing Industry: the rag trade in London's East End* (London: Runnymede Trust).

SHEPARD, G. (1955) *They Wait in Darkness* (New York: John Day).

SIMEY, T. S. (1956) *The Dockworker; an analysis of conditions of employment in the port of Manchester* (Liverpool University Press).

SINGER, H., and JOLLY, R. (1973) 'Unemployment in an African setting, lessons of the employment strategy mission to Kenya', in *Employment in Africa* (Geneva: I.L.O.) pp. 93–105.

SOWELL, T. (1975) *Race and Economics* (New York: D. McKay).

STEERING WHEEL (1976) 22 October.

STEVENSON, O. (1972) *Claimant or Client?* (London: Allen and Unwin).

STIGLER, G. J. (1962) 'Information in the Labour Market', *Journal of Political Economy*, vol. 70.

STOIKOV, V., and RAIMON, R. L. (1968) 'Determinants of Differences in the Quit Rate Amongst Industries', Papers and Proceedings of the American Economic Association, *American Economic Review*, vol. 50.

STORGAARD, B. (1973) 'A delayed proletarization of peasants', in *Dualism and Rural Development in Africa* (Denmark: Institute for Development Research) pp. 103–25.

STYMEIST, D. H. (1975) *Ethnics and Indians* (Toronto: Peter Martin).

SUTHERLAND, A. (1975) *Gypsies: the Hidden Americans* (London: Tavistock).

SWARTZ, M., TURNER, V., and TUDEN, A. (eds) (1966) *Political Anthropology* (Chicago: Aldine).

THURLOW, L. (1968) 'The Occupational Distribution of the Returns to Education and Experience for Whites and

Negroes', *Journal of the American Statistical Association*, vol. 63.

TOMEV, F. (1971) *Short History of Zhelevo Village, Macedonia* (Toronto: Zhelevo Brotherhood in the City of Toronto).

TRIGG, E. (1967) 'Magic and Religion among English Gypsies', Oxford, D.Phil. thesis (unpublished).

VALLADARES, L. (1969) *El Tigre y su Region* (Caracas, mimeo).

VESEY-FITZGERALD, B. (1973) *Gypsies of Britain* (Newton Abbot: David and Charles).

VILLANUEVA, J. (1975) *Production, Employment and Traditional Sectors: Argentina Case (1950–1970)* (Geneva: W.E.P./P.E./10, I.L.O.).

WALLACE, T. (1973) 'Working in rural Buganda: a study of occupational activities of young people in rural villages', *The African Review*, vol. 3, no. 1, pp. 133–78.

WALLMAN, S. (1974) 'Kinship, a-Kinship, anti-Kinship: variations in the logic of Kinship situations', in E. Leyton (ed.), *The Compact: selected dimensions of friendship* (St John's, Newfoundland: Institute of Social and Economic Research, Memorial University of Newfoundland); and in *Journal of Human Evolution*, no. 4 (1975) pp. 331–41.

—— (1977a) 'Introduction' to S. Wallman (ed.), *Perceptions of Development* (Cambridge University Press).

—— (1977b) 'Ethnicity Research in Britain', *Current Anthropology*, vol. 18, no. 3.

—— (1978) 'The Boundaries of "Race": Processes of Ethnicity in England' *MAN*, vol. 13, no. 2, pp. 200–17.

WEBER, M. (1961) *Historia Económica General* (Mexico: Fondo de Cultura Economica).

—— (1968) *Economy and Society*, vol. 1 (New York: Badminster Press).

WEEKS, J. (1973) 'Uneven sectoral development and the role of the State', *Bulletin Institute of Development Studies*, vol. 5, no. 2/3, October, pp. 53–75.

WEEKS, S. G. (1973) 'Where are all the jobs? The informal sector in Bugisa, Uganda', *The African Review*, vol. 3, no. 1, pp. 111–32.

WEISS, L., and WILLIAMSON, J. G. (1972/5) 'Black Education, Earnings and Interregional Migration: Some New Evidence, Even Newer Evidence', *American Economic Review*, vol. 62, vol. 65.

WELCH, F. (1973) 'Black–White Differences in Returns to Schooling', *American Economic Review*, vol. 63.

WILKINSON, R. G. (1973) *Poverty and Progress* (London: Methuen).

WILLIAMS, B. (1976) *The Making of Manchester Jewry 1740–1875* (Manchester University Press).

WILSON, D. (1972) *Dockers: the impact of industrial change* (London: Fontana).

WOODSWORTH, J. S. (1972) *Strangers Within our Gates* (University of Toronto Press).

WOODWARD, J. (1965) *Industrial Organization: Theory and Practice* (Oxford University Press).

WORSLEY, P. (1972) 'Frantz Fanon and the "Lumpenproletariat"', in *The Socialist Register* (London: Merlin Press) pp. 193–230.

WRIGHT, P. (1964) '"Go-Betweens" in Industry – a Research Note', Institute of Race Relations *Newsletter*, January.

WRIGHT, P. L. (1968) *The Coloured Worker in British Industry* (London: Oxford University Press for Institute of Race Relations).

ZBOROWSKI, M., and HERTZOG, E. (1952) *Life is with People* (New York: International University Press).

# Index